THE FAMILY CRUCIBLE

THE FAMILY CRUCIBLE

Augustus Y. Napier, Ph.D.

with

Carl A. Whitaker, M.D.

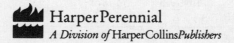

HarperPerennial
A Division of HarperCollins*Publishers*

Epigraph from James Agee and Walker Evans, *Let Us Now Praise Famous Men* (Boston: Houghton Mifflin Company, 1960). Reprinted with permission of the publisher.

First PERENNIAL LIBRARY edition published 1988

Designed by Sidney Feinberg

Library of Congress Cataloging-in-Publication Data

Napier, Augustus.
   The family crucible.

   "Perennial Library."
   Includes index.
   1. Family psychotherapy—Cases, clinical reports, statistics.
I. Whitaker, Carl A., joint author. II. Title.
RC488.5.N36   1988   616.8'915   74-1872
ISBN 0-06-091489-0 (pbk.)

---

98   99 **RRD** 30 29 28 27 26 25 24 23 22

This family must take care of itself; it has no mother or father; there is no shelter, nor resource, nor any love, interest, sustaining strength or comfort, so near, nor can anything happy or sorrowful that comes to anyone in this family possibly mean to those outside it what it means to those within it; but it is, as I have told, inconceivably lonely, drawn upon itself as tramps are drawn round a fire in the cruelest weather; and thus and in such loneliness it exists among other families, each of which is no less lonely, nor any less without help or comfort, and is likewise drawn in upon itself. . . .

JAMES AGEE AND WALKER EVANS
Let Us Now Praise Famous Men

To the Memory of My Parents,
Augustus and Mary Ethel Napier

Contents

Foreword

I began this book when I was in the last stages of training with Carl Whitaker, family therapist and professor of psychiatry at the University of Wisconsin. I came to the Psychiatry Department both to study with Carl and to complete an internship, the last requirement for a Ph.D. in clinical psychology from the University of North Carolina. Family therapy had become my major interest during graduate school, and I was fortunate to find an internship where I could study with such a skilled and widely respected family therapist. A postdoctoral fellowship allowed me to continue the training for a second year, and Carl's generosity extended my apprenticeship through two years of more informal work.

Like many medical schools, Wisconsin honors an old tradition which encourages the medical professor to maintain a small private practice which keeps him abreast of the difficulties of practicing what he teaches. Carl also uses his private practice directly as a teaching medium. Though I attended many seminars and received supervision of my own cases, my most valuable training was in being Carl's co-therapist with a number of families in his private practice. Out of that experience came the impetus for this book.

These interviews were powerful events for me. Some of the sense of power derived from Carl's clinical skill and from his personal force; some of it came from the family's impressive struggle to change its own destiny; some of it seemed to come out of our teaming as co-therapists. I knew that there was a great deal of interest in family therapy among professionals, but little awareness of this exciting new field among lay persons. I wanted to document some of the changes in families that I had witnessed during my training.

In the beginning I went over audiotapes of interviews that Carl and I had conducted together, and I studied videotapes of consultation interviews that he had led in various training institutes. Digging into these interviews was fascinating, but it was also frustrating. I quickly became enmeshed in a nightmare of complexity as I tried to describe the nuances of voice, the peculiarities of phrasing, the intricate sequence of events in the interviews. I wrote fifty pages about a single hour of therapy and felt that I had treated the material superficially! So focused was I on details that I lost all sense of the flow and the drama of family therapy.

I decided to step back from the material and to try to capture the "feel" of family therapy. Choosing a family whose treatment had been recorded on audiotape and which I had studied carefully, I began to write from memory, drawing in episodes from other cases as they seemed useful to illustrate the process of therapy. I added paragraphs and chapters of explanation to clarify both this case and the larger family therapy approach. While every major episode of the Brices' therapy is based on an actual occurrence, their story is truly a composite of various families' experiences in therapy, and is therefore a fictionalized account. Nevertheless, I think the result is a more accurate portrayal of family therapy than was my earlier presentation of the "facts."

The book went with me through a number of experiences. As my own career developed, I shifted from being Carl's student to being his friend and colleague. I found that in my own private practice I began to develop ideas about family therapy that were somewhat different from Carl's; and while my separate views have only served to enrich our association, the book had to change as I changed.

By injecting more of my own view of family therapy into this book, I may have failed to render an accurate portrait of Carl's subtle and indirect artistry. Those who know his work well may feel that I did not capture fully his skillful use of paradox, metaphor, and humor. This omission is the inevitable consequence of the writer's seeing the world through his own eyes. When Carl talks to the family he sometimes speaks the language of the unconscious mind; I tend to speak to the conscious mind and to "teach." Fortunately or unfortunately, the language here is predominantly mine.

Although I conceived the idea of the book and did all the writing, I had a great deal of assistance from several people. Carl's ideas form the real basis for this book. He also collaborated closely with me as I wrote. We outlined the conceptual chapters together, and he offered many helpful suggestions as the book was revised.

Ann Harris, my editor, has been a major contributor to this effort. Her warm, buoyant voice sustained me through periods of discouragement, and her extremely perceptive commentary taught me about much more than the technicalities of writing. Like a good therapist, she not only counseled me to be true to myself, but helped me see more clearly what is natural for me. Ann labored longer and harder over this manuscript than I ever imagined an editor doing, and I am grateful to her.

A number of people read the manuscript and offered useful suggestions, among them my wife, Margaret, my students, and David Keith, a family therapist who is both Carl's and my close associate.

Finally, my thanks to Cindy Hackett and the other secretaries in the Psychiatry Department who spent so many hours typing and retyping this manuscript. They were this book's first readers, and their enthusiasm for what they were typing was very welcome.

THE FAMILY CRUCIBLE

CHAPTER 1

The Question of Structure

"Would you like to see a new family with me?" Carl said. The voice
on the telephone was that of my present colleague and former
teacher, and he sounded less casual and confident than usual. "A
father who's a VIP lawyer, an angry mother, and a teenage daughter
who sounds stormy as hell." His invitation sounded a little like a
friendly dare.

"Sure," I said instantly. "When?" Usually I would think carefully
before agreeing to be someone's co-therapist, but not when the person asking was Carl Whitaker.

We found a joint opening later in the week. "I'll check with the
family," Carl promised. He was about to hang up when I asked,
"Anything I should know before we begin?"

Carl was obviously in a hurry. "Nothing except that the situation
is very tense. The family was referred by a child psychiatrist in town
who says that the girl's getting worse. He's been seeing her individually. The family isn't sold on family therapy, but they say they'll all
come once."

"How many in the family?" I asked.

"Five. There's a younger brother and sister."

"I'll bring my work gloves," I said amiably, letting him go. "See
you Thursday."

Even though the distance from my office to the Psychiatry Department where Carl teaches is only a couple of miles, I was late for
the appointment. It was a cool, beautiful June day, and I had let the
drive be a leisurely one. As I strode into Carl's office, I realized that

I had unconsciously given him time to tell the family why he felt he needed a second therapist and to offer my credentials for the job. He would have mentioned that I was a psychologist in practice nearby and a trusted colleague. He would have talked about the power that families have and how we therapists can be more effective if we work as a team. Since the family had been referred primarily to him, the public relations effort would be helpful. I wasn't sorry for the delay.

Carl introduced me to the family. "This is David and Carolyn Brice, their daughters, Claudia and Laura. We're waiting for their son, Don."

Here was that perpetually awkward moment: not knowing whether to shake hands. There is a social component in the beginning of family therapy, but there is also a professional distance. Uncertain, we wavered between the two for a fraction of a second until the father resolved it by extending his hand to me and smiling anxiously. "Glad to meet you," he said, of course not meaning it. Still, he looked genial enough—a tall, square-shouldered man wearing glasses. He looked directly at me, a sharp, perceptive gaze, yet at the same time he seemed to recoil, as if he thought he might be hurt. He seemed at once assertive, alert, friendly, and afraid. The hesitant posture, the baggy tweeds, the glasses, the keen analytic gaze: clearly his work involved the use of his intellect.

His wife did not offer to shake hands. A slight woman, almost pretty, she looked depressed. Like her husband, she had dark, curly hair. She wore an expensive tailored suit of natural linen, a bright red scarf flaring out of the edge of the neat collar, and a silver pin curled sinuously on her jacket. I sensed that she was angry as well as depressed, her smile token.

The adolescent daughter smiled tightly, nodding to me, but sitting firm and unmoving. She was prettier than the mother, with the same delicate features, the same curly hair. She was very anxious and very angry. After she nodded, she looked down as if in shame, thus identifying herself as "it"—the reason the family was there.

The other daughter, about six, sat in Carl's miniature rocking chair, a little too big for it but pumping back and forth eagerly. "Hi," she said cheerfully. She looked like a happy, active child. The mother made a gesture in her direction to indicate that she should rock less energetically, and she slowed perceptibly.

Carl's office is furnished with two large leather sofas that face each other across the length of the room. At one end three leather-uphol-stered chairs fill the space between them. At the other end are Carl's swivel chair, placed beside his desk, which faces into the corner, and the co-therapist's chair. The seating forms a tidy rectangle. The fa-ther and adolescent daughter sat next to each other in two of the chairs, and the mother sat alone on one of the sofas. The youngest daughter was very near the mother in the little rocker. I noted the seating: each daughter with one of the parents, and the parents separated.

I settled in my chair, looking fondly around Carl's familiar office. It was clearly and comfortably his nest, lined with rows of bookcases, every available surface covered with the memorabilia of his career: sculptures, paintings, photographs, newspaper clippings, cartoons, posters, miscellaneous objects of art or interest, all joined together somehow by the complex pattern of a large Oriental rug.

Carl was sitting in his chair, smoking his pipe, relaxed and wait-ing. In his mid-sixties, he is professor of psychiatry at Wisconsin and is the department's resident family therapist. He is a solidly built man of medium height whose bearing conveys a mixture of casualness and precision, ease and alertness. He has kept the large forearms and hands shaped by his boyhood on a dairy farm, and he has also main-tained the relaxed friendliness of those origins; but in the interim he has acquired a look of scholarly acuity, a subtle, worldly-wise half smile of the person of wide experience.

"So," I said to Carl, my voice relaxed, "can you tell me something about the family?" We deliberately save such briefings until the family is present. In this way they get to know exactly what we know about them, and we establish early in therapy a principle of open communication.

"Well . . ." Carl began, hesitating slightly. I realized he was con-cerned about beginning without the missing son. He resumed, "Well, I'll catch you up while we wait for Don." A pause while he thought. "Mrs. Brice called me last week about an appointment. She was referred by John Simons, who had seen Claudia for a couple of months." The name was familiar; Simons is a child psychiatrist in town who works mostly with adolescents. "John felt things weren't getting any better, and the family apparently agreed." Another pause. "Over the phone Mrs. Brice talked mostly about the problems between her and Claudia: how they had been fighting, how Claudia had begun running away, and how she was concerned about her on a number of counts. Mrs. Brice felt that Claudia has had some strange ideas of late. It sounded as if the stress in the family was quite high, and Mrs. Brice was clear that it was beginning to involve everybody. She didn't want the youngest, Laura, to be exposed to the family struggles, but I thought we had an agreement over the telephone that everybody would come at least once. As I said to you earlier, it feels like a pretty loaded situation."

Claudia glared at her mother, angry at hearing this account of the conversation. She spoke, her voice harsh and strident. "Well, I think you have some pretty damn strange ideas yourself, Mom dear, like I'm supposed to get to bed at sunset and be a good little six-year-old!" Her anger was so intense that it startled us.

Carolyn Brice glared back, stiffening and locking her gaze into the daughter's. It was as if someone had turned on a strong electrical current that magnetized the mother and daughter, pulling them toward each other. The mother: "Well, I think some of your ideas *are* strange, and I *am* concerned." Her response was a blend of attack and worry, and she was defensive about Carl's account of their conversation. The father looked scared, as if he knew what was coming.

Mother and daughter clearly wanted to fight, but it would have been a mistake to allow them to. Carl extended his hand toward them, as if to block the current between them. His voice was firm. "Let me stop you two. Because I really do want to wait for Don." They looked away from each other, and the moment passed.

"Where is he?" I asked, turning to the mother.

"I don't know," she said, sounding tired, discouraged. "A couple of days ago he said he wasn't coming. He didn't want to be in family therapy. Then this morning he said he would come. When we left, he wasn't home from his art class yet. Could we go ahead and begin? Maybe he'll come in. I left him a note to ride his bicycle over here."

Carl answered as I knew he would. "I think we should wait. If we begin now, we don't have Don in on the beginning, and I'd like to start out with us all together." There was nothing unkind about the way Carl said this, but it was pretty clear that he wasn't going to begin without Don. He added, raising his eyebrows in question, "You want to use the phone to call him? Maybe he's home by now."

"Sure," the mother said, rising from the couch and striding toward Carl's desk. A tense silence while she dialed. More silence while she listened to the ringing of the phone. No answer. She sighed and sat down. "I don't know what to do now."

Carl seemed unperturbed, tilting back with a creak of his desk chair, drawing on the pipe. "We have the time reserved anyway. We can wait."

"I'll call the art class," the mother offered, going again to the desk.

With that everyone seemed to relax. We had apparently been anticipating sitting through an hour staring at one another and trying to make talk, and the possibility that Don might be at the art class offered us a moment's relief. The father spoke admiringly to Carl. "I like that tobacco. What is it?" I wondered if he wasn't unconsciously saying something else, like: "I admire your firmness."

While Mrs. Brice tried several phone numbers, the casual talk continued. Claudia loosened a bit and, smiling, pointed toward the coatrack. "What are *those* for?" Hanging on the coatrack were two billy clubs, one painted pink and marked HERS, and the other a longer white one, HIS. A present from a former patient.

Carl, smiling back: "You guessed right. Except I don't let people use them until I get a bigger one for me."

"Oh," said Claudia, intrigued and somewhat horrified.

Then Laura, chirping in her cheery little voice: "And what's that?" She was pointing to the steel abstract sculpture on Carl's wall. It had always looked to me like a billowing tree shape. But I felt like shifting the focus from Carl and his office, and I interrupted before he could tell his story about it. "It's his grandfather." The group laughed nervously, not knowing why it was funny or if, in fact, it *was* funny. I added, "And if you think it's strange-looking, you should see his grandmother!" This time they really laughed, and Mrs. Brice turned from the phone to see what was so funny. When people are anxious, almost any joke will do. I smiled in Carl's direction. "I'm sorry. I interrupted your story."

Carl looked a little flustered, but he grinned. "He can't wait to hear my story for the hundredth time." I shrugged, and Carl began. "Well, when I bought that sculpture, my patients had a lot of associations to it. Everybody saw something different in it. But one day somebody asked me what *I* thought it was, and what suddenly popped into my head was this crazy thought: 'It's the glued-together bones of my grandfather.' And I knew right away where it came from. 'Cause I'm a soft sort of a guy, and my father was the same way. But my grandfather was this tough character who, when he got gangrene in his big toe, took a pocketknife and cut it off. He didn't need no damn doctor! Well, I figured out that I bought this sculpture because I was trying to get for myself some of the iron that was in my grandfather, some of his toughness."

Even though we were still waiting for Don, therapy was well begun. We were engaged in a subtle, often predictable, and very important contest with the family about who was going to be present at the meetings. Carl and I had revealed some of what our relationship had to offer: a good-humored liking for each other, an ability to cooperate, and an insistence on remaining ourselves. I was clearly not going to be the reverential assistant to the older man. And perhaps most important, Carl had intuitively modeled some of the process of therapy for the family. By sharing insight into his own personality, he was saying by demonstration, "It's important to search for your own unconscious agenda."

Meanwhile, the battle over whether or not we were going to have an "official" meeting was becoming more serious. Don could not be found at the school where the art class was held. The mother, worried, spoke with a kind of grim insistence. "Why can't we meet now and have Don come next time?"

It was my turn. "I agree with Carl. I think it would be a mistake. What we are talking about is the prospect of the family as a whole changing. And to start that process with one fifth of the family absent would be unfair to Don and I think unfair to you. He's part of the family, and we need him here if the family as a whole is going to change." There was an edge of toughness in my voice.

Mrs. Brice didn't give in easily. "But Don isn't the *problem*. The problem has to do with Claudia." Her voice was chilly, too. We were definitely having a fight.

Nor was I giving in. "But you see, that's *your* initial definition of the problem. We assume that the problem is much more complex and much more extensive than Claudia. And the whole family just *has* to be involved." I hesitated, gazing with level intensity at the mother. I realized that pushing the family might mean losing them, but I knew that it had to be done. "Now, maybe you guys aren't up to this kind of major job that we're talking about. We really can't decide that for you. But it's clear to us that we need the whole family." A very large and imposing silence.

"I agree," Carl said quietly, adding a final nail to the argument.

The mother spoke in a soft and faintly bitter voice, "It's easy for you to say that, but as her mother I have to worry about tonight and tomorrow." Anger crept back into her words now. "I mean, I don't know what's going to *happen* if we go back home now. And frankly, I'm worried."

Carl was losing patience, too. "But you're missing the other side. If this is such an emergency, why didn't somebody get that message to Don and make sure he got here? Because it was perfectly plain over the phone that we couldn't meet unless the whole family was here." He backed away slightly from the tough statement, softening his words if not the position he had taken. "Or was I not clear?"

"You were clear," Carolyn said, resigned. "Don just didn't keep his part of the agreement."

Carl smiled, easing still further away from the anger. "Not as I see it. And let me try to explain." He was friendly now, but speaking with conviction. "My view is that Don is not acting just for himself, but that through a very complicated unconscious process he got *elected* by the family to be the one to stay home. That way the family wouldn't have to face the full electricity of this thing, and you'd find out if we really meant business about working with the whole family."

"Elected?" she said with skepticism.

I explained. "Probably something in your and your husband's voices that let him know you really didn't mean it when you said he had to come." I could see her feeling cornered with the responsibility. "We're not trying to blame *you* personally," I said. "It's really the *family* that has the anxiety about everybody's getting together, and the *family* he's acting for." She looked relieved at the shift in focus.

David Brice entered the conversation with a quietly argumentative rationality. "I don't really understand what you mean by all this, but how do we deal with this practically? What do we do now? We *are* concerned about Claudia, and I think we have reason to be." I could feel the husband-wife coalition against us, realizing that Carolyn had been fighting not just for her own view, but for a thoroughly unconscious agreement between the couple that they would keep the focus on their "sick" daughter. The force of "concern" which both parents directed at Claudia did not feel very loving; under the surface of caring was a steely attack. As they talked about her, Claudia cringed.

Somehow we had to get around the immediate problem of the parents' accusation that we were being professionally irresponsible by delaying the appointment. I turned to David, the father. "Can you say what you're concerned about that can't wait till tomorrow? Because we can find the time to meet if it's that urgent. Are you afraid she will run away or that she's suicidal?"

"The latter is what *I'm* worried about," the father said.

"*Yes,*" the mother resounded softly. What a dilemma. We were being given the choice of surrendering our insistence on meeting with the whole family or perhaps acting irresponsibly in the face of a suicide threat. With every added minute of interaction with the family, we were weakening our case for not having the interview, yet there seemed no alternative but to deal forcefully with the suicide issue.

"How about it?" Carl said to Claudia. "Are you suicidal?" The girl started with the directness of the question. She looked pale and tense and very angry.

"I've thought about it," she said with mysterious intonations that had to be pursued.

"How about my question?" Carl said. "Are you suicidal now? Or do you think you might be tonight?"

The slightest of smiles crossed the girl's face, like the sudden but tiny flash of brightness that occurs when a distant car strikes a reflective angle with the sun. "I don't think I'd do it." A pause. "But I have thought about it."

"How would you do it?" I asked. If the fantasy was explicit and well worked out, there was plainly greater immediate danger.

"I don't know—maybe sleeping pills. There doesn't seem to be any really good way." I didn't like the passivity in her voice.

"You still didn't answer my question about now," Carl reminded her gently. "Do you think there's any danger you might kill yourself before we can meet again?"

"No," Claudia answered firmly. Then she glanced angrily at her parents. "Especially if they will leave me *alone* for a while!"

Carl turned to me. "What do you think we should do? How do you see Claudia?"

I was momentarily surprised by his question, but it was obviously an appropriate time for a conference. Pausing as I tried to collect my thoughts, I felt exposed to the family's scrutiny. The situation called for decisive action, and Carl and I had to be together in whatever we did. "Claudia seems pretty alive to me," I said. "I like the fact that she's angry and fighting with her parents rather than taking the anger out on herself. I feel that Claudia is very stressed, but that suicide right now is an option that she keeps open rather than an obsession. As a fantasy, it seems very much a part of her battle with her parents." I summarized. "She doesn't feel suicidal to me." Claudia seemed to brighten with the words.

Carl turned back to the parents. "I agree with everything that Gus said. And while I might not trust either one of us alone, I trust the 'we,' the stereoscopic vision." He breathed in deeply, then out, and with this long breath seemed to relax. "Tell you what I think we ought to do. You guys go home and think about whether you want to be in this as a family. And if you do, call me and we'll set up a time tomorrow or Monday or even Saturday if it's absolutely necessary."

The father settled the question with a move that seemed authoritative, all the more so since he had remained so hidden in the "interview." "I don't think we need to do that. I think we should make an appointment now." Then he turned to his wife. "Don't you?"

"Yes," she said, sounding a little disconcerted, as well as relieved. "Do you have an opening in the morning?"

"We'll make one," Carl answered positively. "How about you?" he said to me. "You have time?" Since I had an opening at nine, Carl agreed to shift his appointment.

With the decision made, everyone relaxed, and it was not until the tension began to ease that I realized how caught up in the family's battle I had been. But just as the family was getting up to leave, Carl again did something surprising: he sat down on the floor beside Laura and began to talk with her. "What do you think of all this crazy stuff?" he asked with confidential warmth. "You think we can all stand one another for a year or so to work this out? How about you? Can you stand it?"

Laura looked at her mother for a response, and Carolyn merely smiled back. Half the group was standing, the other half sitting; everyone was both interested in the dialogue and a little confused by it. "I don't know," the little girl said hesitantly. Then she somehow found the courage to add, "But I don't like it when they fight."

"Think you and I could teach them how to love?" Carl asked.

" 'Cause I've got a feeling that you already know how. And if you and I teamed up, we might teach the rest of your family."

Laura was embarrassed, but she also liked Carl and couldn't avoid smiling at him.

"Maybe we could start with something easy like shaking hands. You want to shake hands?" Carl extended his hand to her, and she offered her own. "Very nice," he said. "I liked that." And so the interview ended. Though Carl had not planned to sit down with Laura until it suddenly occurred to him, it was a useful moment. The family could see that in addition to strength, we could offer them warmth.

Fortunately, most families do not present us with such a crisis in the first interview. But many families do engage in some form of struggle over membership at the meetings. So predictable is this challenge that we have given it a name: the battle for structure.

When Carl asked the Brices to bring their whole family to therapy, everyone in the family knew intuitively what that meant. Their whole world would be exposed: all its caring, its history, its anger, its anxiety. All in one place at one time, subject to the scrutiny and invasion of a stranger. And that was too much vulnerability. With its own unconscious wisdom, the family elected Don to stay home and test the therapists. Did we really mean everybody? Would we weaken and capitulate if they didn't bring Don?

They had something to gain by the strategy. If we were hesitant and unconfident in our approach to their defiance, they would know that they could not trust us with the boiling caldron of feeling which their family contained. If we were decisive and firm, they would guess that maybe we could handle the stresses which they intuitively knew had to be brought out into the open. One way or another, they had to find out how much power we had. In the meantime, they postponed facing that mysterious electricity, that critical mass, the whole family. Perhaps they thought they could be spared what Zorba called the full catastrophe.

Don, of course, had his own questions to pose. "How much do I matter?" their middle child was asking. "Will you undertake changing the whole family without me?" Every member *is* important. I remember one mother who said in a session, "I just don't understand it. When one member of the family is missing, we get along fine. But let the missing one just walk in the house, and all hell breaks loose. I just don't understand it."

It has been a long road for us as family therapists to reach an understanding of just this phenomemon—the sense of the whole, the family system. While we could have explained the theory of meeting with the whole family to the Brices, at that anxious moment it would not have touched them. There are situations where, in the words of Franz Alexander, the voice of the intellect is too soft. The family needed to test us. They needed the *experience* of our being firm. As unpleasant as it was, our response must have reassured them. They knew, and we sensed, how difficult and desperate their situation was and how tumultuous it could become. They simply had to know that we could withstand the stress if they dared open it up.

The individual psychotherapy patient comes to the therapist with an almost automatic deference, a sense of dependence and compliance. The role pattern is old and established: the dependent child seeking guidance from a parent figure. There is no such traditional image for the family, no established pattern in which an entire family submits to the guidance of an individual. And the family structure is simply too powerful and too crucial for the members to go trustingly into an experience that threatens to change the entire matrix of their relationships. If the family therapist is to acquire that initial "authority figure" or "parent" role that is so necessary if therapy is to be more powerful than an ordinary social experience, he has to earn it.

Families come into therapy with their own structure, and tone, and rules. Their organization, their pattern, has been established over years of living, and it is extremely meaningful and very painful for them. They would not be in therapy if they were happy with it. But however faulty, the family counts on the familiarity and predictability of their world. If they are going to turn loose this painful predictability and attempt to reorganize themselves, they need firm external support. The family crucible must have a shape, a form, a discipline of sorts, and the therapist has to provide it. The family has to know whether we *can* provide it, and so they test us.

CHAPTER 2

A Beginning

The next morning Don entered the room first. He had the practiced sloppy walk of the young adolescent who is in the process of becoming a picaresque character. Unlike the rest of the family, his hair was long and straight and blond, and he wore the current adolescent uniform—body shirt, jeans, and sandals. He walked across to shake hands with Carl right away, saying with apparent confidence, "So you're Whitaker."

Carl smiled. *"Dr.* Whitaker, if you don't mind."

Don: "I don't mind, Dr. Whitaker." Carl wasn't overly serious, of course, but he was slipping almost instantly into a posture with Don, at once teasing and challenging, which was to continue for most of the therapy.

Don, a little flustered, turned to me. "And who are you?"

I decided to play it straight. "I'm Dr. Napier."

Don extended his hand, and suddenly he was straight, too, the ironic tone dropping from his voice. "How do you do?" He looked like an interesting person, alternatingly serious and skeptical, brash and hesitant, wavering between boyhood and adolescence.

The family seated themselves, Claudia and her father in the center chairs, facing Carl and me, and the mother and Laura on the couch to the left. Don sat alone on the other couch. For a while we were social, that process of reassuring ourselves that we could be casual with one another, a ritual protection from the intensity that was to follow and perhaps a necessary prelude to it. How could we risk getting involved if we didn't know we could be superficial and distant, if we didn't know we could escape if we all wanted to? We complained together about the parking lot attendants at the hospital. We remarked how wonderful and clear and cool the weather had been. We talked about the crazy painting propped up against the rear wall of the office, a group project done at the end of a workshop Carl had conducted with the staff of a mental health center. It was certainly abstract, and it was certainly expressive, and it was so awful that it was interesting. Obviously any single person who had done it would have been crazy. Then a silence, marking the border between our being social and our getting to work.

I spoke to the mother. I was smiling, but the content of my question was clearly leading us toward the task at hand. "I see that you found him."

She managed, just barely, a smile in return. "Yes. He was walking home from the art class, apparently *very* slowly." She sounded as if she were blaming Don for not coming to the previous session.

I spoke to Don. "Do you have any sense of how you got chosen by the family to be the one who was absent last time?"

He answered as if he understood the language I was speaking. "I don't know—just my lucky day. Maybe so they could yell at me."

"Don't sell yourself short," I said. "I think you were up to more than that. You were helping the family make up its mind about whether or not it wanted to be here. And now that everybody has decided it's worth trying, we're ready to get moving." His earlier bravura was gone now, and he looked scared; I wanted to say at least a few supportive words to him before we got embroiled with the family.

David sounded irritated. "So could we begin?"

Carl jumped in quickly. "Sure. Could you start us?"

The father: "I think I would rather my wife start. I think she's really closer to the situation."

Carl: "All the more reason for *you* to start. We fathers are often on the outside in families today, and I'd like to hear how the family looks to you. Maybe you have an overview." Carl was doing something interesting: he was directing the interview, in effect pushing the father around, at the same time that he was complimenting him, attending to him, and in the process making it hard for him to resist.

Fathers usually *are* the outsiders in the modern family, and often they find coming into family therapy very uncomfortable. This father was typical in attempting to shift the focus away from himself. It would have been a mistake for us to let it happen, because although he was eager to defer to his wife, he would probably have resented it if we had allowed this. Most of the time, the mother is the psychological center of the family, and our moving quickly to her would have given the father an excuse to feel himself more and more removed, until he had become as isolated and alone in the therapy as he felt in the family. If anyone were likely to pull the family out of treatment, it was the father, and by bringing him in early, we were deliberately attempting to bias the start slightly in his favor. Women are more sophisticated about the interpersonal world, the world of feeling, and we were trying to compensate for this kind of cultural inadequacy in men. We were also making it clear that we were assuming responsibility for leading the meeting, and that included who spoke when and to whom. Again, the uncomfortable—but necessary—quality of abrasiveness, of struggle over power.

The father hesitated. "Well, all right." A pause while he thought. His shoulders sagged under the burden, his brow furrowed, his face pale with tension. "Claudia," he said, pausing again, looking for words, "has been in trouble, and I mean psychological trouble, for some time. I don't know quite when it began or how it began, but for the last year it has been getting worse and worse. Lately it has just been impossible."

I had expected him to talk about Claudia, but I was glad to hear a glimmer of something else. "You said 'it' had been impossible. That sounds like something more than just Claudia. Can you say what the 'it' is?" The father looked a little disconcerted at finding himself being interviewed by two people working in close coordination. But since Carl and I were sitting together, he had only to turn his head a degree or two to look at me.

He sighed. "The 'it' is constant conflict. Usually the fights are between Claudia and her mother, and they seem to be about just *everything*—Claudia's room, her schoolwork, her friends, her dating, the way she dresses. Claudia does exactly the opposite from what her mother wants."

"And how are you involved in this?" Carl asked.

The father was troubled by the question. "I'm not sure. Often I find myself thinking Carolyn is too hard on her, and sometimes I defend Claudia. And, of course, that makes Carolyn furious. Then sometimes I get very angry at Claudia, particularly lately, and I join in with Carolyn, and that seems to be just devastating for Claudia. Sometimes I try to stay out of it, but that doesn't work either. Things have gotten too desperate for that."

"Desperate how?" I asked.

"Well, Claudia came home last night at two-thirty. And it was the first time in a week she had been home. We don't know where she sleeps, or with whom for that matter. And when she's home, she locks herself in her very disorganized room and turns up her radio. A month ago she took off hitchhiking across the country with her boyfriend." The father looked pale, scared. He glanced furtively at his daughter.

Claudia sat stiff and silent beside him, her eyes cast down. She wore a short-sleeved faded denim shirt and dirty faded jeans. She had tied her long hair behind her head with a handmade silver clasp. A piece of abstract jewelry hung from a thin silver chain around her neck. How different the mother and daughter looked: the mother as beautifully dressed as before, the daughter following almost as carefully the casual style of her peers. Yet both wore the same unusual silver jewelry. I wondered about the parallel.

The father continued, his voice now stronger, almost aggressive. "But if it were just a fight, just Claudia's lashing out and running away, I wouldn't be so worried. It's more than that. Claudia has been talking for some time about her philosophy of life, and it sounds to me, while very complex, also very troubling. She talks about five levels of reality, and the deepest levels seem to be pretty despairing ones, bleak. Claudia is a poet, as well as a talented musician, and recently most of her poetry has been about death." What had sounded almost like anger in his voice was, in fact, anguish, a pushing toward his daughter in order to reach her. And he seemed to be doing so, for as he talked, tears began to stream down her face. As she cried silently, the tears collecting around the bottom of her chin, I saw that her eyes were puffy because she had already been crying that day.

The father was ready to continue, as if once started on his disclosure, he had to proceed to an end. "And there's more. Claudia has a lot of physical problems. Mysterious aches and pains, a ringing in her ears that doesn't seem to have any physical cause." As the testimony about her accumulated, the girl grew visibly more depressed and confused. She had stopped crying and sat there glassy-eyed and vacant. I found myself wondering: is she schizophrenic? Or is she just very depressed and anxious? The aches and pains could be depression, and the ringing in her ears could be anxiety. But the five levels of reality sounded ominous.

We had focused quickly on Claudia, the "patient," and the interview seemed to be moving inevitably toward questioning her next —about herself, her symptoms, her view of the problems.

Because the family's attention was so structured around Claudia, Carl's next move surprised the father and the family. I expected it, though, and would have done it myself if he hadn't. "I'm pretty clear about what's going on with Claudia," Carl said, a thin, tough edge to his voice, "and I'd like to get away from her for a while. Can you talk about the family as a whole? How do you see it?"

Our asking about Claudia had produced, you see, the same kind of pressure on her that she sensed in the family at home. She felt scrutinized, blamed, on the spot. And Carl was trying to give her some relief, not by accepting her status as "patient" but by dodging her, passing her by for the time being. He would get to her later.

The father was confused by the question. "What do you mean?"

Carl, rapidly: "What is the family like? Quiet or noisy? Organized or confused? Angry or loving? How is it structured? What are the teams, the coalitions? What are the various roles?"

The father still looked confused. "Which of those questions would you like me to try to answer?"

Carl's voice relaxed a bit. "Any one you like. I'd just like to get a sense of how you see the whole team."

The father was trying hard, thinking now about Carl's questions. "I guess we're a pretty quiet family generally and fairly traditional. I'm a lawyer, and busy, and I suppose I expect things to run smoothly at home. Usually they have, very smoothly." He seemed to be musing, almost to himself, as he wondered about the family. "My wife and I have gotten along well, agree on most things except, I guess, Claudia." Then he stopped and couldn't seem to go any further. Clearly he had come to talk about Claudia—everybody had—and it was strange to think about this other subject, the family as a whole. He wasn't prepared.

Don was fidgeting with the strap on his sandal. I spoke to him. "Can you help him? How do you see the family?"

He looked up. "It's OK. Only moderately lousy, I guess."

"How is it lousy?" I asked. So much of what we do is prod people to talk. Don complained about the fights. They just went in circles. Did he have any idea who started them, or did everyone do his or her part? His cynicism was very helpful; he agreed that everyone did his or her part. We asked him if he could identify the different steps in the family's dance. How did it begin?

Don seemed to know what we were asking for. "Well, Claudia will do something, like leave her room an extra-special mess, or leave her books at school, or stay out too late—this was in the days before it got this terrible—and Mom will yell at her. And Claudia will sulk off to her room. Then Dad will come home, and Claudia will be up in her room, and Dad will try to go find out what is wrong with her. Then Mom will say something to me about Dad taking Claudia's side, or she will just get real quiet. Dad will come downstairs, and then in about a half an hour Claudia will come down looking weepy, and nobody is speaking to anybody for quite a while. It makes for a wonderful dinner." An eleven-year-old who really knew what was going on.

We asked about how things had changed in recent months, and he knew about that, too. "Nowadays Claudia doesn't hang around. When she gets mad, she may yell about two words to Mother; then she's off. She goes out the door and slams it and may not come back for two days. It almost always happens when Dad is home, and before Claudia is gone ten minutes, Mom and Dad are in a fight. Well, I wouldn't really say a fight. A sort of medium-warm argument. Mom wants to call the police or some such thing, and Dad says let her go, she'll come back." We asked him what *he* did to help the fight along, and he said there wasn't much he could do at times like that except pick on his little sister. "Sometimes if she starts crying, they'll stop arguing."

Carl and I glanced at each other briefly, smiling faintly at a pattern we both recognized. Then Carl said, "Sounds like Claudia is in charge of getting Mom and Dad to start fighting, and you and Laura are in charge of helping them stop." Don tilted his head and smirked as though he were thinking it wasn't a half-bad idea.

We asked Don if Claudia was the only thing his parents fought about, and he said yes. How long had they been fighting? Six months. Before that he saw no fights? No, none. And what were the fights like that he saw now? How noisy did they get? Don: "Not very noisy. Like I said, medium-warm. Mom grumbles loud, and Dad just grumbles."

Then we asked him if there were other things besides Claudia that his parents were mad at each other about but didn't fight about. Don thought that question was interesting, and he took a minute to think about it. Finally: "Yes, I think so. Mom doesn't like it a bit that Dad works so much. He's *always* working. And when he comes home, he goes up to his study and shuts himself in and works some more. He sure does love to work. But Mom doesn't complain to him about it. She tells me."

Suddenly, I saw a parallel. "So that's one reason Mom gets so mad when Claudia goes and hides in her room—she's being like her dad." Don said, "Huh," in a sort of studious way, and it was evident that both the parents and Claudia had heard me. I looked at the parents, and they had a look of retreat, scared, as though they had suddenly stumbled over a snake and weren't sure whether it was poisonous. Carl and I were the snake, grilling their son about their relationship. It must indeed have been disconcerting, and Don's willingness to talk must have been one of the unconscious reasons they hadn't wanted to bring him to the first session. He was just old enough and observant enough and uninvolved enough to be a terrific asset to our probe into the family.

"And what," Carl asked Don, "is your dad mad about that he *doesn't* confront Mom with?"

Again, Don thought. Then he seemed to have it. "Her mom." A pause. "You see, Mom's mom is a really old lady, but she's pretty hard to please and pretty nosy. She calls Mom a lot, and Mom has to go see her a lot. Dad gets mad that Grandmother can tell Mom what to do, and he gets mad about the telephone bills and the airplane bills."

"How did you find that out?" Carl asked.

"I overheard Dad talking to Claudia."

Carl: "So Dad complains to Claudia, and Mom complains to you. Is that the way the teams go in the family? Claudia is on Dad's team and you're on Mom's?"

Don: "I guess so, but I try not to be on anybody's team, really. I want to stay out of it." He looked worried at the mention of teams, sensing as he did the deep divisions within the family.

"I know," Carl said, with a curious mixture of empathy and teasing. He understood, but clearly he wasn't the captive of his empathy.

At this point, he was keeping his distance, and the distance, like the occasional abrasiveness, was necessary. Without the perspective that allowed Carl to pull back and shift emphasis, we might still be breathing down Claudia's neck, trying to find out what was wrong with her. Instead, we were exploring the family, trying to uncover the structure, the tone, the patterns in the family that were deeper and more significant than Claudia's problems, serious as those were. This was exploratory surgery, and for the family, especially the parents, it was no fun.

But for Claudia the experience was different. Since we had moved away from her and her problems, she looked different: more alert, more curious, and relieved. She was quietly composing herself and hearing every word.

Laura had found the rocking chair again. Carl had quietly handed her a tablet and pencil, and she was rocking very slightly as she drew. She looked completely oblivious to the discussion.

The next question was an obvious one, and Carl asked it, his voice warming as he turned toward Laura, smiling. "Whose team are you on?"

Laura had apparently been waiting. She answered with a little-girl pout. "Nobody's."

Carl, still smiling: "What's the matter? Can't you get somebody on your team? How are you going to stand up to your brother if you don't get some help? He's bigger than you are."

"Mom will help me," Laura said, smiling a little herself. "And sometimes Daddy."

Carl, a blatant flirt: "Oh! That's not fair! Mom *and* Dad on your team. No wonder your brother gets upset." Then he continued, more serious now. "Say, how do you see the family? What do you think of these disagreements between Mom and Dad and Claudia?"

Laura's face clouded, and her voice retreated into quiet apprehension. "They worry me."

Carl spoke almost as softly as Laura, his words quite warm. "Who do you worry the most about?"

Laura thought for a while; then: "Claudia."

Carl, concerned: "What do you worry will happen?"

Laura, even quieter: "That she'll be gone, won't come back."

Carl: "And then what?"

Laura, beginning to cry a little, a few tears, her voice strained under the intensity of her feeling: "Mommy and Daddy will be so mad at each other they'll divorce."

I had heard her talk about Claudia's "leaving," and I wondered if it was related to still another fantasy. I asked Laura, the concern clear in my voice, too, "Do you worry that Claudia will kill herself?" And with that Laura burst into tears. She had moved quickly from an entertaining petulance to quiet seriousness to open grief. I was amazed. I hadn't guessed that the apparently happy little girl was hiding such deep and painful fantasies. Divorce, suicide—what else was she worried about?

Finally, she calmed down and said, again quietly, "Yes. I worry about that, too. I heard my mommy and daddy talking about it, and I keep thinking about it."

Carl reassured her. "Well, I guess that's why we're here—so she won't need to kill herself to change the family."

Laura seemed to accept what Carl said, settling into the rocker with a look of relief, snuffling softly still. The feeling in the room had changed: gentler, less suspicion and tension in everyone. We all shared a tenderness for Laura. Some therapists might say that a child the age and status of Laura in this family could well stay home. She wasn't the "problem" after all, and she might be hurt by what she heard. Yet in the space of a few minutes she had changed the entire emotional atmosphere of the interview, had, in fact, helped all of us feel warmer. The inflection in Carl's voice as he spoke to Laura was what allowed her to cry, and it was not lost on the family. Here was a warm "parent," as well as a tough one. It was also important for Laura that she was able to expose her painful fantasies and cry about them. She probably hadn't shared those thoughts with anyone.

We all were silent for a moment, and in the silence I thought about the secretive quality in families. This family appeared no different from several hundred others I had seen. They worked hard at maintaining certain secrets, but apparently everybody knew everything anyway. Even Laura knew about the suicidal poems. What they were able to hide, and thus avoid sharing, was their pain. In their isolation, they all were very lonely.

The silence was a watershed moment in the interview. We had drifted from exploration toward an attempt to define the problem for the family—perhaps in a way they hadn't seen before. Now we were ready for the mother. Because she was such a crucial person in the family and was bound to have so much feeling about everything, we had postponed her comments. It was her turn now.

Carolyn Brice was angry. Sitting in attempted composure on the edge of the sofa, her legs crossed, she nevertheless betrayed both physical and emotional discomfort. While the father seemed weighed down by some invisible burden, the mother appeared to be pushed from all sides, her dark eyes flashing a warning that she felt both trapped and resentful.

Carl began: "Mom, could you talk about your view of the family?"

She bit her lip just slightly and turned toward Carl. "I guess I find it hard to talk about the family, I'm so upset about Claudia and so angry at her."

"Wish you'd try," Carl said.

The mother sighed, a long, deep sigh that spoke of her discouragement.

Carl: "You could start with your sigh. Say what it was about."

Carolyn: "Oh, I just thought about the family, and suddenly I felt depressed. It's a mess. It's so complicated that I don't even know where to begin."

Carl: "What's the worst part for you?"

"The struggle with Claudia."

"What else?" I asked. She shifted her eyes slightly to look at me.

"The thing with David, my husband. I knew that would come out —it had to."

I was surprised she was talking so easily about it, and I followed her lead. "What's wrong with the marriage?"

A thin rim of tears formed in her eyes. "Oh, nothing," she said. "Just that sometimes I wonder if it's ever really existed. I thought it was fine until the last year—he'd go to work, I would take care of the children and the house, and everything seemed to go smoothly." Then her voice dropped, and she was musing. "Maybe too smoothly."

"And then?" I asked.

She looked up, resuming her normal tone. "Then everything fell apart. This thing with Claudia, it has just ruined everything we had. We fight about it all the time now. We blame each other; we don't know what to do."

Carl seemed curious about something. "How about the time before it blew up? You didn't see anything wrong with the marriage then?"

"No," she said.

Carl: "How about right now, when you look back at it? See any-thing now? How about the stuff Don was talking about?"

"You mean about his working too hard and my problems with my mother?"

"That's right," Carl said. He smiled. "Because, if I could use the language of therapy, it sounds as if he were having an affair with his work and you were carrying on with your mother."

Carolyn frowned, confused, trying to see what Carl was getting at. "I suppose it's true that I resented the work. I still do. And he has always resented my mother."

I saw where Carl was going, and it was important. One of the joys of our working so much together is that we know each other so well. We can function as if we were one interviewer. I jumped in again. "Do you have a sense of how separated you were even before Claudia's troubles came up?" She said yes, she guessed she could see it. She certainly felt unhappy with how much she was alone with the children. I wanted to know when this emotional divorce between them began. Was it there from the start? No, she didn't think so. They were very close and very happy in the early years of their marriage. When did it change? When the children came along, she guessed, and when his work load got so heavy. And when was that? She thought it was when they had been married eight years or so. Did she think it was just the demands of a job and children that had caused them to drift apart? She did.

I wasn't satisfied, though I was amazed at how easily she con-tinued to talk about the marriage. This would never have happened if we had begun the interview with her. She would have insisted on fighting with Claudia. I made a guess in my next question to her. "How about the dependency between you and your husband in the early days? Were you aware of that?"

She seemed surprised that I should know about it. "Yes, I think we were very dependent on each other. In a strange sort of way we still are."

"I agree," I said, not offering any explanation. "Maybe that's what made you two get so separate, made him get so overinvolved in his work, and you get so overinvolved with the kids and with your mother. The dependency in the marriage scared you. It may have felt as if it were going to gobble you both up." I said this with a special tone in my voice, as if I were speaking not directly to her, but to some sensitive and elusive part within her that could hear it, somewhere behind the usual rational level of understanding. And hear it she did, though she clearly didn't *like* hearing it. I saw her wince at my words. This kind of invasion of someone's life is very threatening. The fact that we were being relatively gentle at the same time that we were forceful made us seem doubly dangerous. Our intrusion was difficult to fight.

Carolyn may have thought that I had some kind of special power that let me guess correctly that she and David had been very dependent on each other early in their marriage, but not so. You don't have to see even as many as a hundred families to realize that the dilemma is predictable. Most of us—and psychotherapists are included—get married to the great American marital dream. Marriage is going to be that happy state in which we get all the nurturance and care and love and empathy and even the good advice that we didn't receive in our families. Marriage is going to help us feel better about ourselves; it is going to make life easier and more secure. And behold, usually it does—for a while. We form a very tight, dependent unit, and we help each other in all sorts of ways: advice, sympathy, mothering, teaching. We have a lot to give each other.

But sooner or later this psychotherapy project, this at first delicious mothering, fails. It fails for a complex set of reasons, most of which we will deal with later, but the major reason is that the protagonists get very scared that they are each going to lose their individual identities in the dependency, in the same way they lost them in the families in which they grew up. The marriage begins to feel like a trap, a replication of the old family of origin. So the couple begins to back away from each other, mistrusting. They are right to mistrust. How can you safely depend on someone with whom you're struggling for dominance in the relationship?

If the partners could stick with the backing away and endure the aloneness for a while, the problem might be solved. They would get over being so dependent, and marriage wouldn't feel so threatening. But it rarely happens that way. Instead, they usually find a substitute for the dependency.

Carolyn nodded her head very slightly, her eyes fixed on the complex tangles of color in the Oriental rug. Then she looked up, puzzled. "So what happened?"

I smiled at the dimensions of her question and at her naïve assumption that I somehow understood it all. But if I couldn't answer the question, at least I could relate to it. "I really don't know what happened, but I could make a guess. I imagine that both of you got scared by the closeness, backed away from each other, and found a substitute closeness. He got overinvolved with the work world. You got overinvolved with the children and maybe reinvolved with your mother. But the dependency and all the other problems didn't change. They were just submerged, waiting to catch up with you."

I was beginning to sound theoretical, something I dislike in myself. One of my weaknesses as a therapist is that I intellectualize, and I was at it again. There would be plenty of time to explain the dynamics of marriage. There was a pause while Carolyn was thinking about what I said or waiting for another question to occur to her. Carl saw the opening as a way to move us on. He turned toward Claudia. "You look sort of bored," he said. "Can you say how you fit into this? How do you see the family and your part in it?"

Claudia blanched. She had become comfortable with not talking. Her eyes flared wide in fear; then she calmed a bit. She began to talk quietly, obviously trying to contain her feeling. "I don't think I have a place in this family, or at least I can't find it." I asked what she meant, and she continued. "Well, I can't seem to please anyone, at least not my parents, especially my mother." An edge of anger had come into her voice, and she glanced quickly at Carolyn. The mother shifted her posture ever so slightly, toward her daughter and toward the argument which she sensed was coming. It was as if they had been waiting for this moment, for a word that would give them permission to fight.

But Carl was not interested in their having a fight, nor was I. Not that we are against fighting—far from it—but it simply isn't productive for the family to come into a first interview of therapy and have their usual fight. They leave the interview with the feeling "What's new?" We wanted them to hold off on the fight so we could worm our way into the family's analysis of its problems. Maybe the family could come away with at least *one* new idea, as well as some impression of who we were and what we were up to.

Carl: "Can you talk about this other thing that's so hard to get a handle on—the whole family? How do you see it?"

Claudia faltered, as puzzled as everyone else had been by the

question. "I don't know what you mean. What do you want to know?"
She sounded irritated at being deterred from attacking her mother.

Carl had apparently heard something in her initial words. "You
said something about not having a place in the family. Did you mean
that literally? Do you have no territory in the family that feels like
your own? Not even your room?"

Claudia glowered at her mother. "Especially not my room." She
sounded very bitter. "My mother owns my room. Nothing in it is
mine. She is *constantly* on my back about it and the way I keep it."
Then she added as an afterthought, "And she is an incredible snoop."

This time the mother couldn't resist. She leaned toward Claudia,
her gaze locking into her daughter's, that strange anger magnet
pulling the two toward each other. "Claudia, that's simply not true.
I only complain about your room when it gets absolutely, *intolerably*
messy. And I *resent* your comment about my snooping. I have not
done that. I have just cleaned your room up occasionally, when I
couldn't stand it any longer."

Claudia, beginning to flush with anger: "And you had to read my
letters from John while you were cleaning!"

The mother sounded defensive. "Well, I was concerned about
you. You never tell me anything about your life, and as a mother I
have a right to be concerned!"

Claudia: "But not a snoop!"

Mother: "Call it what you will. I call it concern."

I moved my hand to attract their attention, reaching toward the
mother as if to grasp her wrist. "Mom, can I stop you? We'll get back
to you in a minute. Right now we need to hear some of Claudia's story
about this thing."

Carolyn was still angry at her daughter, but she was beginning to
focus the anger on me. "But she misrepresents it."

I: "I know. Each of you knows quite well how to get the other's
goat and how to get into a fight. But we're trying to find out what's
going on, and we can't do it if you insist on fighting."

The mother settled against the couch, looking depressed. "Well,
all right."

Carl had apparently been thinking over the situation while I was
breaking up the fight. He emerged from his thought and smiled at
Claudia. "Maybe that's an example of what you were talking about."

Claudia looked puzzled again. Carl does this often, saying something enigmatic to get people's attention, then explaining himself. He continued, still half-musingly: "Well, we asked you to talk about yourself, to define *your* view of the family. Which is sort of like giving you some time and space in this interview. And you seemed almost eager to turn it over to Mother or to this fight the two of you have."

Claudia: "I don't understand. You mean I gave up my chance to talk?"

Carl: "Of course. All I could hear was the fight. I couldn't hear *you* at all after the first few sentences."

Claudia struggled with what Carl was saying. "What do you mean, you couldn't hear *me*?"

Carl: "You as separate, as a separate person. You seemed lost in the fight."

Again, her eyes withdrawn as if she were looking inward, Claudia grappled with this strange idea.

Carl: "Did you feel that way? Caught up in it?"

Claudia, very quietly: "Yes, I guess I did."

I had become interested in the idea too, and I ventured in, addressing myself to Carl, "You know, it seemed to me that Mother was just as caught up in it as Claudia."

Carl nodded, continuing with Claudia. "How about that? You think Mother is as intimidated by the fight as you are?"

Claudia: "Intimidated?"

Carl: "By the need to fight with you, assuming she can't help it either. Or do you think she goes through this agony because she wants to?"

Claudia: "I think she wants to. She provokes me all the time."

I: "And you don't think you provoke her? You don't have a sense of the things *you* do that make her mad? Your step in the family dance, as it were?" Claudia didn't see it that way. She saw herself, and I think she really felt it, as the victim, the helpless one, her mother as the one with free will. She said that her mother *chose* to persecute her.

Working in close synchrony now, Carl and I explored Claudia's view of the family. It looked to us as if both mother and daughter were thoroughly helpless in the face of this fight. They were itching to get at each other at the same time that they abhorred the process of fighting. Each of them was focused on the other as the source of the trouble, and it was difficult for either to look at her own feelings and actions. We had taken Claudia's initial words about a lack of personal space in the family, had seen an example of it in the power of the fight itself, its power to "take her over," and we were using this fight as a metaphor for defining the family problem. What we wanted to do was get away from the simplistic notion that Claudia was the problem. At the least, the family should come away from the interview with a little more complicated view than *that*. We were working to show them that the real problem was family-wide and that it involved their helplessness to avoid a complex and thoroughly painful pattern or, as we phrased it to them, "a family dance." They winced when we said they were doing a "dance" because it felt to them as if they all were wearing steel shoes and dancing mostly on one another's toes.

We asked Claudia what she thought was behind the fight, something more significant than her messy room. And on that question she drew a complete blank. It had never occurred to her that there might be anything beyond the issues themselves, unless it was simply her mother's ill will toward her. Claudia was working hard to answer our questions, but as gentle as we tried to be, she still must have felt a bit accused, much as she felt at home. While she talked, she kept shifting in her chair, looking nervously at her mother and her father. She sat between them, and it was not easy for her to keep monitoring the way each responded to what she was saying. I had the sense that she was not talking to us at all, but that everything she said was directed at her parents. It is a feeling I get frequently in the beginning stages of family therapy: though the family wants to talk to an outsider, they are so caught up in their war with one another that they can't manage it. Every word is subtly targeted at someone in the family. You can't always tell who the intended recipient is, but you get to feeling used after a while, since the words are being bounced off you toward someone else.

I had that feeling as I asked Claudia about her mother's resentment. "What do you think is behind it, Claudia?" I watched Claudia's face, angry and sullen as she thought about her mother, and I realized that in spite of our civility, the interview was just barely under control. The fight between mother and daughter hung over us like a threatening cloud.

Claudia looked angry. "I don't know. I wish I did."

"What would you guess?" I asked.

As hard as she tried, Claudia could not simply discuss the issue. She had to hurl herself into it. Her voice gathered fury as she turned toward her mother. "I think she's jealous! She's afraid I'll do something, meet somebody, have a little fun. Because *she* certainly never does *anything* that I can see except ride me and ride me and ride me!" The words sprang out of her like a hand flung wildly, and they had the immediate effect on her mother of a slap in the face.

Carolyn flushed and snapped her gaze toward Claudia. "No! That is *not so!* But you want to know what it is? Do you want to know? It's your *defiance* of me. Every action you take, every look you give me is *defiant!* You act as if *you* were the parent, the one in control, instead of me. Well, I'm tired of it! *Tired* of it, do you hear!"

Her daughter yelled back at her. "And I'm tired of *you!* You think you are the only one who can get fed up! I'm fed up, *too!*" The two of them sat on the edges of their seats, straining toward each other, all the while looking frightened.

The father had been silent for a long while, but just as Carl and I began to try to get the two women to calm down, he spoke. "Now, Claudia, I can't tolerate your talking to your mother like that. You know you defy her, and she has a right to resent it." It was a pathetically weak statement, pale by contrast with the fury of the women. But it had a peculiar effect on Claudia. She had turned and bent all her anger on her mother, so the words from her father came from behind her. She tried to turn to face her father, and just as she did so, her mother said something else angry to her. For a moment Claudia wavered between her two parents, trying to decide whom to face.

Then inside her something happened; some tolerance reached its end. She turned cold white and stood up. Moving quickly, she said in real panic as she strode rapidly across the room toward the door, "I can't stand this. I have to get out of here." She slammed the door hard as she left.

The family was stunned, and Carl and I were surprised and unhappy. But we had dealt with the same situation many times before and had a sense of what to do. Our "battle for structure" would be lost if we continued without Claudia, and the interview would certainly feel weak and chaotic to the family if we stopped. We suggested gently that they go get Claudia so that we could continue. The father realized that he was the only one who could do this, and he shrugged and left. The rest of us sat there, still feeling the shock, waiting. David returned, Claudia walking in behind him, her eyes bleary and red with crying. She collapsed a bit theatrically into her chair, avoiding her mother.

Everyone looked dreadful. Claudia was limp and exhausted and still weeping a little. The father sat upset and tense on the edge of his chair, and the mother leaned against the back of the sofa, confused and still angry. Don and Laura were silent and somber. After Claudia and her father sat down, there was a very difficult silence.

Carl broke it, and as he spoke, he looked at Claudia and smiled very slightly. "Could I guess?"

Claudia managed a weak smile and a nod.

Carl turned to the father, apparently not wanting to put any more pressure on Claudia. "She was doing all right with Mother alone, but when you got into the fight, it was too much. She was caught between you and Carolyn, in the cross fire as it were. Did you see it?"

The father looked embarrassed. "I didn't then; I guess I do now."

Now I interrupted. "May I make a suggestion? Why don't you trade places with your mother, Claudia?" Mother and daughter looked at each other, both puzzled, and then did as I asked. Now the parents were sitting together in the chairs, facing us. The children were on the couches. As soon as they were in their places someone, I think it was Claudia, sighed. I added, without explanation, "That feels better to me, too."

It wasn't an ordinary seating change, just as the family's original seating position wasn't ordinary. They had unconsciously portrayed the structure of their family in the way they sat, and in changing it, I was making a symbolic shift in the family structure. Both Carl and I realized that part of Claudia's dilemma lay in her being caught between her parents, and we were working, on different levels, to help the family deal with the pattern. I was asking them to make the shift physically, while Carl was beginning to define the need for it verbally. I didn't interpret my effort to get the parents together because I wanted to leave it implicit, a sort of preconscious suggestion.

Carl went back to the father. "Could you try again? We really didn't give you much chance before to talk about your view. How do you see this situation, this conflict?"

The father didn't like this process at all. "As I said before, I have felt torn between the two sides. For a long time I felt that Claudia was the underdog in the fights, and I suppose I have defended her. I've tried to get Carolyn to ease up on her, and sometimes I've given Claudia permission to do things that her mother denied her. And I think that has created a lot of conflict."

The mother, very quietly and angrily: "It certainly has."

The father continued. "But lately I have tried, I have really tried, to support Carolyn."

I remembered then the timid way he had scolded Claudia just before she left the room, and I turned to him. "I guess I heard you 'trying' in the way you spoke to Claudia just before she ran out. You sounded hesitant, as if you were making an effort to scold her but didn't have your heart in it."

The father looked chagrined. "I guess that's right. I see my wife's point, but I also feel sorry for Claudia."

I looked at Claudia. She was listening again, reflective, appearing much calmer. I didn't want to make her say anything, so I just spoke my thought aloud to her. "Maybe that's why you panicked the way you did. You were still caught between Mom and Dad, but Dad seemed to be betraying you, going over to Mom's side."

Carl, to the father: "How about that? You think Claudia feels that you've betrayed her? That she's lost her ally?"

Father: "It's possible."

Carl, to Claudia: "How about that? Have you lost your ally?"

Claudia looked sad, drained of feeling. She nodded. "Yes. I thought I could count on Dad."

Almost simultaneously, Carl and I looked at the clock and realized that our time was almost up. First interviews are so difficult. We were trying to control things, or at least keep them from getting *out* of control, and trying to learn something about what was happening in the family, and trying to communicate some of our ideas to the family, trying in fact to invade the family with our "reinterpretation" of their dilemma—and all within an hour. As usual, we didn't have enough time.

Carl, at ease and putting away his pipe which had long ago gone out: "Hey, we've got to get to work. We're almost out of time. Let's see if we can sum up." The family was silent, waiting. Then Carl turned to me. "You want to, or shall I?"

"Go ahead," I said. "I'll sum up your summary."

Carl smiled back at me. "The younger generation always gets the last word."

He paused then, reached for his pipe, tamped some fresh tobacco in, and lit it. The smoke curled upward and out into the room like a weed drifting in a lazy stream. Though Carl may have been in a hurry to finish, he certainly didn't show it. Actually, I think this kind of ritual is very important. I'm convinced that psychotherapists are basically people engaged in the art of making suggestions; they just use fairly subtle ways of making them. Carl wasn't consciously practicing hypnosis as he lit his pipe, but the rhythmical way in which he did it had the effect of gathering everyone's attention and of calming and focusing all of us on what he was about to say. When he finally spoke, the family was sitting in a churchlike silence.

"Well, it feels like a pretty standard family triangle, and a very tight one at that." A pause while he took another puff on the pipe. "It sounds in a way as if the family has been working for a long time on a fairly serious problem, and I don't mean Claudia." Another pause. "The most serious problem seems to have been the slow, quiet drifting away of the parents from each other and the gradual cooling of the marriage. In a way, Claudia's crisis may be a way the family has evolved of trying to deal with this bigger problem of the coolness." Pause. I knew Carl was choosing his words very carefully. He could have said "deadness" instead of "coolness," but he didn't dare.

Now the father took the lead in questioning Carl. "What do you mean, Claudia's crisis is a way of dealing with our coolness? She has made things *worse* between us."

Carl: "Yes, I know. Let me finish." The father shifted in his chair, and Carl went on. "It sounds as if the basic thing that has happened is that the two of you, the parents, agreed to get Claudia between you as a way of helping you heat up the marriage. Dad could team up with Claudia, and Mom would get jealous and very angry. Then Mom and Claudia agreed to heat up their fight as a way of finding out what it was like to really fight things out." Carl glanced gently at Claudia. "And maybe you were just trying to teach Mom how to fight!" Claudia smiled weakly back, looking embarrassed.

I was impatient with listening, and I wanted to add something. I spoke to Claudia. "I think the really painful part, though, is that the family intuitively agreed to escalate things to the point where Mom and Dad *had* to get together if they were to cope with you. Dad even said it was happening—he was beginning to support his wife against you."

Carl replied in a single syllable, but it had an emphasis to it; he really meant it. "Yep." He glanced at me. "Claudia sure is the family Christ, fighting to get her parents together and to get them all to a therapist. And it's a big job."

I realized that we were elevating Claudia to the status of family saint and making her parents sound like villains. I spoke to the father. "Of course, the real accomplishment may be that the family as a whole agreed to create a situation desperate enough so that something had to change. Agreeing to push things that far takes real guts."

Carl: "That's right. Most families let things rock along unhappily forever. They never see the possibilities of escaping what Thoreau called quiet desperation."

The family looked a little puzzled that we were praising them for being desperate, but we were serious. Their unconscious decision to escalate their conflict is probably one that is made in the context of the availability of outside help. They tried to resolve their problems within the family, using the resources they had. When this attempt failed, rather than settle into the resigned hopelessness that many families feel, the Brices began an escalation process that was intuitively calculated to bring in someone from the outside world. Trite as this sounds, the conflict was a call for help from the entire family.

Because a family comes into the therapy with such a sense of failure, it is important to show them that they are unconsciously "up to something" that is basically constructive. Their *method* of trying to grow has its obvious faults, but the will to live is intact. It is, in fact, the driving force behind their crisis.

We were winding up. Carl had taken his appointment book out, and I reached for my briefcase to get mine. Don had sat quietly through the storm of the last half of the interview and now came out of his reverie. He spoke to Carl. "Wow. Do you do this all day?"

Carl, smiling: "Yep."

Don: "How do you stand it? Don't you get tired of all this fighting?"

Carl: "Nope. I like it. I find it very exciting to be in the midst of people's trying to grow. And you know why?"

Don: "No, why?"

Carl: "Because it pushes *me* to grow. I'm here for me, not for you guys. This is just part of my plot to try to be a more alive person. You didn't think it was for charity, did you?"

Don, a slight smile crossing his face: "I thought it was for money."

Carl: "Touché. But only partly true. I would have made more money if I had stuck to being a real doctor, delivering babies and stuff. Hey! We've got to quit."

The family looked relieved, and you could see them warming visibly to Carl's banter with Don. Now we were being social again, leaving the symbolic and intense inner-family world, returning to our ordinary roles.

Carl turned cheerfully to the father. "Well, do you want to meet again?" He spoke with apparent confidence and with complete neutrality, as if he really didn't care whether or not they came back. Some therapists would either simply assume that the family wanted to return or even try to persuade them to continue, becoming in effect salespeople for their own work. But if the family senses the therapist is trying to rope them into therapy, they immediately become suspicious: "Why does he need us? Doesn't he have enough patients? Is he overinvolved? Has he some personal need that only *we* can satisfy?" And they back away. Carl and I try to be as effective as we can in each hour, and when that's over, we leave the question of continuing completely up to the family. Otherwise, the parents begin to wonder if we are just like *their* parents—possessive. If people are really going to get deeply into therapy, they need to know that they can escape easily. So at the end of every hour we implicitly give the family the option of not making another appointment.

David and Carolyn Brice looked at each other askance, not knowing what the other thought about continuing. He took the step. "I would say yes." His wife nodded, relieved. She was right to be relieved, since fathers are so often afraid of the process of psychotherapy and are reluctant to continue.

We found a time for the next appointment, but not without some fumbling with schedules and contingencies, the inevitable hassle of trying to assemble seven people, *any* seven people, in a world of complicated commitments.

The family was collecting their paraphernalia when I interrupted. "Could I caution you about something?" They looked startled. "Try not to carry this fight on at home. Save it for in here, so we can help you with it, and so we can get to be a part of it." I smiled broadly. "Don't fight!"

The father smiled, too. "Do you hear that, girls?" He glanced fondly at his daughter; Claudia, after hesitating for a moment, grimaced and stuck her tongue out at him. The mother saw it, and she too managed a smile.

I turned to Carl, smiling. "And that, *Dr.* Whitaker, is my last word."

And then they left, the father shaking hands with both of us, Laura handing over her pencils, waving as she backed out of the door.

Cautioning them not to fight at home was important, because often families will take home from the first interview a sort of vague message: "Be more open with each other." Then they get into a really bad, destructive fight and come in black and blue to the next interview, saying, "See, it doesn't work." If we could get them to do their fighting in the interview, we could help make it a more constructive process. We would also get involved much more quickly than if we had to sit and listen to a blow-by-blow retelling of last week's altercation.

It is an anxious step, inviting a family to bring all their long-accumulated tension into your office. But then, where else can they take it?

CHAPTER 3

Origins

Several months after we had completed therapy, I sat down with David Brice in his law office and we talked about the therapy. We reviewed the time period before the Brices began family therapy: the crisis that led to their seeking help, the brief individual therapy Claudia received, and the eventual referral to Carl. While this information had been solicited during the first telephone contacts and their first "history" visit, and while I knew the general outline of events, it was the first time I had had a chance to focus directly on the family referral.

As he spoke about Claudia's problems—the running away, the great stress between her and her mother, the "ringing" in her ears, the despair and the fantasies of death in her poetry, the confused "philosophy" which she had formulated—David's face grew tense, remembering. He was recalling the feeling of increasing desperation in the family, a sense that the crisis was out of control and intensifying. Finally, he and Carolyn faced the fact that they were helpless to change this process and began to look for outside help. They went to their family physician, and he suggested that they take Claudia to a child psychiatrist whom he knew. It was a logical step, and having this referral afforded the family an immediate—if short-lived—sense of relief.

Claudia went to the psychiatrist reluctantly. She felt badgered and coerced at home, and to be sent to a therapist, albeit one specializing in the problems of adolescents, seemed like another in a long series of indignities. Still, she went. She would sit morosely in the big chair, saying little. What she did say, however, disturbed him, and he asked a psychologist colleague to do a complete evaluation of her, using a standard battery of psychological tests. Eventually he and the psychologist sat down with Claudia's parents and gave them a lengthy report.

The report was somber, and though it was delivered with concern and sensitivity, it frightened them. The psychiatrist and psychologist reported that Claudia was in all probability suffering from schizophrenia. They defined schizophrenia as an illness, one that was admittedly poorly understood and with, at best, a guarded prognosis. If Claudia recovered, they said, it would probably be after years of intensive treatment. They were sorry; they understood how upsetting this news must be to the family. They recommended that Claudia continue in individual therapy for an indefinite period of time.

David and Carolyn went home depressed. But David was angry as well. Something in the whole picture didn't fit. The Claudia he knew didn't seem that hopeless: she was very bright, she was obviously fighting for things that she believed in, and in spite of the turmoil, she was still at times the strong, forceful person he had always admired. He refused to accept so bleak a prognosis. For a time, however, he kept to himself his misgivings about Claudia's treatment.

Claudia would go to the therapist, talk a little, and come home. Then she would go to her room or out with her friends. The sense of alienation within the family continued; there was less fighting between mother and daughter, but no more warmth. Then Claudia began to get angry with the psychiatrist; she would be late for her appointment, or she would refuse to go, or she would pretend to go and not show up. Some of the anger she felt toward the family began to be transferred to the therapist, but instead of communicating this anger to him directly, Claudia again acted it out, for the most part nonverbally. Finally, she complained aloud to her father about the whole process. "All he does is ask me nosy questions! He wants to know about my *fantasies*, whatever those are, and my dreams. Strange stuff like that. Wants to talk about my *childhood*, and about my *feelings* about everything, but especially about you guys. It's really weird."

Part of the problem was that Claudia was very, very sensitive to pressure from adults. She felt pressured by her parents, and the therapy felt like more pressure. She began to see the therapist as a special kind of policeman who had been hired by her parents to "shape her up." The fact that he had met several times alone with her parents made her doubly suspicious; she wasn't sure she could say anything to him in confidence.

As Claudia pulled back from the individual therapy, the battles started all over again. This time they focused on Claudia's going to therapy. Mother would push, and Claudia would push back. As Claudia's relationship with her mother worsened once more, the family's sense of desperation increased because their attempt at help was failing. One night after Claudia had run out of the house, crying, David felt a great wave of despair sweep over him. "It just seemed like the end, as if my family was collapsing before my eyes and there was nothing I could do about it. For the first time I had a fantasy of killing myself—I felt that helpless, that bleak. Then, all of a sudden, I thought of my psychiatrist friend, Ed, and I wondered why I had never thought of him before." Ed and David had been neighbors and casual friends for some time, but David had apparently "forgotten" what Ed did for a living. He called him immediately, at one o'clock in the morning, "and Ed must have heard the urgency in my voice because he said he would come right over."

The two men talked for several hours. Ed had been trained in the Department of Psychiatry at Wisconsin, and he had had some experience in family therapy. He explained at length that he thought Claudia's problems had to do with the family stresses. He treaded lightly, but since he knew the family, he was able to point out what some of those stresses were. David listened hard. At the end of their talk, about four in the morning, the psychiatrist suggested family therapy and recommended they see Carl. He couldn't see the family himself because he felt too close to them to ensure the necessary professional distance. David and Carolyn talked at length the next day, and she volunteered to call Carl. Carl was reluctant because Claudia already had a therapist, but after a phone conversation with the child psychiatrist, who was discouraged and said his work with Claudia was going badly, it was agreed that Carl would see the family. And so we began.

It is tempting for the reader to assume that in seeking out a family therapist, the Brice family was trying a new *technique* in treating their emotionally disturbed daughter. And while they did look at it in this way originally, a family therapist has a very different view. In giving up on Claudia's individual therapy and calling a family therapist, the Brice family made what we consider a radical shift. They did not merely elect a new maneuver for solving *Claudia's* problems. The whole family stumbled into an approach that called into question some of their most basic assumptions about individual autonomy, about causation and motivation in human relationships, and about the nature of psychological growth. In entering family therapy, they leaped a wide conceptual and methodological gap that has developed in the mental health professions, one with profound implications for mental health care. The transition didn't merely occur by placing a telephone call, of course; it took a great deal of effort for them to make the conceptual change.

What is so different about family therapy? As we concluded our talk in his office, David seemed to be grappling with this very question. "Well, one day after we had been working for a month or so, I found myself sitting back and just watching what was going on. I was thinking about the individual therapy that both Carolyn and I had during the early years of our marriage, and I wondered what was so different about this family business. We were all there together, of course, but it was more than that. Suddenly it occurred to me that a big difference was the way you guys *thought* about people and relationships. I mean, the two of you have some interesting ideas, if a little strange at times." We grinned at each other before he resumed. "But there was also something—a kind of electricity— going on between us Brices. Always. And it always felt intense, as though something important were at stake. What struck me that day was that this process that was happening between us was bigger than all of us, that it had a life of its own. I remember the moment so clearly, sensing the power in that room and feeling a little anxious in the face of it."

If we are to sharpen this definition of family therapy as being so "different" from individual therapy, we need to look at its origins. And no description of a contemporary therapeutic approach can have the necessary perspective without at least some reference to the source of the entire psychotherapeutic movement: the pioneering work of Sigmund Freud.

The essential discovery of psychoanalysis is that every person's rational orientation to the world is underlain by a very powerful and primitive nonrational component, the old animal brain of our distant ancestors. Freud felt that this nonrational component not only supplied the motive force for most human activity, but also dominated much of human action and thought. Outside of conscious awareness, this primitive brain function, which Freud called the id, tricked us into doing its will. We had always felt that reason controlled the individual; Freud said that reason was controlled *by* this other part of the person, an inconsiderate beast that demanded for man his essential needs: food, water, sleep, sexual satisfaction, aggression.

Freud pointed to a dichotomy between the primitive urgency of an individual's "unconscious" needs and the demands of social living. Society required that man delay gratification, that he plan, think, and accommodate himself to others' needs. We had been so long in discovering the unconscious need function, Freud postulated, because the individual had had to develop very powerful *inhibiting* functions in order to be able to live as a social being. Freud spent much time describing these inhibiting functions: some he felt were deliberate and conscious, and these he termed suppression; some he felt were unconscious, and these he termed repression. Through these restraining mechanisms, the individual was able to delay gratification, to hold at bay these powerful urges while working at finding "civilized" ways of satisfying them.

Freud went even further in classifying the inhibiting functions: one function he identified as similar to the "conscience"—a largely nonrational adoption of social mores and codes "because the parents said so." The child blindly internalized the moral teachings of the parents because of the power of the parental model. Another function he saw as a more rational, analytic one, an intelligent attempt to accommodate the individual's needs based on a realistic appraisal of the environment and its demands. This rational function Freud thought was the strongest asset of the personality, though subject to occasional overthrow by the nonrational components of the mind.

Freud's access to the unconscious mind was through the disturbed individuals who were his patients, and his attempts to discover what went wrong in these lives make fascinating reading still. He was convinced, and probably accurately, that the most powerful determinants of personality are active during childhood. It is then that our character and our personality take their unique shapes.

There is an interesting story about how Freud developed his ideas concerning the trends in childhood that lead to emotional disturbance.

Some of Freud's most crucial early work focused on the condition termed hysteria, in which the patient often had symptoms such as paralysis or deafness that had no physical cause. Influenced by Jean Charcot's view that hysteria was due to early traumatic experience, Freud formulated the thesis that many of these patients had been sexually molested or seduced in childhood. Freud found in his patients' confessions what he felt was ample evidence that these events had actually occurred. Furthermore, when patients "uncovered" these painful memories, they often improved dramatically.

After Freud had published some of his ideas about hysteria, he made a shocking discovery. Some of the "seductions" which his patients reported had in fact never taken place. Faced with this embarrassing evidence, Freud was at first bewildered and depressed. Then, with characteristic tenacity, he rethought the entire problem. His brilliant solution led him to assert that the source of the patient's dilemma lay not in actual events, but in the motives that prompted them to "invent" these seductions. He postulated that children have sexual drives and feelings and that much psychological torment later in life lies in an effort to conceal and defend against these impulses.

Disillusioned with the influence of the environment, Freud began to place strong emphasis on the *internal motive state* of the patient. External conditions, such as parental training that led to an overly severe conscience, were still deemed important. But increasingly Freud focused on the inherited, biological drives in the individual and on the defenses which he or she developed to cope with these "socially unacceptable" drives. The intricacies of how the mind dealt with these polarities *within its own system* preoccupied Freud for the remainder of his career, and his elaboration of the defenses, the fancy footwork which the mind must perform as it steps delicately between innate desire and social conformity, remains perhaps his most brilliant achievement.

Freud was a practicing neurologist, and most of his ideas were developed as he attempted to help his emotionally disturbed patients. At the same time that he was evolving a revolutionary view of humanity, he was also creating a new method of treatment: psychoanalysis. This treatment grew out of his early work with hypnosis,

and it was designed to help the patient recall—through free association and the reporting of dreams—the "forbidden" material of the
unconscious. His basic assumption was that if the patient could become conscious of, understand, and "forgive" particularly his sexual
motives, he could then search rationally for satisfaction of his needs
rather than deny the existence of these virtually irrepressible emotions. The tyranny of repression could then be lifted, and the relief
of biological "pressure" through greater life pleasure should cure the
symptom.

As this family therapist looks back on Freud's work, I share the
admiration of many others for his bold intelligence. I can understand
his passion to explore, once he discovered its existence, the murky
and fascinating realm of the unconscious, the very foundation of
man's psychological world. But while I remain dazzled by the search-
light brilliance of his mind, I regret that he did not also turn it in
other directions. He looked deep *inside* the person; he hardly looked
at all at the social environment.

Rereading Freud's case histories, I am surprised that he could
avoid seeing that his disturbed patients were members of disturbed
families and that while they might not have been *physically* seduced
or assaulted by these families, they were nevertheless subject to often
subtle psychological pressures from them. Once Freud turned away
from external forces as a causative factor in neurosis, he never looked
in that direction again. Perhaps he was so chagrined at having been
wrong that he could not compromise his thinking; he had to revise
it entirely. Thus we are left with a strange sense of the man's naïveté
in the world of interaction between people, especially within the
family.

Modern historians have begun to fill in some of the unexplored
familial context in Freud's own cases. *Soul Murder*, a fascinating
work by Morton Schatzman, demonstrates very convincingly that
the psychotic "delusions of grandeur" suffered by one of Freud's
most famous cases are directly traceable to the *actual* persecution
which this patient endured in childhood. Texts by the patient's father, a well-known child-rearing expert of his day, outline all manner
of blatantly sadistic "techniques" which were undoubtedly practiced
upon the child, which appeared vividly in his later psychotic "delusions," and which Freud explained by postulating complex *internal*
constructs in the patient. Freud's view of paranoia is still widely held

today, and it is one that largely confines the dilemma to the patient. But perhaps the paranoid patient is being truthful: at some time in life, he *has* been a real victim of persecution at the hands of his family.

How unfortunate that Freud's exploration of early family experience as a possible cause of emotional disturbance ended in disillusionment. If he had only interviewed the parents! If he had only looked harder, he would certainly have confirmed not just the power of early family incidents, but the continuing influence of the family throughout the individual's life cycle. In the process, he would have dramatically shortened our quest for better theories and better treatment. If one thinks about the implications in such a move, however, one wonders if Freud's focus on the individual was perhaps all society could tolerate at the time. Exploring the unconscious mind was threatening enough! Perhaps Freud unwittingly spared himself the additional storm of controversy which would have occurred if he had turned his attention toward the entire family.

A great deal has since happened that has made us more aware of the larger context of human life. The ecological movement has sensitized us to the interdependence of living systems, and the new sciences of sociology, anthropology, and psychology have helped us understand the interrelatedness of human social systems. Family therapy is merely one wave in this new tide of consciousness of the interconnectedness of life.

Yet in spite of these changes, the power of Freud's example still dominates the practice of psychotherapy. In turning away from the family, Freud took generations of therapists with him. Or rather, they followed him. What besides the fear of violating Freud's example could have induced Claudia Brice's first therapist to ignore all that was occurring in her family life and to concentrate solely on her? How could so many otherwise able therapists avoid seeing the profound implications which the family has in the lives of their patients? They have betrayed Freud's sense of quest and inquiry by following his example so slavishly, for so long, and with so little question.

There is more to regret in Freud's thought: the tendency to look down upon people as well as only inside them. In Freud's day Darwin's theories had recently linked the human being with the animal kingdom, and science was busy explaining human behavior by reducing it to simpler functions in animals and in the physical world.

Society was becoming industrialized, and the machine was a dominant metaphor in scientific thinking. The mind was postulated as indeed machinelike, an intricately whirring device of motives and countermotives, all designed to keep asleep—and sated—the beast within. Still to be discovered was the science of the higher person: the psychological study of creativity, of curiosity, of the drives toward growth and integration of the personality, of our instincts for parenting and caring. The image of the person became that of a creature content with homeostatic somnolence, all nobler efforts—art, music, poetry, thought itself—merely contrivances to placate the not-so-human animal.

This scornful attitude toward humanity that is inherent in Freudian thought has been exacerbated by the almost coincidental fact that Freud was a physician and worked within the medical tradition of diagnosis and treatment. Though it is a tradition that richly deserves its place of honor in our society, medicine (and its stepchild, psychiatry) sometimes unwittingly collaborates with a society that treats emotional disturbance punitively. Look at Claudia. She was pressured and scapegoated by her family to the point of desperation. Then she was sent to a therapist, given the label of schizophrenic, and pressured further to go for treatment. The process of diagnosis and treatment felt to her like a further form of punishment, and indeed, one can understand her objections. Why take people who are already under stress and put them under further pressure to change in treatment when it is not they who are the problem? Claudia did not have a disease inside her life; she was surrounded by a troubled family. By trying to treat her in isolation from the real source of her problems, the first psychiatrist was unknowingly collaborating with the scapegoating process in the family; he was, in fact, a well-meaning agent of that process.

One final regret. Freud had hoped that the patient's awareness and insight would lead to cure. As Claudia's scorn for her first therapist's analytic probes might indicate, insight is often a feeble tool in the face of life's pressing urgency. All the major new therapeutic approaches in recent years have arisen out of a basic dissatisfaction among therapists with long-term, individual, insight-oriented therapy, the basic derivative of psychoanalysis. We know all too well by now the syndrome of the patient who is interminably in therapy, understands a great deal about himself, and doesn't change. Our misgivings about this approach to therapy are also being confirmed by a growing body of research that indicates that it is not very effective. While insight was very helpful to Freud the scientist (and thus informs us all), the patient needs more.

CHAPTER 4

The Concept of the System

In the early 1950s a group of researchers on the staff of a large mental hospital became interested in an observation they made about the behavior of schizophrenic patients. Although the schizophrenic is supposedly responding to his own internally warped view of the world and is reputedly "out of contact with reality," these observers noted that when a patient's mother visited the hospital, the patient would often be acutely upset on the ward for days afterward. They wondered what was happening between the patient and the mother. Obviously the acute disturbance didn't come out of the patient's fantasy life. So they brought schizophrenic patients and their mothers together in the hospital and observed them interacting over a period of time.

They were fascinated by what they saw. Far from being out of contact, the patient was deeply involved in an intricate and disturbed pattern of communication with the mother. One of the interesting findings was that communication seemed to take place on two levels—verbal and nonverbal—and that in the case of the schizophrenic and his mother, the messages on each level were often in conflict.

For example, the schizophrenic son sees his mother coming toward him on visiting day at the hospital, and he smiles broadly, glad to see her. He opens his arms to give her a hug. Mother allows her son to embrace her, but she is uneasy about the physical contact and stiffens slightly, though her words to the son are the same warm words of greeting that he offers her. The son, sensing his mother's *nonverbal* rejection, backs away from her. The mother then says, coolly, "What's wrong? Aren't you glad to see me?" Now confused, the son gazes vacantly.

The son in this situation was in what the researchers began to call a double bind—trapped between two conflicting messages. If he responded to the verbal warmth, he had to ignore the nonverbal coldness. When he responded to the nonverbal message, his mother denied its validity. They couldn't talk about the ambivalence in their relationship, and the son couldn't avoid responding in a way that placed him in conflict. So he became confused in order to deal with the ambiguities of his situation.

And the researchers were off, into an exciting arena in which much schizophrenic behavior began to make sense in terms of some very disturbed communication patterns between mother and child. While this particular research developed into what has become known as the communication school of family researchers and therapists, there was during this time focus from a number of other theoretical viewpoints on the mother-child relationship. "We discovered," says Jay Haley, one of the most astute researchers in the family field, "that schizophrenics had mothers!" And for a considerable time the mother-child relationship was viewed as *the* culprit in "mental illness." One psychiatrist used the term "schizophrenogenic mother" —that is, the mother who creates a schizophrenic—and another psychiatrist used the term the "perverse mother." Mothers, of course, loved this period of psychiatric history.

Then the researchers discovered that disturbances in the father-child relationship were also important. Many of the fathers in these families were very distant from and uninvolved with their children, allowing the mother's overinvolvement with the children to hold sway. Why were the fathers so uniformly distant and passive? The researchers weren't sure, but it was clear, as Haley said, "that schizophrenics had fathers, too."

Then a most interesting observation was made. As the families of schizophrenics were studied, it became evident that in almost every case there were long-standing and severe marital difficulties between the parents. Furthermore, the psychotic episodes of the "patient" seemed to be related to the cycles of marital conflict. The parents would get into a battle, and as it began to intensify, the son (or daughter) would begin to become psychotic. Once hospitalized, the couple would call off their war in order to be, again, the parents of "a sick child." Actually, their child's psychosis seemed to have a very practical result: it helped the couple deal with their conflict by giving them a way of avoiding it. The family's very stability seemed to be maintained by the periodic "illnesses."

Through this research the scientists began to think of the family in a new way. Rather than look at it as a collection of individuals, they began to view the family as having almost the same kind of organized integrity that the biological organism has. The family functioned as an entity, as a "whole," with its own structure, rules, and goals.

Another way of saying this is that the observers began to see the family as a *system*. And what is a system? Well, brace yourself. A family theorist, Lynn Hoffman, comments: "The question of what a system is is a vexing one. The most common definition seems to be: any entity the parts of which co-vary interdependently with one another, and which maintains equilibrium in an error-activated way." Vexing indeed: a "something" with parts, these parts behaving in a predictable relationship with one another, thus creating a pattern that maintains a stable equilibrium by making changes in itself.

Perhaps an example borrowed from Paul Watzlawick, another family therapist, will make the systems concept clearer. Assume that we are studying the population of rabbits in a western state. After taking counts for a considerable length of time, we notice that there are regular undulations in the frequency curve. Now there is a bounty crop, now a scarcity. The undulations in the curve are so regular that we must wonder about the cause. We can continue to study rabbits to find the reason for the fluctuation, or we can look at other variables, other influences surrounding the rabbit, that may be affecting its population figures.

After a proper period of casting about, we hit on the idea of charting the population of foxes in the area. We find, interestingly, a similar rhythm in the fox population—except that the foxes are plentiful when the rabbits are scarce, and vice versa. Finally, we realize what has been happening: as the plentiful rabbits are harvested by the foxes, the food supply of the foxes declines and they in turn eventually decline. The decline in foxes permits the population of rabbits to expand again, but then the foxes again become more abundant as their food supply increases. And so the cycle is repeated, over and over again.

An interesting transition in thought takes place in this example, one that also took place in the way the researchers thought about the origin of schizophrenia. In both instances the investigators went from studying an individual or an individual species to studying a set of relationships that seemed to be influencing the subject. We shifted from thinking about one species, the rabbit, to examining a configuration of relationships within an ecological system. And the hospital researchers shifted their focus from the individual schizophrenic patient to the patterns of interaction in the individual's family, discovering that the patterns of acute disturbance in the patient, like the fluctuations in the rabbit population, made much more sense when examined in relationship with other "outside" forces.

Of course, the fox-rabbit cycle is only one part of a much larger system on the prairie that includes the soil, the weather, the insects, the other animals and plants of the area; and the family is a much more complicated system than a husband-wife-child triangle. But the idea of the system is the common referent, and it is a very exciting idea.

The systems concept is interesting because it gives us a method of conceptualizing a great deal of complexity. The entire universe, in fact, can be thought of as a collection of systems. Within this universe of systems, there are two major types: living and nonliving. A nonliving system, such as a planetary system or a weather system, is not "dead," in the sense that it is active and exhibits what might be called in a general sense "behavior." Planets move, and weather fronts sometimes make their presence known very forcefully. But there are dramatic differences between these nonliving systems, whose behavior can often be predicted from the laws of physics, and living systems, whose behavior retains many elusive processes.

All systems are organized, and they maintain some kind of balance or equilibrium. Our planetary system has a precise order, and its equilibrium is maintained by well-understood physical forces. Even weather systems maintain a certain balance over time.

Living systems are organized, too, but in very different ways. Look at a very simple organism: the amoeba. It is a system, but a system with clear boundaries. Within these boundaries there is an organization of sorts. This organization is active, and it "works" to maintain its structure. If the amoeba encounters a hostile chemical or organism, it may dodge or attempt to elude the intruder in order to protect the integrity of its life.

This is an interesting characteristic of living systems, one which we will find useful in later discussion: they make changes in their own behavior based on information about their environment. This mechanism, called feedback, permits the system to alter its activity, its structure, its direction, in order to further its own goals. Of course, nonliving systems can operate according to feedback, too—as in the rocket system that alters its course on the basis of information gathered concerning altitude, speed, and direction. But these systems can do so only if carefully instructed by human beings.

The comparison may seem strained, but the systems concept allows one to compare the simple organism like the amoeba with the more complex system like the family. And indeed, there are similarities: the family has boundaries, and within the boundaries it has an organization which its members work very actively to maintain. The researchers we cited were pointing to a psychotic episode as one way the family might "adapt," thereby maintaining its stability.

An interesting aspect of systems is that they are organized *hierarchically*. For example, one can look at the individual person as a system. As one looks "down" from the level of this system, one sees that it includes a number of *subsystems* in a decreasing order of size and complexity:

PERSON OR ORGANISM
organ system
organ
molecule
atom
atomic particle

Of course, one need not stop with this hierarchy. One can look "upward" into still more complex systems which influence the individual person. Just focusing on some of the other human systems to which the individual is related expands the chain of influence considerably:

world community of nations
national alliance
nation
state
county
city or community

community subgroup (work, friendship)
extended family
nuclear family
PERSON OR ORGANISM
organ system
organ
cell
molecule
atom
atomic particle

While this rather crude hierarchy of systems leaves out much that influences the individual person (weather or food supply, for example), it illustrates a perspective, one in which the individual is part of a vastly complex chain of influence. Generally, the larger, more complex systems tend to exert control over the smaller and less complex systems. But influence moves up and down the entire chain, and if we are to understand human behavior, we must integrate knowledge from many different levels. The individual is influenced from "below," for example, by a genetic code which originates at the atomic and molecular level. But he is also influenced by learned patterns which are transmitted by the social network which hovers "over" and surrounds him. And within these two large spheres of influence—physical and social—there are many other component influences acting on the person.

A wife sits down to a family dinner. True, strong physical needs compel her to eat. But so many of the forces impinging upon her are social forces. Her table manners are learned from the society, as is the role definition which led her, rather than her husband, to prepare the meal. Other things influence her: she may be angry at her husband for being late for the meal, and she may avoid speaking to him even though she is aware that he was kept late at the office for legitimate reasons. But her anger flares unusually strongly at her five-year-old son, whose squirming irritates her. Both husband and wife may be silently anxious about the family's finances as they eat, brooding about the rising cost of groceries and other essentials. The tension at the table may be increased by a telephone call from the husband's mother that interrupts the meal, edging up the wife's anger. At the end of the meal the teenage daughter gets a telephone call from her boyfriend, and she wants to be excused from her chores so she can go to what the mother is sure is an X-rated movie. The wife-and-mother, who has not been out in the evening for a month and who by now thoroughly resents what she says to herself is her "housewife role," finally loses her temper.

The pressures on the wife and on the whole family appear to swirl around them in a very chaotic manner. The wife may feel that she is being repeatedly stung by invisible insects, so randomly intrusive do these tensions seem. But if one looks more closely, all these tensions operate on certain *levels* in the hierarchy we listed above.

Today the largest societal system pressuring the family is perhaps the inflationary world economy, but there are other systems influencing it as well: the work system, the teenage peer group, the extended family, and, of course, the dynamics of the nuclear family, including subsystems within the family such as the mother-daughter relationship or husband-wife relationship. And the fact that there are conflicts within the larger society influences this family. The Arab-Israeli conflict has a bearing on the family through the price of oil set by the Arab world, adding significantly to world inflation. Ideological conflict within the society concerning the woman's role, the man's role, the degree of independence of adolescents, questions of censorship —all these issues that are unresolved by the society bear upon the individual family's conflicts. When the mother wonders whether to allow the daughter to go to the movies, she can turn to no sure guideline, no consensus in the society. She can't even turn to her husband because she is having a fight with him.

Parceling out some of these tensions as systems problems and as problems operating on different levels gives the observer a way of simplifying some of the complexity and perhaps a means for setting some priorities in solving the problems. This family might resolve one of its mealtime problems, for example, by becoming a little less of an "open system" during the meal hour. They could take the phone off the hook. The other problems might take a little more work, but they could be approached, too, if one subsystem were taken at a time, probably beginning with the smallest and most accessible systems: the nuclear family relationships.

Once one begins to think about systems, they seem to be everywhere: at work; at home; in the community; in the world at large. One's body is a system, as is the clique of gossipers at the office, as is the ecology of the garden or the lawn, as is our—now we notice it!—world economy.

It is daring and exciting to see groups of scientists from different backgrounds finding their interests converging in an attempt to develop a general theory of systems. Imagine, a theoretical structure that would allow science to unify the behavior of, say, political systems with atomic behavior! That day is far, far away, but the work is in motion: biologists are contributing, as are engineers and space scientists, sociologists and anthropologists, economists, mathematicians, physicists, chemists, and many others. For *all* these systems have certain properties in common, and a theory of systems may be a way in which all scientific knowledge can be structured and related.

But this is a very big jump: from a few behavioral scientists interested in family relationships and schizophrenia to general systems theory. While therapists today find general systems theory a very helpful framework for thinking about their work, the background for this shift in focus didn't occur overnight, and it didn't happen simply from the study of a few patients labeled schizophrenic and their families. Researchers and clinicians alike *groped* their way toward the idea that families were somehow influential in the lives of psychiatric patients and the later realization that these families behaved as systems. And they groped in many different ways.

Research continued, of course, and the interest in schizophrenia was crucial in this effort. While the dream, in Freud's words, provided "the royal road to the unconscious," the complexities of the schizophrenic's family provided a model for thinking about covert influences in the family in general. The schizophrenic's family became a royal road into the subtle, sometimes terrifying interior of the family. But research included other kinds of families, and a wide variety of questions were asked in the research; many questions are still being pursued.

Clinicians also became much more aware of the family. Some therapists discovered the family system by being bruised by it. They had some of the same experiences that Carl and I have had: working with an individual and being totally defeated by the family's power over the patient; or seeing a client "recover," only to witness all the progress undermined by the family; or treating the scapegoat child "successfully," only to find another child in the family dragged into the role; or working with an individual patient and feeling the fury of the family's sudden explosion just as the patient improved. All too often divorce seemed to follow successful individual therapy with one of the spouses. This kind of learning about the family system was powerful and painful. The therapist learned about the family by being allied with one person or one subsystem in the family, and by being literally induced into the family's conflicts. Being tossed around by the family is one way of learning about its force, and the lessons are indelible.

But some clinicians didn't take defeats like this passively. Feeling the power of the family, they began to bring family members into the therapy process. If they had access to the family, perhaps they would have more power to influence it. A psychiatrist encountered his patient's family at the hospital bed, and he was intrigued by what he saw happening between them. He started meeting with the family regularly right there at the bedside. A worker in a child guidance clinic began meeting with a mother and child; then, sensing that the problems between the parents were contributing to the child's problems, he brought the child and its parents together. Another psychiatrist had heard *enough* about his patient's husband, and he asked her to bring him to the next interview. The husband came, and soon the doctor was meeting regularly with the couple and listening to their problems. Then he got tired of hearing about the children and asked the couple to bring them in too. In many different settings and in many different situations, therapists discovered the power of the family and assembled them in order to try to be more competent in the face of this power.

These therapists did not stop with the nuclear family. Some therapists today work with "networks" of as many as thirty or forty people, including friends, neighbors, extended family, employers, past therapists, schoolmates, and other involved people. But it was when the nuclear or immediate family was finally cajoled into treatment that the therapists found a new level of energy and excitement in the consulting room. And they began to learn a lot about families.

As therapists and researchers started to interview and study a wide range of families, their initial reaction to these families was a fairly uniform "Ye gods, *everybody* in the family is sick!" The language was still the medical model, but the idea was interesting. Investigators had to poke around a bit to discover that the "perfect"

older sibling of the "disturbed patient" was really a very tense, troubled youngster beneath the veneer of conformity and achievement.
And they had to look for a while to see that the wife of the alcoholic
was not the paragon of health and virtue she maintained she was.
Once they looked, they found stress from all directions in those
families in which a single individual had sought psychological help.
*And it didn't seem to matter what the complaint was, or the tradi-
tional diagnosis.* Troubles, it seemed, came in families.

Of course, this conclusion in itself didn't mean very much. It said
nothing about what *caused* the troubles. Unhappy people came from
families where there were a lot of other unhappy people. So what?
Well, a little more looking produced the idea that what was wrong,
or at least a major portion of it, was in fact quite visible. It was not
buried in the deep complexes and superegos and egos of the individuals but was evident in plain daylight to the therapists. It lay in
the family system: in the way the family was organized; in the way
its members communicated; in the way they worked out their daily
interactions. Like the communication between the schizophrenic
patient and his mother, once the therapists looked at what was happening *between the people,* some formerly mysterious things began
to make much more sense.

As these investigators tried to be more specific about what was
wrong, or inefficient, or unproductive—and increasingly this became
the focus rather than "sick" or "well"—they had to develop a whole
new way of viewing people and a new language system for describing what they saw. They had to look at the way the family was
organized, at their implicit "rules," at their communication patterns,
and at much, much more. We will examine this new style of thinking
about the individual as influenced by family process as we look further at the Brice family and at other family situations.

But while the investigators' focus shifted from individual dynamics to family process, an awkward problem remained. What to do
with the individual "patient," the person whose complaint first called
attention to the troubled family? Where did he or she fit? Well, the
easiest thing was to label this person a simple victim of family
stresses. The identified patient was family scapegoat, whipping boy,
Christ—someone who agreed to suffer openly the stress of the entire
family so that the family could remain stable.

Even this limited idea was interesting, and as its scope dawned on investigators, they asked themselves, a little horrified that they could have missed it for so long: *are all individual psychotherapy patients simply scapegoats of family stress?* The harder they looked, the more it seemed possible. While the idea was, as we shall see, too simple to be entirely true, it was close enough.

Because if it were true, if every person who thought of seeing a therapist was really responding to stresses in his or her family system, then—at least ideally—every therapy patient should be a family. If the problem was the family, the family should be the focus of therapy. The family, in fact, should be the patient. And for a professional world accustomed to thinking of individual distress, this would mean a radical restructuring.

Imagine the analyst as he tried to visualize his patient's family all somehow perched like pigeons on his couch.

Or the medically oriented therapist who uses tranquilizers frequently, trying to reconcile writing out a prescription for a whole family. (One early family therapist actually prescribed a tranquilizer for an entire family in an effort to persuade them that they all were indeed the "patient.")

Or a psychiatric hospital trying to structure its staffing and its rooms and its conceptual framework to justify admitting whole families that were in the process of having a "breakdown." (This is not a funny issue at all, but a badly needed service, so terrible do family stresses sometimes become. Indeed, there are a few hospitals which actually do it.)

Think of the insurance company, trying to tell its computer that the patient is, in this case, not an individual but a family. "No, it doesn't have an age, or a height or a weight, or a blood pressure. It's a family."

Computer: "Date of birth, please. And diagnosis."

"Listen, it's not a person. It's a group. An organization. A system!"

Computer: "Date of onset of illness?"

Or think of the community mental health center, where families are being seen in therapy. It quickly becomes evident that there is nothing particularly medical about communication processes in families and that the certified social worker may be more qualified in this area than is the medically oriented psychiatrist director of the center. Why then is the psychiatrist officially in charge and making three times the salary of the social worker? This discrepancy in status and pay may be tolerable for the staff as long as medical and non-medical approaches coexist. But if the clinic began seeing *only* families? Would there be a revolution in the hierarchy? Indeed there would, and in some settings it is already occurring.

One of the difficulties the family systems approach created was to expose the fallacy of thinking of human emotional problems as medical problems, as being analagous to or connected with "sickness." But this was just one of the troubles.

The therapist also had problems. Imagine yourself, if you will, in a room with little of interest to look at except an entire family of eight seated before you who are wondering why they are all there when it is really John who has all the problems, and waiting not-so-patiently for you the therapist to do something immediately to remedy the situation. You have no alternative but to do battle with a very powerful social-biological group over its damaging misconceptions and practices, often a rather frightening prospect.

What therapists did when they were literally confronted with this situation was reach for help—into any available theoretical model for understanding and toward any available technical approach for methods. And for any available colleague, finally, as a co-therapist. The discovery of co-therapy by Carl and his colleagues at the Atlanta Psychiatric Clinic was pivotal in the development of family therapy, for it gave the therapist much more comfort in working with families, and in our view it has made treatment much more effective. We will discuss co-therapy in more detail at a later point.

Family therapy was then, and still is, difficult for families, too. It was one thing for the family to be willing to assemble to answer questions about poor John or Mary. But when the therapist's questions began involving the whole family as not only part of the problem, but as *the* problem, the anxiety in the room rose very dramatically.

Picture the family's distress when the psychiatry resident began an interview with a family in which the father had nearly succeeded in killing himself with a drug overdose the previous week. One of the children said in response to a routine question, "Well, we all fought with Dad about a lot of things until about three weeks ago."

Therapist: "What happened then?"

Child: "I don't know. We just all quit. Maybe we got tired of it, always fighting with him."

Therapist: "You think you gave up on him?"

Child: "Maybe."

Therapist, to the father: "So maybe the family gave up on you, and you sensed it. And you then gave up on yourself and took the pills."

The father: "Maybe I did. I had never thought of it that way."

Could the family have decided, silently and without anyone's really realizing it, that they all would be better off with the father dead? Whatever the presenting problem, it is very disturbing for the family to find their entire structure involved *and to discover that they are all in some measure responsible for their problems.* Sharing good times is easy. But sharing the blame for the bad ones is more difficult.

The development of family therapy to this point has required more than a quarter of a century, though the field is still only in its adolescence. Its infancy took place during the frenetic, growthful years of the early 1950s, a time—like the present—when divorce rates were very high and there was an obvious need to help the family. The first family therapists worked in virtual isolation, meeting experimentally with families, but with little support or encouragement from their colleagues. In fact, when they eventually announced their work through journal articles and lectures, they were met with hostility and skepticism. Psychoanalytically oriented psychiatrists were particularly scornful of the outrageous idea of meeting with the whole family, probably because they intuited the long-term threat this approach presented to medical control of the psychotherapy process.

The early family therapists were strong, independent people, and they had to be, for they found themselves opposed on every side. They were also isolated from one another. As these leaders began to develop an individual therapeutic style and a conceptual framework, they also accumulated followers and trainees and the beginnings of a local "clan." Fritz Midelfort worked in private practice in La Crosse, Wisconsin; Murray Bowen trained psychiatry residents in Georgetown University in Washington; Nathan Ackerman built a dynamic program at the former Jewish Family Service in New York City. An outstanding group of people were associated with Don Jackson and Gregory Bateson in Palo Alto, California, and many of this group have gone on to become widely known themselves; they include Virginia Satir, Jay Haley, and Paul Watzlawick. Carl and his colleagues at the Atlanta Psychiatric Clinic were among the first to work with families. Gradually these clinicians—and many others whom I haven't space to mention—found one another and began to develop a nationwide network of family therapists.

During the 1960s family therapy became firmly established as a national movement. Journals were started, books published, and conventions and workshops initiated on a larger scale. Mental health trainees discovering this new approach found it met an almost instant need in their search for clinical skills. And this was what happened to me. In 1968 I was one step away from my doctorate in clinical psychology at the University of North Carolina. I visited the Psychiatry Department at the University of Wisconsin to consider it for my internship year, the final requirement for the degree. I happened to attend a seminar at which Carl Whitaker, who had moved to Wisconsin in order to be able to devote more of his time to teaching, was interviewing a family. I found the interview so exciting that I became a family therapy enthusiast within a matter of minutes.

Increasing numbers of young people had this "conversion" experience, though many were not able to find positions in a training program as fine as the one I entered at Wisconsin. The demand for experience was so great that in many larger cities private institutes were opened to supply postgraduate instruction in the new specialty. These institutes were necessitated in large measure because the faculties of traditional academic programs remained unsure, skeptical, or downright hostile toward family therapy. However popular it was with students, family therapy was still an underground, rebellious enterprise.

The 1970s have found family therapy in an interesting and complex situation. If the sixties comprised our early adolescence, in which therapists discovered their peer group and utilized support from one another to rebel against their "elders" in the psychoanalytic establishment, the seventies find us in late adolescence. The angry search for identity is over. Family therapy has come of age, is accepted by universities across the land. There are several journals which devote themselves exclusively to marital and family therapy. The best-selling professional books in the mental health fields are about family therapy. We have been given a job to do by the society, and we are rather anxiously trying to do it.

Some significant problems remain, however. Family therapy is relatively unknown to the general public. When people look for a therapist, they still tend to go as individuals seeking individual therapy. While there is a great clamor among students for adequate training, there is still a real scarcity of experienced family therapists to provide that instruction. There is also an increased awareness among family therapists that we have taken on a very difficult job. Initially, family therapy seemed so exciting to many of us that we hardly noticed how hard we were working. Now we realize how much energy, knowledge, and interpersonal skill are demanded of the family therapist, and we are more cautious about whom we accept as students and more aware of our own performance. We also confront an increasing diversity of approaches within our own movement. The original clans that gathered around strong individuals in the fifties and sixties have solidified into schools of family therapy. We will attempt to delineate some of these differences in approach at a later point.

Despite the problems and the diversity of approaches, family therapy remains a simple idea with a good future. Like the ecological movement, whose growth it has paralleled, family therapy is likely to increase in prominence in the years ahead. Both orientations are based on the concept of the system and a consciousness of the interdependence of life and the conditions that support it. Working directly with the totality of the forces that influence the individual is such a logical idea that it is hard to deny its validity. And while the family therapist of the future may be called a systems therapist and may include among his clients a corporation or a school, we believe he will still be meeting with families. In our view the unit in human life with the most powerful dedication to growth is not the individual, or the work group, or the social group, but the family.

CHAPTER 5

Initiative

Our next interview with the Brice family was at nine on a Thursday morning, and when I arrived, early, Carl was puttering around, watering the plants in his office windows, collecting the coffee cups from the day before, and humming. The sun streamed in the windows, and the big coffee urn was groaning softly as it began to heat up. We said hello, glad to have a few moments before we began to work. Then I picked up a handful of coffee cups and headed toward the small kitchen near the front door, almost colliding with Don. Running full tilt, he was being chased by a gleeful Laura.

Don drew up short, uttering a mock-apologetic but smiling "Oh, excuse me, sir."

I smiled back, barely managing to balance the cups. "Hey, you're supposed to run away from therapy, not toward it!" I said.

"Sorry about that," he said, darting past me into the office. Laura glanced up shyly as she too slipped into the room. In the hall I passed Claudia, walking alone, and then her parents. Her face was serious, and her parents were talking quietly to each other as they walked. They greeted me; Claudia was silent.

When I returned, Carl was asking Laura about some jacks she held out toward him. How many could she pick up? Could she do it on the first bounce? While David poured coffee, they talked about where in the room she could practice.

When we all were settled, I realized that there was an entirely different feeling about the family. They seemed happier and more relaxed. But it was most evident in Claudia. She wore a long cotton dress in a flowered pattern, cut in peasant style and freshly clean. Her hair was arranged in a bun on the back of her head, and she looked older. I told her I liked the dress, and she was faintly embarrassed.

This time the parents sat together in the center chairs, and Carolyn began. "Well, Doctors, I'm not sure we have a lot to talk about today. We've had a pretty good week. No crises, no fights, and Claudia has been in on time, or almost on time, every night. I don't know what went right."

"Congratulations," I said.

Carl smiled, adding, "Don't worry. It won't last."

Carolyn smiled back and her husband made an amused sound; but she looked disturbed by Carl's remark. "What do you mean?"

Carl: "It's a honeymoon. When people decide to go into therapy, things are usually better for a while. I was just warning you so you wouldn't be surprised when it didn't last."

"Oh," she said, falling silent. Outside, in the bright summer morning, we heard the sounds of a truck loading trash from the cancer research building next door, a high whine as the truck did its job. Then Carolyn said, "Well, whatever the reason, I'm glad it was a good week."

"Of course," Carl said. Then the silence returned. For a long minute nobody said anything.

The father broke the silence. "I guess we're waiting for you guys to start us off."

Carl tilted back in his chair casually and took a puff on his pipe. "And we were waiting for you to start with each other. Bet we can wait longer!" His tone, though pleasant and teasing, had a serious quality. The father laughed slightly, and then the silence returned.

This time it was stronger, more determined, and more threatening. A subtle contest was taking place, everyone waiting for someone else to take the first step, as if taking that step implied a degree of responsibility that no one wanted. Carl and I had sat through this moment many times before and were confident about waiting, though it made us a little anxious, too.

During the previous interview we had worked hard, taking a lot of initiative and essentially directing the whole hour. Now we were shifting our approach suddenly, demanding wordlessly that the family begin to assert itself, the members begin to talk to one another. If we had continued in the same vein as before—questioning, prob-

ing, interpreting—we would have set a dangerous precedent by implying that we were assuming the responsibility for pushing for
change. And that would have been very unfair to the family. If
therapy was to succeed, they had to know, early in the process, that
their initiative, their will to fight and struggle and push and try, was
essential to a successful outcome. By withdrawing from the arena,
Carl and I were not-so-subtly coercing them to start relating to one
another. Carl joked about our waiting, but it was very serious and
very important.

Not all therapists would sweat out the family's discovering their
own initiative in this way. Some assume that therapy is a teaching
process and that the therapist, like the traditional teacher, has to
direct, assign, dig, and explain, in fact, lecture, on a pretty constant
basis. But we are convinced that successful therapy isn't something
that is "applied to" the person or the family. Therapy, for us, is
related to a growth process that takes place naturally in lives and in
families. We assume that the will and the need to expand and integrate experience are universal; and the family that enters psychotherapy is simply one in which that natural process has become
blocked. Therapy is a catalytic "agent" which we hope will help the
family unlock their own resources. Therefore, we place great emphasis on the family's own initiative, assuming that if they cannot discover their own power to change themselves, therapy will have no
enduring effect. Like the parent who teaches the child to do things
for himself, we are thinking ahead to the end of therapy even in this
early struggle over initiative, saying implicitly that the family must
learn to find their own resources, do for themselves, learn early to
care about their own fate.

In the early part of therapy we also want to avoid any repetition
of the initial interview. In that interview we took the initiative, and
we focused on the *structure* of the family—the pattern of relationships that all could agree was fairly predictable. We got our information by asking the family to tell us what happened at home. Now we
were insisting that the family begin to relate to and struggle with one
another in our presence. This was a definite escalation of our demands. We wanted to *see* how they interacted, not hear about it. And
that was a factor in their current tension, sweating as they realized
the implications of this demand, wondering if they dared expose to
us the actual process of their relating. We were asking to see something that no one outside the immediate family had probably even

seen before: the way they fought; the way they lived.

The second silence lasted perhaps five minutes. It seemed longer, even to me. For a while we looked at one another. The children snickered anxiously. The adults shifted in their chairs. Then it became difficult for anyone to look at anyone else. I fixed my eyes on the rug, its complex pattern growing larger and more elaborate as I stared at it, and I had the feeling that if I watched it any longer, the lines would begin to curl and waver in my sight. The father looked at the books in Carl's bookcase. The mother placed her hands palms down in her lap and surveyed them. Claudia simply stared meditatively, at that moment perhaps the least anxious of anyone in the family. Don had taken out a *Mad* comic book and was nervously turning the pages, not really reading. Laura played jacks in the corner, off the edge of the rug. And Carl puffed on his pipe—quietly, slowly, deliberately.

The longer the silence endured, the more tension it generated. I could feel my chest tightening slightly as I waited. *I* was tired of waiting, and I was seized by a strong need to say something, anything, that would bridge my sense of aloneness. I looked anxiously at the family. Now Claudia's eyes were down, and she appeared alone and depressed. Everyone in the family seemed solitary and edgy.

I began to coach myself silently. "Relax. Breathe deeply. Relax." And I did—slowly and purposefully, letting go of the struggle to speak, settling down in the chair, feeling myself breathe more and more evenly. As I relaxed, I began to enjoy sitting there, my body now all of a piece, at rest. Almost simultaneously, I sensed a flood of feeling that I had not experienced before. Instead of feeling distant from the family, I felt close to them, as if I had entered a warm pool of water in which we all were immersed. I was enjoying the fantasy of the entire group sinking slowly into this pool when the father spoke.

"Well, I'll talk, if no one else will." His voice had an edge of true panic and more than a little irritation. "I want to talk about my relationship with Claudia." He had turned toward Carl, as if he were pleading with Carl to talk with him.

For a brief but significant moment Carl didn't say anything. Then he stirred in his chair, took his pipe out of his mouth, and spoke. His voice was calm, but it carried a feeling of personal concern. "Can I help you with this?"

David: "I wish you could."

Carl: "Talk to *Claudia* about your relationship. Not to us."

David: "I've tried that at home. We don't seem to get anywhere."

Carl: "Try again. Maybe it'll be different in here."

The father sighed, then said, "All right. I'll try." He turned toward Claudia. As he did so, she stiffened visibly, as if she were about to be punished. David began, "I guess all week I have been thinking about their remark, one that you agreed with, that I had somehow abandoned or betrayed you. It's bothered me." His voice was tender and a little sad, and he struggled to say the words, as if he were ashamed of the emotion he was revealing.

Claudia attempted diffidence. "Well, so what's the big deal?"

David: "I thought maybe it was important to you."

Claudia: "Well, it was, but I've gotten over it. I'll live." She clearly didn't want to talk to him, at least not now.

David, shifting in his chair: "Well, I'd like to try to talk about it. How did I betray you?"

Claudia, who had been trying to avoid looking directly at him, now flared in response to his pushing. "I don't want to talk about it!" And she turned away.

The father spoke to Carl and me. "See what happens? We can't have a real conversation about this, or about anything."

And it was true. Their effort to work on their problems was so feeble and short-lived that it was pathetic. David did try, genuinely, but gave up easily when Claudia backed away. Now he was asking us to help him. Perhaps he expected us to probe further or to extract some meaning from what we had heard so far. As in the situation where a child looks up pleadingly and complains that he is having trouble tying his shoe, we were very tempted to intervene.

Yet the interview was actually going fairly well. Our long silence had had an interesting effect. Stripped of words for a while, everyone had been in essentially the same dilemma as mine: forced back on his and her own internal resources. We all were panicked at first, but then we all began to *feel* more, to gain access to the realm of feeling that our glib use of words often prevents us from experiencing. While words are our chief means of communication, they can also be used, and frequently are, to conceal or defend against feeling. During the silence some of the emotion that the family was afraid of facing began to become more obvious to them. When we started talking again, it was with more genuineness. The personal note in Carl's comments, the urgency and sadness in David's voice, the hurt petulance in Claudia's responses—all were valuable because we were closer to the sharing of feeling.

Still, there was a profoundly "blocked" quality in the family's communication. Last week, when we were trying to hear about their life at home, they had been eager to fight. This week, when we invited them to begin negotiating and struggling with one another, they froze. And when the father made an attempt to be genuine, the daughter refused to talk. A very powerful, restrictive force was operating in the family, which kept them from moving toward a resolution of their problems.

Carl and I were not about to intervene now. When David turned back to us after Claudia had refused to talk to him, I said, a note of toughness in my voice, "Well, try some more. Maybe you can take it a step further this time."

David looked at Claudia, his shoulders slumping. He seemed to be saying, "Do I have to do this?" I wondered for a moment if *he* was going to get up and walk out. But he began again, this time sounding deeply discouraged. "Claudia, how can I talk to you if you don't want to talk? Obviously I can't. But *why* don't you want to talk?"

If there was a "blocked" quality in the family, Claudia epitomized it. She looked thick, sleepy, obscure, as if all the force in her life were dammed up, sluggish and deep, behind the impenetrable mask that was her face. She didn't speak.

David tried again, almost pleading. "Well, can you at least tell me what I have done that amounts to a betrayal? I don't even know."

Now Claudia's face was angry, though she kept her words cool and controlled. "I've *said* it *before*. I think some of the things Mom wants me to do and some of her rules are *just ridiculous*. And you used to sometimes take my side and talk to her about it, and she would let up a little. But now you are always agreeing with her, at least around me."

David, his voice tensing, the lines in his face tightening: "Claudia, I have to. I just can't agree with some of what you are doing. Your running away, your refusal to obey even the simplest rules—I just can't agree with it. You say I have betrayed you, but you've let me down, too. It's almost as if you *force* me to toughen up with you." A pause. "But it's not that simple. As Don said last time, I do fight with your mother about you. And I do defend you to her. Most of our fights have been about *you.*" The anguish in his face revealed both caring and stress. He glanced furtively at his wife.

At that moment Carolyn, who had been listening quietly, interrupted, speaking curtly to Claudia, though the remark was really directed at her husband. "He certainly does. I don't know if he has betrayed you because he takes your side with me as much as he ever did. He may take my side when *you're* around, but as soon as you're gone, he's arguing for you."

David shifted sharply in his chair to be able to look at his wife, who was sitting beside him. "Well, what do you expect?" he asked her angrily.

It seemed to be my day to be the disciplinarian. I spoke gently to the mother, using her first name for the first time. "Carolyn? Could I stop you? They were just getting into this, and although they may have invited you to step in and rescue them, I think they need to struggle with it themselves." She retreated visibly, taken aback by the reprimand but apparently not resenting it. Then I gestured toward the father and daughter. "Go ahead."

It was a simple but important maneuver. There was a lot of tension between Claudia and her father, and as they began to face each other, they were tempted to find something to save them from the encounter. When David looked furtively at Carolyn, it may have been a nonverbal signal that she was to rescue him, and she had cooperated nicely. A bit more, and they would have been in a convoluted, triangular tangle, and the moment and the feeling between father and daughter would have been lost. Carolyn's intrusion was another of those involuntary blocking maneuvers in the family, an unconscious agreement that whenever a conflict began to be too personal or too difficult, someone would intervene to distract the protagonists. By forcing Carolyn back, I was attempting to keep the discussion as simple as possible, a *dyadic* transaction, in hope that left to themselves, the pair might get more movement, at least some new element, in their relationship.

Now they had no choice but to continue. I could see they were afraid at the thought of going further, yet drawn to the prospect.

"All right," David said, gathering determination, "let's talk about *the* issue."

Claudia: "What issue?"

"Oh, come on," the father said, irritated now, "you know very well what I mean."

"You mean my staying out?" Claudia sounded bewildered.

David: "Your staying out as long as you choose, with whomever you choose, and doing whatever you choose."

Though Claudia looked afraid, she too was becoming increasingly angry. The good mood in the family had collapsed, as Carl had foreseen. "Well?" she prodded.

David: "Well, we don't like it. You are not even sixteen yet, and we don't seem to have any control of what you *do!*" For a moment he sounded assertive, strong rather than pleading. Then he faltered. "Of course, I realize that it's not simple, that you have stresses on you that make you do what you do. But still, we're your parents, and we should have more influence than we do." Having made a stand, he abandoned it as soon as he saw his daughter's confusion and pain.

And Claudia heard the retreat. Her voice grew stronger as she seized the initiative that her father had surrendered. "And you know what happens to me when I hang around home! Mom gets on my back about my room and my homework and my boyfriends and just about everything in my life, and we get into a fight. And I have to leave. I just *have* to." She spoke with an edge of panic, as though she really didn't know what might happen if she stayed for very long in the same house with her mother.

Either the father didn't hear the panic or he ignored it because he went on talking about his daughter's behavior. "What concerns us is where you go, Claudia. You don't tell us where or with whom, or what you are doing, and we have no choice but to jump to conclusions. And they aren't pretty conclusions."

Claudia turned ironic, mocking her father's concern. "And what kind of conclusions do you reach? That I'm going to get *pregnant!* That I'm going to get on *drugs!* That I'm going to slip out of school and smoke *dope!*" The singsong falsetto of her voice was a decoy, designed to make fun of a topic which she obviously didn't want to discuss.

David: "Well, yes. Those are very real possibilities. In fact, they seem like probabilities right now. Those, and others."

Claudia flared, still mocking. "What else is there? VD? Do you think I might get VD?"

David blushed, embarrassed that his daughter could articulate the words which he could only imply, but he answered quietly. "You wouldn't be the first person that it happened to."

Claudia continued to parody his words. "You wouldn't be the first person that it happened to!" Then she added, "Well, you wouldn't be the first parents that didn't know anything about anything." Her mockery was barely sustainable, crowded as it was by anguish. She was nearly in tears.

Again her father seemed to ignore her tears, just as she seemed to miss his concern. By now her taunting voice angered him. "Well, dammit, Claudia, you can make fun of me, but I have a right to insist that you obey the rules of the house. I'm your father, and I have rights, too. And they aren't unreasonable. They have your best interest at heart." Yet for all his anger, he spoke wearily, as if he were saying the words for the hundredth time, with no hope that he would be heard. He sounded, in fact, half-dead, lost in a deep, discouraging struggle not just with his daughter, but with himself.

As David finished his speech, something happened to Claudia. Perhaps she had heard it too many times before, or perhaps she heard something new in it. She flushed, her body tensing, and she leaned toward him, her fists clenched. "Well, what do you want me to *do?*" Her voice rose steadily toward a yell. "Sit in my cleaned-up room like a goddamned statue? Just sit there with my hands folded and go *crazy?*" The feeling she had pent up for so long flooded through her body, giving her limbs, her face, her voice a super-charged quality, as if she might indeed explode. Nor did this feeling emerge easily; it erupted in bursts, fighting itself free from another force in her, perhaps similar to the force that kept her father so even and controlled. But her final words were explosive and agonized, hurling out at him: *"Is that what you want me to do? Sit home in my room and go crazy?"*

If David had been cool before, he was now even cooler, his voice under rigid control; he was frightened of his daughter's fury. "Of course, I don't want that, Claudia. You know that."

His retreat did not calm Claudia at all; in fact, it exacerbated her anguish. She continued, her voice still trembling with rage. "That's what *happens* to me when I stay home! *I feel like I'm going crazy!*" And then she collapsed into tears, her sobs flooding into grief, all the other emotions dissolving their knots into a long, deep flow of crying. She cried for three minutes or so, while the room sat in awed silence. Gradually the sobs became softer, less jagged and painful, more a tender self-consolation than a statement of agony. Claudia kept her eyes down as she cried, and she crossed her arms and clasped them just above the elbows, pressing them to her sides, perhaps in an effort to feel less alone. As she hugged herself, her hair fell across her tear-streaked face, and wisps clung to her wet cheeks.

The father looked shaken, the mother extremely upset. Neither could say a word. Don's face was blank. Laura finally broke the silence, raising her childish voice as she stood beside her mother. "Mom, what's wrong with Claudia?"

Carolyn spoke softly. "She's upset, darling. She'll be all right."

Suddenly I heard myself saying to Laura, without having thought about it at all, perhaps because I wanted to do myself what I was advising Laura to do, "You could go comfort her, you know."

Laura looked up at me, startled. "Me?"

Then the little girl went over to her sister and extended her hand, touching Claudia on the arm. Claudia half sobbed, half laughed, sweeping her hair off her wet face and turning to hug Laura. The two sisters embraced for a moment, clutching each other tightly, and Claudia emitted a couple of sounds that were laughter, tears, and relief all at once. At their embrace, the whole room of people seemed to relax, as if a deep wound of aloneness and grief had been healed. Then Laura sat down beside Claudia, still holding her hand.

The father, shaken, turned to me. "I wish I could have done that, could have hugged her like that." Unlike much else he had said, these words came through fresh and unrehearsed, with the appealing quality of utter caring that children possess so easily and adults achieve with such difficulty.

"You still could," I said.

Claudia stiffened at my words. Her father blushed. "No, I couldn't. Perhaps if I could, this would be a lot easier. I'm sitting here still angry, wondering what I did, wondering what it is that Claudia is talking about that is driving her crazy, wondering what is wrong with our home."

Claudia started to speak, again with a note of anger. "Well, I don't know what you did that made me break down like that. . . ." For a moment the argument seemed about to resume, but then Carl spoke to her, to prevent the discussion from returning to its impasse, to preserve what had been achieved.

"Maybe I can help you with that, because it's pretty clear to me what happened."

Claudia looked toward him, a little frightened, and then she saw his slight smile and was relieved.

Carl: "What I thought threw you, pushed you so hard, was your father's *painful reasonableness*. You were mocking him, remember?" Claudia nodded slightly. "And I thought you were doing it to avoid crying or to get your old man to come out of hiding and react to you in some way." Carl shifted slightly in his chair, leaning forward. His unlit pipe was balanced carefully in his hand, and the hand was resting on his knee. "But what your dad did was give you a lecture about how he was your father and how you had to obey the rules of the house. He had lots of very real feelings, but he kept them all covered. I think that was what threw you, that he wouldn't admit what he was feeling, that he kept trying to be reasonable, trying to be a father rather than a person." Then Carl paused, and Claudia waited for him to finish. Finally: "It was the process of Dad's *destroying his own feelings*, his own personhood, that I thought got you so upset. And it was appropriate for you to get upset. I think it's a very serious problem."

Carl relit his pipe, then resumed. "Part of the problem is also the way the argument is phrased. Dad talks to you as though you were a seven-year-old who is expected to jump just because he says so, rather than negotiates with you about questions that you can help decide." He looked quizzically at Claudia. "And I must admit, you do respond in kind at times. It's as though neither of you has realized that some years have passed since you last took a look at your relationship, and you need to work out a new system for relating. You obviously can't be *controlled* the way you could be when you were seven, but neither side has worked out a new set of agreements for living together and a new language system for negotiating your differences."

Claudia started to speak to Carl, but her father interrupted her. "Did you think that I meant to—"

Carl was almost curt with David. "Wait, would you? I'm talking to Claudia." Then he turned back to her, speaking warmly. "You were saying?"

Claudia began slowly, hesitantly, but with obvious warmth for Carl. "I don't know what got me so upset. I guess I'm just upset."

Carl: "I'm not sure it's necessary to understand it. The *experience itself* may be what is most valuable. And what I thought was good about your getting upset is that you said 'I.' So often in families we tend to talk about behavior, about what people are *doing*. But you talked about yourself and what you were *feeling*, and it sounded hopeful. If everybody in the family could learn to do that, this problem would be half-solved."

Claudia was quietly delighted by what Carl was saying, surprised that there was something positive contained in her getting upset. Still, she had questions. "But my father isn't really the problem. He and I usually get along pretty well, or we did until lately. It's Mother and I who seem to have the problems."

Carl: "Or you and the family."

"Huh?" Claudia was confused.

Carl: "It may be the family's process of deadening itself to its own feelings, just as Dad did, that threatens to drive you crazy." He waited for a moment. "I thought your fantasy of sitting in your room, sort of turning yourself into stone, was what frightened you, as if you were responding to the *family's* tendency to keep its feelings muffled, half-alive." I had a sudden, very clear image of Claudia, sitting in her room, statuesque, going quietly crazy. Carl was now eager to finish. "Because Mom has some of this same feeling of painful reasonableness, too, as if she's trying so hard to be *good* that it's hard to be *real*." Then he stopped, waiting for a reaction.

I looked at the parents. They were distressed, feeling both accused and left out. One of the advantages in co-therapy is that when one therapist gets locked in with one person or one relationship in the family, the other therapist is available to shift the focus. I spoke to David since he had been the most involved person in the hour. "You look unhappy."

David, a little perplexed, irritated: "I don't understand. Claudia is screaming and upset because my wife and I are so reasonable, because we try hard to be *rational* about all this? I don't see how that's wrong."

I waited for a moment before trying to answer him. I felt some sympathy for the parents, and I wanted to help them get over their sense of being blamed. "I don't think it's something you and Carolyn are doing by yourselves. What's in control here is a situation, a set of *relationships*, that is more powerful than any single individual. And I think there is a struggle in the family over two systems of relating to feeling. The question of how conflict began is a complicated one, but what's happening now is that you and Carolyn are overcompensating for Claudia's hot rebelliousness by being cool and controlled, and she is overcompensating for your coolness by becoming even more emotional. The more each side goes in one direction, the more the other is forced to compensate in the opposite direction. The hotter she gets, the cooler you get, and the cooler you get, the hotter she gets."

David was growing curious about what I was saying. "But Carolyn and I sometimes explode, too."

I glanced quizzically at Claudia. "And I bet Claudia cools off then or escapes. When you guys turn up the temperature, she turns it back down. The basic problem is that the whole family wants to turn up the temperature of its living but is afraid to. So you work out an arrangement so that when somebody turns up the thermostat, somebody else will yank it back down."

Claudia, with a sly good humor: "I escape when they start yelling; you're right."

I had liked something that Carl had said a few minutes back, which the family had ignored. I wanted to make sure that they heard it, so I turned toward Carolyn and David again. "I want to raise something else, a point that Carl made a moment ago. He talked about your talking to Claudia as if she were seven years old. Does that sound accurate to you?"

David remained the spokesman of the skeptical older generation. "I just think of it as our parental duty, to give her some direction."

"I'm not quarreling about that," I said, "but about how you give it and how she responds to it. It feels to us as though you are locked into an authoritarian system that is much more appropriate for a younger child. And I think one reason you and Carolyn don't put more of yourselves into these edicts you give is that you don't really mean them. You have the remnants of an old disciplinary system that isn't working anymore, so you keep plugging away at it sort of half-heartedly."

David: "Well, what alternative is there? Should we let her make *all* her own decisions?" I felt the sting of his question, an obvious setup in which I was expected to expose myself as an impossibly permissive psychologist.

"What you do is you grope for a transition between the old system, in which you were parents in control of a child, and a new one for the future where she will be on her own, in which you and she will be more person-to-person. At best you can be the consultants she'll be able to turn to." I had avoided being pinned down.

But David wasn't through with his pseudoquest for practical advice. Actually, he was being defensive and a little playful with me as the younger member of the therapy team. "So how can we grope better? We *are* already groping."

This time I answered with greater firmness. "One way would be to expose more of the personal side of yourselves as parents. You say 'parental' things, but you don't talk about yourselves, your feelings. If you are going to have a person-to-person relationship someday with your adult kids, you ought to begin to try to reveal more of yourselves than the disciplinarian who is always supposed to know what is right. You too have doubts, and fears, and questions. If Claudia knew about those, she would be more likely to see something in you that she could identify with, not just things she needs to fight against."

I glanced at Claudia. "Of course this isn't one-sided. Claudia will obviously need to change, too. A lot of the solutions will have to come out of a negotiation process in which Claudia takes more and more self-responsibility. Right now she can blame all her troubles on you."

As we talked, I could see the family warming to my implicit suggestion that the family's mode of relating could change. The parents were obviously going to be forced to relinquish some of their "control" of Claudia, control which they didn't really have. And Claudia was going to have to acknowledge and *own* more control of her life. At the moment neither side was eager for this transition. To some degree both parents and daughter were still dependent on their painful tangle of angry interdependence. The parents did not yet realize how much they needed Claudia to be in the midst of their lives, and Claudia had no idea how grateful she was to be able to blame the struggles in her life on her parents.

As Carl spoke to David, he wore an enigmatic half smile that revealed some mischief in his question. "Of course, the question of why you and Carolyn got Claudia to stay in this archaic battle with you is an interesting one. Did you ever wonder about it?"

David was more serious now. "We certainly did, though I never thought of it quite that way."

Carl, point-blank: "Did you ever think that it had to do with your marriage?"

David was now puzzled. "Our marriage?" He and Carolyn looked at each other.

Carl: "Sure. It may be the unexpressed tension between the two of you that Claudia feels, a tension that makes her feel she's going crazy. Because she's very close to both of you, though in different ways."

Carolyn was amazed. "Claudia and I *aren't* close." She sounded incredulous and looked a little frightened. I wondered if we weren't moving too fast.

Carl didn't hesitate, though. "Of course you are. You don't think all this anger comes because the two of you are distant, do you? The flip side of all this anger is a lot of involvement and, I assume, a lot of caring." Mother and daughter looked askance at each other.

An interesting thing was happening. Carl had raised the question of the couple's marriage, and immediately Carolyn tried, unconsciously, to shift it back to her battle with Claudia, as though she were afraid to look at the marriage. I brought them back to the issue. "Carolyn, you seemed perturbed at the question about the marriage."

Carolyn looked at me timidly, as though this were strange territory for her. In her conflict with Claudia she had sounded strong, almost tough, but when I spoke to her directly, she was shy and unconfident. "I guess I was," she said. "You alluded to it last time, and I have thought about it—or tried *not* to think about it." This new dimension seemed too much for her to deal with.

I spoke gently to her. "Marriage problems are pretty universal these days, though. And the creation of this sort of triangle is a common way of dealing with them."

Carolyn looked still more troubled. "Triangle? What do you mean?"

I half smiled. "That's the way most conflict in families is organized, in a triangular pattern or in a series of triangles."

Carolyn: "I guess I don't follow you."

I shifted in my chair. It was important to say this right, say it so that she heard it. "Your marriage began to cool off some time ago—right?"

Carolyn: "I would agree."

"But I would assume that, underneath, it wasn't all coolness. You and David have struggled with a good deal of stress between you."

Carolyn: "I agree, though I don't think we were always aware of it."

I nodded. "I know." A pause while I assembled the words. "Well, one way of dealing with both the coolness and the tension was to elect Claudia as a go-between." I paused again. "Can you feel that? Can you sense that Claudia is somehow *between* the two of you?"

Carolyn spoke with a peculiar emphasis. "I certainly *can.*"

I leaned forward in my chair. "Can you hear the anger in your voice when you say that?"

Carolyn, slightly embarrassed: "Yes."

"Let me take it a step further. Even though it has been painful, can you see that in some way this arrangement has been useful to everybody?"

"No," Carolyn said, shaking her head.

"Well," I said, with a rise of confidence in what I was saying and relief at my sense of nearing the end, "it's very clear to me that at least in the beginning it was. Claudia could help David simply by being close to him, by trying to fill some of the empty space in his life. But their closeness could also make you jealous, and that was probably useful, too. It helped heat up some of the conflict between you."

Carolyn ventured a sly, slight smile. "Not between *us*. Between *Claudia* and me!"

"That's the other part," I said, somewhat cryptically. "By fighting with Claudia, you could express some of your anger at David without having to risk open conflict in the marriage." I paused, wanting to emphasize what I said next. "In a way, both of you expressed your anger at each other and your caring for each other *through Claudia*. That's why I called her a go-between."

Carolyn sat silently, then looked directly at me, as though she had decided that she could risk asking the question. "And why did we do this?" She appeared naïve, dependent, offering me a strange kind of implicit trust. I knew it wasn't that simple, that inwardly she was questioning everything I said.

"I don't know," I said frankly, not wanting to get into the trap of pretending to have knowledge that I didn't. "But I would assume that it was because you and David mean so much to each other. You couldn't risk exposing all that you feel about each other for fear that it would disturb the tenuous security you have. You couldn't risk the chance of losing each other."

"Oh," she said, as if surprised by the positive note.

There must be a strange perversity in therapists that never wants to leave things simple and clear, for suddenly I found myself tilting my head to one side and saying, with a smile at Carolyn, "Of course, the question of how the two of you got so insecure is, you know, another agenda for another day." It was a slight put-down, but it was also a joking reassurance that their fear of being direct with each other was really exaggerated.

Carolyn smiled back, but she didn't say anything. Then she turned to Claudia, apparently ignoring my last comment. This time her voice had a new quality of gentleness, as though the way I had been talking to her were now influencing the way she talked to Claudia. There was also a touch of remorse. "I guess if we did that to you, it wasn't entirely fair."

Carl had been quiet for a good while, giving me rein to go where I wanted with the family. But he stirred with Carolyn's last remark, as though something in it bothered him. When he moved, it was in synchrony with the theme I had been developing. "Let me help you with that," he said. "It wasn't what you and David did to Claudia. You all agreed on it, I would guess. And I would imagine Claudia didn't only suffer in this arrangement. She also gained a lot of power and influence, not to mention the status of being an honorary member of the older generation." He smiled at Claudia. Then he asked her, "What do you think of all this?"

Claudia looked confused, but she laughed. "It sounds pretty crazy to me!"

Carl just kept smiling. "Well, you know about us family therapists, we're naturally a little that way." A pause. "What's the matter, don't you like crazy ideas?"

Claudia, guarded now: "No. They scare me."

Carl: "We'll have to struggle about that, because I think craziness is where life really *is.*" He clearly wasn't kidding, though the tone was light. "That's why I got a little excited when you said the family was driving you crazy. That's part of what this family needs—to be able to be crazy. Of course, nobody wants to be *driven* crazy, but if you could help the family learn to be crazy *voluntarily* and enjoy it, it might be quite something. In fact, I think that might be a factor in the family's pressure on you. If you could break out of this dreary reasonableness, they might learn how to go crazy, too." Carl was close to saying that the family was driving Claudia crazy because of their own needs to be less controlled, and he obviously didn't want to stand around and answer questions about his oblique comment. He glanced at the clock. "Hey, we've got to quit. I've got to get to work."

Carolyn looked at me, somewhat irritated. "Maybe there's something wrong with me, but I'm very confused. Just as we were starting to focus on one thing, a new topic came up."

Carl was standing, about to reach for the telephone to check his messages, and the rest of the family was rising and assembling themselves. Laura had nestled against Don for the latter part of the hour, almost going to sleep, and she was drowsy and bewildered in the clatter of departure.

At the last possible moment Carl turned toward Carolyn, and the family stopped while he answered her objection. "At the risk of seeming flip, I think your confusion is good," he said. "Confusion is the beginning of creativity, and if you're going to develop something new in the family, you almost *need* to get confused. But let me give you some advice. Don't try to sort it all out rationally. Let it cook in you, and don't talk about this stuff at home. The things that are valuable will sort themselves out and begin to make sense to you as we go on." A pause, everyone suspended. "Same time next week?" Carl asked.

The parents nodded, and we said our good-byes, Carl gently tousling Laura's sleepy head as she passed. David and Carolyn looked a little dazed as they left, and I didn't blame them.

The basic form for all the interviews that were to follow had been established. We asked the family to take the initiative, and they did. They not only risked exposing some of their interaction to us, but allowed the conflict to "heat up" more than they dared do at home, provoking one another into new levels of open anger. Though we intervened occasionally when the process became blocked, our function for much of the hour was to observe and to provide a sense of safety. Then, toward the end of the hour, we told them what we had seen. This is the fundamental pattern: the family makes a move, and we react to it in a way that we hope will catalyze further growth.

Their confusion over our comments was actually a positive sign. It meant that they had stopped "policing" themselves for a time and had turned that function over to us. Our vantage point outside the family allowed us to perceive patterns which they simply couldn't see—not because they weren't intelligent, but because they were in the midst of the conflict. The confusion represented an edging toward still greater involvement as the family entrusted to us the function of monitoring and interpreting their struggle.

A family can go to see a therapist, or they can be "in therapy." This family was in therapy.

CHAPTER 6

The Basic Conflict

When we are working, Carl and I have a good reason for sitting together, facing the family. Even though the family has come for help, and we are trying to help them, we are also at war with them, and they with us. From the very beginning we are "fighting" with the family: about who will come to sessions; about who will get to chair the meetings; about who must take the major initiative. We are also fighting about the diagnosis. The family usually comes with a conscious intent to help one of their members, and while we are interested in helping that person, we are also busy redefining the problem in a way that necessitates change in the entire family. Just how we think the family should change isn't entirely clear to them or us yet, but it *is* clear that they often don't like our diagnosis of the problem.

Eventually family and therapists should form a group with considerable unity in working toward common goals. But in the beginning neither subgroup in this tenuous new system really knows or trusts the other, and there is bound to be tension. Two different worlds are trying to cooperate.

Every family is a miniature society, a social order with its own rules, structure, leadership, language, style of living, zeitgeist. The hidden rules, the subtle nuances of language, the private rituals and dances that define every family as a unique microculture may not be easy for an outsider to perceive at first glance, but they are there. The wife *knows* what it means when her husband looks at her that way, and he knows what that curling inflection in her voice signifies. But the neighbors may not know what these signals are conveying, and you and I, outsiders, may not know either—yet. The family has established their world through years of living together, and the roots of their present experience go deep into their unique link with history. As the family walks into the therapist's office, everything that has ever happened to them—including some things that have not happened to them but to their antecedents—is alive in their system.

Nor does the family have to *tell* you everything about their world; you can see evidence of it in the way they relate to one another: the way they sit; the way they talk to each other; their tones of voice; the ideas and assumptions they hold about life. Out of the forces acting on them and out of their own decisions, they have shaped a model for living that is organized, predictable, and has unique and irreplaceable meaning for them. They experience predictable tides of feeling. The family members move in precise planetary orbits around one another. They are a world, a solar system, a small universe of experience.

The therapists also have their own world. They have known each other for some years, they have accumulated experiences separately and jointly, and they have a certain perspective on life. Some of this experience is professional, some of it personal, and some a combination of the two. The therapists' world is somewhat less likely than the family's to be modeled on the prescriptions and values of the larger society. There is a slightly radical tinge in the therapists' world view, something not quite accepted by the social order within which the family lives, an order the tenets of which the family has in the main accepted until this point. In fact, one of the therapists' major tasks may be to help the family question what they have been taught about relationships.

By coming to the therapists, the family has formally admitted that their model for living has at least temporarily failed. The rules, the order, the sense of coherence in their life are disintegrating or threatening to do so. The therapists have formally acknowledged to the family that they *may* have a superior model, a world view that contains *something* the family could learn from. And so, formally, the family is submitting themselves to the therapists' guidance.

But all this is only surface. The family isn't at all sure that the therapists have anything to offer. And even if it turns out that they do, the family isn't sure that they *want* to change. After all, this system—these people, this subtle language and tonality and pattern derived out of years of life invested together—is all they have. It is the central continuity in their lives, the bridge between their past and their future. If they change, what then? Does change threaten this continuity? Will their life be worse still?

Therefore, though there is a contract in which the family agrees that they need to change and will allow the therapists to help, the family knows they will resist change, and the therapists know it too. So the battle is formally joined, system against system, with the therapists given permission to invade the family with their own world view, but knowing all the while that the task is far more complicated than that. The final outcome will depend on *so* many variables, among them the family's courage and willingness to risk and the therapists' real adequacy as people, both inside and outside their professional roles. If the family situation is very difficult, it may even be necessary for the therapists to grow personally in order to respond adequately to the crisis. There is great complexity on both sides, then, the two systems deliberately allowing themselves to collide and mingle and generating a chemistry that is not always predictable.

Let us attempt to sharpen this polarity, looking at each side of the underlying tension between family and therapists, including the abrading surfaces where they touch. First, the family's dynamics.

Once the initial pleasantries are over, Carl and I sit there listening to the family talk, and we usually notice things that make us uneasy. We begin to see the family's faults, their problems, their distress. This faultfinding is part of our job, but it has deeper roots, because the family's style of living often threatens our own. We see a good deal in their world that we don't like and don't want to be a part of. Some of these things may merely appear unpleasant and unproductive. But some elements in the family may strike deeper chords in us, resonating with problems in our own lives. Whatever the source, in the beginning we find ourselves looking around for the origin of the uneasiness that the family generates in us, asking: just what is wrong here? In almost every family we find certain general patterns.

1. *Stress.* All families live with stress, and in our society with lots of it, but families that come into treatment have much more than their share. Often the origin of the stress seems mysterious. The fact that there was a great deal of stress in the Brice family was obvious: in their tense postures; in the smoldering anger that brooded and

flared among them; in the vigilant defense which they maintained. Their faces were worn and tired under the stress, their voices sagging and discouraged with it. It stayed and stayed, crackling around the room like an electrical charge.

As Carl and I begin to look for the sources of the family's tension, we are aware of several general categories of stress. There is, of course, what might be called the normal wear and tear of living. We go to tense jobs, worry over the mortgage, and pull a muscle straining to lift a sofa. As the noted authority on stress Hans Selye has pointed out, even breathing, walking, and talking constitute a kind of stress that contributes to the eventual wearing out of our bodies. Living itself involves stress, and it always will.

The *acute situational stress* is a predictable crisis for everyone at some time in life. A serious illness, a job change, the birth of a baby, a move to a new city, the death of a family member—all involve coping with a life suddenly altered by new circumstances, and all produce an acute sense of stress. Researchers have shown that we are most likely to get physically sick at times of sudden transition like these, largely because of the body's adverse reaction to stress.

Interpersonal stress involves conflict and disunity between people who are normally expected to cooperate with one another. Rather than cope with life's innumerable practical problems and minor emergencies, we make war with friends, fellow employees, and family. The schisms within the family can be the most complex and mysterious because they are often related to events that took place in previous generations, the emotional residues of these events being passed down as part of the family's heritage. It may seem strange to think that a family's sense of identity may be tied to maintaining certain patterns of conflict, but just as children learn values and facts from their parents, they can also learn emotional patterns of conflict and tension.

Intrapersonal stress is the person's war with himself. Conflict within the individual doesn't begin there; it is the product of external pressure which the person internalizes. The child who is repeatedly attacked by a parent grows up attacking itself internally, and eventually this self-attack spills over into relationships with others.

While all levels of stress are significant and worth our attention, family therapists begin by looking hardest at interpersonal stress, particularly the war within the family. Family relationships are so crucial, and often so threatened by outright dissolution by the time therapy gets under way, that solving these schisms has the highest immediate priority.

2. *Polarization and Escalation.* The Brice family simplified things a bit by presenting us with an organized version of the larger and more diffuse stress. The ultimate simplicity—"Claudia is the problem"—we rejected from the beginning. We knew the problem was bigger than that, and we refused even to entertain the possibility of dealing with the family's problems through their scapegoat. When we got the whole family together, we were presented with a second-order simplification: "The problem is a war between Claudia and her mother." Better, though we were still suspicious.

No question about the war: Claudia and her mother were engaged in a painful duel that was escalating toward possibly tragic levels. We all know intuitively about this process: one person offers a provocation, the other retaliates with one of his or her own, and this brings about a reciprocal provocation by the first person. Each person adds a little more force to each response, and the process of attack and counterattack increases rapidly to higher and higher levels of intensity. We have all performed in this way on the playground as schoolchildren, daring one another toward some crisis that ended in bloody noses and torn jackets. It happens in families. It happens between service stations in a price war. It is one way that nations get into ultimately tragic wars.

This process of polarization and escalation is very familiar to systems theorists, and they call it by various names. I'll choose one: *positive feedback spiral.* Assume, if you will, that any system has a certain degree of stability and balance, a homeostatic level which is its usual pattern. Assume, too, that the system needs information about how it is doing in maintaining that pattern or balance. This information is called feedback, and it comes in two kinds: positive and negative. Positive feedback tells the system that things are changing, that the system is deviating from homeostasis. Negative feedback tells the system that it is returning to its usual pattern, "to normal" as it were.*

For reasons that were initially mysterious to us, the Brice family,

*In systems language, the words positive and negative are not used in the usual evaluative sense, but indicate the *direction of change,* either toward or away from the norm.

particularly Claudia and Carolyn, were caught in a spiral where most of the feedback was positive. Every step brought the relationship farther and farther away from its once-stable pattern. Of course, every system needs to change, needs positive feedback at times. But the vicious cycle between mother and daughter had gone so far that the changes threatened the stability of the whole system. Interludes of balance, or stasis, grew rarer and rarer. Claudia refused to let herself be supervised by her parents, and they refused to let her supervise herself, and around and around they went, spinning toward a fate which everyone both feared and was unable to alter.

It was difficult to make sense of this mother-daughter war. The issues didn't seem that serious, certainly not worth suicide or insanity. Yet those seemed to be the stakes. We simply *had* to suspect that something more was happening, that there were hidden issues that had to be discovered if this bitter spiral were to make any sense to us. And making sense of it was a necessary prerequisite to changing it.

3. *Triangulation*. We didn't have to look far to find what Jay Haley has called the basic problem in emotional disturbance: the triangle. In almost every instance of "symptomatic" behavior, Haley finds this simple, sad, common story: two parents are emotionally estranged from each other, and in their terrible aloneness they overinvolve their children in their emotional distress. Then these children grow up disturbed and repeat the pattern in their own families.

There was no question that Carolyn and David's marriage was in trouble, though until we mentioned it, this trouble had been only a flitting shadow across their consciousness. But when we brought it up, they admitted it readily: their marriage had been cool and distant for years, and it was getting cooler. There also seemed to be little question that Claudia's troubles were intimately related to the problems in the marriage, though the nature of the connection and what could be done about it remained in doubt for a while.

One way of looking at the triangle between the couple and Claudia was to see it in old-fashioned sexual terms. As in Freud's description of the Oedipus and Electra complexes, David, estranged from his wife, began to lean too heavily on his daughter for emotional closeness, and with time this relationship became tinged with an inappropriate sexuality. David didn't recognize it, but he was using Claudia as a wife substitute.

Carolyn didn't realize why she was so angry with Claudia, but it was partly because of the way David stroked Claudia's hair, the way he spoke to her first when he came home in the evening, the fondness in his voice when he talked to her, the amount of time he spent helping her with her homework. Carolyn was, in fact, furiously jealous of her own daughter.

As far as it goes, this analysis of the situation was correct. But there are some obvious problems in this view. One problem is the language of causality: "David became overinvolved with Claudia, and this was the cause of Carolyn's anger." David did something *to* Claudia. But to put it this way is to make David the real villain and the two women mere reactors. This is the old cause-and-effect language of physics, a language that is old-fashioned even in physics. And it is definitely inadequate in helping us analyze the beehive of complexity and complicity in the family.

Look at it this way: David and Carolyn evolved a mutually agreed-upon distance in their marriage. For the moment, never mind *why*—it just happened. David didn't do it; Carolyn didn't do it. They both did it—by gradual degrees, over a period of years, and unconsciously. But the psychological space between the couple didn't remain a vacuum. Into it moved their children, most prominently Claudia. Nor were the spouses merely cool and aloof from each other. As Claudia grew, she became a pawn in the unspoken but intense conflict between her parents. David could meet some of his needs for emotional closeness by snuggling up to his daughter, and Carolyn could express some of her anger at David indirectly—by yelling at Claudia instead of at David. The couple lived vicariously, indirectly, through their daughter. And this situation was obviously very confusing and painful for Claudia.

But Claudia was more than victim. On some level, she too agreed that she would participate in this folly, partly, one suspects, because she gained power by doing so. Claudia was "promoted" into semi-adult status by her parents, and this induction into their marriage gave her a powerful leverage. If Mother said no to a request, Claudia could count on her father as a covert ally, and she would readily defy her mother and get away with it. At times Carolyn was imploring and inadequate in the face of her daughter's defiance, and this came about precisely because of the split between the couple, a split which Claudia knew about and used to her advantage.

So they all were guilty in the unconscious collusion that produced this absurd situation, even Claudia; yet at the same time no single person was guilty *by himself.* It took everyone performing a particular step to produce the whole dance. For a while the dance seemed mutually advantageous, but a point came when it lost its usefulness to the family and became the painful caricature of family life which we saw at the beginning of therapy.

But *why* this crazy war between Carolyn and Claudia that threatened to tear the family apart? Why couldn't Carolyn and David address their conflicts with each other directly? Why destroy Claudia's life by fighting through her? Because, we assume, the couple was simply too frightened of the implications of an open war between them. They loved each other enough, and were dependent enough on each other, for it to be too risky to acknowledge their hostility. Although they appeared distant from each other, beneath the surface they had formed a tight, frightened togetherness. The clear-cut, honest divergence of a good fight was hazardous to this togetherness. The tension had to emerge elsewhere: between Carolyn and Claudia.

An interesting hypothesis about the escalating war between Claudia and her mother is that it was really part of increased tensions within the marriage and that it *helped stabilize that tension.* For various reasons, there was a largely covert increase in the conflict between Carolyn and David, and the family agreed tacitly to help the two of them deal with it by the creation of a war between Carolyn and Claudia. What is more, the war between mother and daughter, however disruptive and tragic it seemed, actually did result in the parents moving closer together. They couldn't help it; they had to cooperate in order to cope with their daughter. Claudia even complained about the result she had helped expedite: "Dad, you're agreeing more with Mother these days."

As in the case of the schizophrenic patient who went to the hospital when the marriage war heated up, this is a terrible price to pay for marital stability: the expulsion of one of the children, with great pain, from the family.

4. *Blaming.* An integral part of the family's agony is its fascination with finding someone to blame. Blaming is a very powerful process, the members not only hurling accusations at someone else, but defending themselves in turn. Carolyn is sure that if Claudia would only change, the family would relax. Claudia is certain that if only her

mother would change, the family and she would relax. Each feels herself powerless, victimized; she sees the "other" as the one in power, the one who controls her fate.

As Carolyn and Claudia sit looking balefully at each other, each pressuring the other, they betray more than a misunderstanding about issues and ideas. Each reveals an intense awareness of the other person, but a profound lack of awareness of herself. They are not aware of their own feelings, nor do they recognize their own potential for action and change. In the beginning they can't even *talk* about themselves very well, much less consider the possibility that they themselves can be different. It is always the other person whom they talk about, the other person who must change.

Claudia and Carolyn really fail to see each other as separate human beings. They are abstractions to each other: powerful entities; threatening forces; wild images; symbolic strangers in a jungle of anxiety. For Claudia, her mother is Punitive Authority, or Betrayal, or Smothering Fog. To her mother, Claudia is Rebellion, or Ungrateful Scorn, or Intimidation. Who knows what they *really* see as they stare? Does Carolyn see her husband as she looks at her daughter? Does she see her own mother? Herself? A sibling? Enormous complexity is mixed into this fight, giving it a supercharged quality that almost completely obscures the real people. Carolyn certainly doesn't see very clearly the scared, lonely, confused daughter whom Carl and I see, nor does the daughter perceive the painful intimidation and shyness in the mother, or her loneliness. Caught in the storm of anger, each is Threat to the other, not a person.

We are talking about much more than a perceptual problem based on misunderstanding, however. The trouble is far more serious. Perception of Other is rooted in experience of Self, and the limitations the family members have in seeing one another as truly human are really limitations in self-experience. We can't teach people intellectually to see one another differently. First, they must experience *themselves* differently. And that is what this approach to family therapy is all about: experience.

5. *Diffusion of Identity.* There is an even more serious problem in families than a political war between various family antagonists. The assumption that this is only a sexual-political conflict may overestimate the maturity of the family members. Carl and I believe that in a family where there is a problem of any seriousness, the family

is likely to have a tense, difficult kind of relatedness in which no one member is free to be autonomous and independent. They may not be grown up enough for that, adult though some of them are. There is often a *family-wide symbiosis* which inhibits the individuality of every member. They are so dependent on one another, so afraid of losing one another's support, that in this fear they all agree intuitively not to "rock the boat." They fall into rigid patterns with one another, contriving intricate and tortuous routines that preserve their unity at the expense of their individuality. Carolyn might like to say something direct and challenging to David, but she is afraid to. He might like to go camping alone for a weekend, but he doesn't dare. The family's spontaneity, their creativity, their very liveliness are compromised again and again in the interest of pleasing one another and keeping the peace. None really dares be himself for fear of—what? They don't even know what they are afraid of.

Instead of a family of five separate persons, there is a conglomerate person, *the* family. And instead of the members controlling the family, they are rigidly controlled by their roles in the family system. The family rules them all with a steel hand. This symbiotic togetherness, which is probably basically a response to stress, produces a stress of its own because of the fact that *it threatens the individuality and autonomy of the family members.* Everyone is panicked by the fear of losing his or her individuality in the morass. One of the methods the family evolves to deal with this fear of loss of self is to create conflict. The battles indicate the family's need for separateness, and a war with somebody is one way of developing independence from him or her. The problem is that sometimes the war isn't enough or that it becomes far too destructive and costly.

By the time the family has entered treatment every one of its members is usually crying out about being intimidated by someone. It is clear that each means it. They really do *feel* intimidated. But the husband and wife or mother and daughter who point accusingly at each other, saying, in unison, "You are intimidating me," are not intimidated so much by each other as individuals as by their *mutual need for each other*. Their insecurities are profound enough that, in the interest of security, they subjugate themselves to the relationship and its demands. *It is the relationship, the system, the dance that intimidates them, enslaves them. It is the family itself from which they beg freedom.*

But more than freedom and independence are at stake, because the family's unity is a false one. As the family begins treatment, its members usually feel a frustrating combination of personal isolation and tight restrictiveness. They do not enjoy either the freedom of genuine separateness or the exhilaration of real intimacy. They suffer a seemingly unending purgatory of solitary imprisonment in a family that they love but cannot fully enjoy.

6. *Stasis.* There *is* a greater fear in the family than the fear of losing one another, and this is the fear of immobility and stasis, which is really the fear of death. The awareness of death underlies all our experience, and this consciousness is a crucial family dynamic.

David and Carolyn Brice felt the years of their lives beginning to roll by them rapidly, and with every unfulfilling year there was less life left to enjoy. Although they didn't say it to themselves in so many words, they began to feel panicked that they would never have a satisfying life together.

Like that of so many couples, their relationship seemed to become cooler and cooler as time passed, more and more distant. But on a deeper level, their feelings about one another were far from cool. In fact, with every passing year their investment in each other was greater and their total feeling about each other more intense, just as we assume it is for every couple. But if this was so, why the distant, cool exterior? Why the solitary, bored unhappiness?

The basic fault lay in the model for intimacy each had learned in his and her respective family of origin. Neither of them had been allowed to be fully alive when they were growing up. They learned early and well to set their "emotional thermostat" low, and when emotional pressures began to build up in their marriage, the only alternative allowed them by their family models was to cope with these tumultuous feelings by creating emotional distance. The emotional "lava" didn't disappear; it merely traveled silently under a layer of surface rock, looking for an outlet.

In time, Claudia became the expressive agent for the couple; the sexuality, anger, and pain which the parents attempted to squelch in her were part of their own, and she was the symbol of all they hoped to liberate in themselves but dared not even admit to awareness. So the family behaved *as one personality* at war with itself: one part (Claudia) crying for freedom and searching wildly for life, the other (the parents) fighting against the first, saying lie down, be quiet. If you will, life against death.

Claudia was more than an expressive symbol for the parents. She was their provocateur, mediator, and messenger to the outside world. By saying, "I want to be me!" she became their model for individuation, the person most challenged to become a person. Thus, while Claudia expressed much of the family's despair, she also represented their hope for breaking the terrible inertia and silence which had settled over them. Since she had come to represent so much to them, it was not surprising that they would resist any change in her role in the family. Small wonder we collided with the family over the issue of diagnosis; redefining the problem meant redefining the family.

Fortunately, the sense of crisis and confusion in the family represented a real, if temporary, break in their impasse and presented a point of entry for the therapists. Without therapy, they would probably reestablish their chronic conflicts in familiar patterns. But for the moment they were relatively open to "invasion" by the therapists.

Let us turn briefly now to the professional side of the therapist-family relationship, the world of the two co-therapists.

Carl and I have offered to represent the family's need for contact with an "outside" social system, and we ourselves are a social system, too. Before that, though, we are separate individuals, with our own professional and personal histories, our own families, and our own separate views of the world. All this separate experience is part of what we bring to the family.

I grew up in a small town in southern Georgia, while Carl was reared on a farm in northern New York. I went away to Connecticut to college, became an English major and aspiring poet, and returned to Georgia to teach English at a small college. Carl went from the family farm to college and then to medical school at Syracuse. He was in the process of becoming an obstetrician when the experience of being a patient in therapy turned him toward psychiatry. I was on my way toward graduate school in English when a similar experience with therapy led me to become a psychologist.

Carl's distinguished career has included a great deal of clinical experience with delinquent adolescents, schizophrenics, couples and families; the chairmanship of a department of psychiatry; and many years of lecturing and consulting nationally. While my career has really just begun, I have also tried my hand at administration and teaching, and most of my clinical work has been with families and couples. I have a wife, Margaret, and three children, the eldest just entering adolescence. Carl and Muriel have six children, the youngest of whom has recently left for college.

Elaborating the details of our lives is not essential. What is important is the fact that each of us brings useful experience to the therapy. That Carl learned to "talk crazy" (and indirectly) while working with schizophrenics and children is very helpful. His years of psychiatric experience with severely disturbed patients have given him a contact with the world of the unconscious and the irrational that is essential when the family is quite disturbed. My background in psychology, where more emphasis is placed on normal development, provides a good complement to Carl's more clinical background. My classroom teaching experience helps me explain something logically to the family, at least on good days. My seriousness is often appreciated by the family, but they also learn from Carl's sense of humor and his love of spontaneous play.

We credit our own therapy experiences with much of what we are able to bring to the family (Carl has been in therapy five times, and I have had three therapy ventures). The basic models for intimacy which we draw upon are those in our own marriages and families, relationships which we feel are very good ones. The fact that Carl is in his sixties and has survived the experience of helping bring up six children is useful, as is my relative youth and current immersion in child rearing. Carl's tough paternal qualities and my more maternal leanings complement each other nicely, though we may unconsciously reverse these roles a number of times in any given session. The important point is that we bring to the therapy a complex and sturdy relationship, a mixture of separateness and togetherness that makes a good professional "marriage."

We assume that therapy is really a symbolic *parenting* experience and that our co-therapy relationship is the basic instrument of therapy. Whereas the family contains divided parents with a tenuous bond between them, we have a firm and comfortable bond between us, and it is our capacity for teaming that provides the power we need for working with the family and that provides the family with the reassurance they need that they can trust us. Later in therapy, at the point where their own individuation is greater, the family will be interested in the ways in which we are separate, individual, different. But in the beginning the strength of our togetherness is what matters.

A note about sex. Some therapists would maintain that one of us should be a woman, and they may be right; ideally, the therapist team should probably be husband and wife. But it doesn't seem to be essential that the co-therapists be of the opposite sex in order to establish themselves as symbolic parents to the whole family. What really helps is that both therapists be ageless and sexless, free, as a marvelous therapist named Asya Kadis was fond of saying, "to play all the keys." Carl can be a very big-breasted, tender mother at times and a stern, tough grandfather at others, and I myself don't make a bad rebellious adolescent at times. It's a lot more complicated than the simplistic way in which we often identify personality with biology.

As we start to work with the family, we have several immediate goals. We want, first, to steal the scapegoat's job. In the Brice family, Claudia has been the family therapist in a sense, and one way we can gain entry to the family is to do what she does—fit ourselves into some key triangles in the family. One of us will plunge into the family, become embroiled in an issue or with a person, and then retreat back to the safety of the co-therapy relationship. We begin the kind of "in and out" movement that Claudia was attempting by running away and coming back home, and in this way we hope to help break the stasis, just as she was trying to do. And because Carl and I have each other, we can plunge in with more impunity than if he or I were alone.

We are always fickle in the coalitions we establish with family members; now we support or push one person, now another. Thus, we avoid getting caught in the trap of becoming the permanent advocate of one person or one position. We work as the agent of the family as a whole, and we can't afford to get locked into a particular relationship.

As the agent of the whole family we have some general goals in these early stages. As the family begins its long struggle to break the grip of stasis and stress, we are convinced that the most significant breakthroughs will occur in moments of peak experience. These moments may or may not take place during the therapy hour, but it is hoped that they will be stimulated in part by therapy. Two kinds of experience seem to be crucial: the moment in which the family risks being more separate, more divergent, perhaps even angrier than usual, and the moment in which they risk being closer and more intimate than they have been in their everyday living.

The sequence usually goes like this. The family begins to trust the therapists to supply some cohesiveness and takes advantage of this support by exposing some of their long-accumulated anger. Lo and behold, nobody drops dead or files for divorce. In fact, the opposite usually occurs—everyone feels a strange exhilaration and peace. The outburst of anger is often followed by moments of greater intimacy and warmth, though sometimes there is a long wait before the warmth appears, especially if a lot of anger has been stored up in the family archives.

We feel that the family's capacity to be intimate and caring and their capacity to be separate and divergent increase in careful synchrony. People can't risk being close unless they have the ability to be separate—it's too frightening to be deeply involved if you aren't sure you can be separate and stand on your own. They also can't risk being truly divergent and separate if they are unable to count on a residual warmth and caring to keep them together. The more forceful and independent they become, the easier it is to risk being intimate and close. The more closeness, the easier it is to risk independence.

But how to get this moving, how to get the family to risk taking a first short step out of the deadly, cloying compromise of pseudo-closeness and pseudo-separateness? How can we help break the sticky net of frustrating entanglement? In part, we have to model the process for them. We need to show the family they can begin to take risks in being intimate by taking some risks ourselves. If we want the family to make an "existential shift," in which they become more real, more direct, more alive, then we have to be real, and direct, and alive ourselves.

In helping the family move toward individuation (and closeness), we expect the first separation to come between the generations. Claudia Brice was terribly overinvolved in her parents' affairs, and they in hers. Before the individuals in the family can be separate and distinct, the generations probably need to be separate and distinct. This is not a simple problem. Claudia's parents were not really individuated from *their* parents, as we eventually discovered.

David and Carolyn could not allow Claudia to be really separate from them until something happened *within* their generation. That is, some of the marital tension had to be resolved before they could afford to let Claudia go and be herself and live her life. Until that point she was stuck with being very badly needed by her parents.

And though the couple seemed willing enough to look at their marriage and to talk about it, helping them change it was a much more difficult task than we originally guessed. It was not unlike trying to untangle a ball of yarn that had been played with by a mischievous cat for a very long time.

CHAPTER 7

Grandmother's Ghost

Carl and I knew that approaching the couple's marriage problems would be sensitive work, a little like delicate surgery. Carolyn and David were anxious about their marriage, and we had to be careful. We also knew, simply from her face, that Carolyn Brice was a troubled person. Behind the obvious scapegoat, Claudia, there flitted the image of a deeper family victim, her mother. Somehow we were not as concerned about David; his persistent smile, his efficient "let's solve it" approach to the family's problems reassured us that he was not going to pull back from therapy. In fact, after we had been working for a while, he took on the role of shepherding the family along: negotiating with us for time for the next appointment, asking helpful questions of the other family members, even interpreting what he heard. We were somewhat suspicious of his motives for being so enthusiastic and helpful, of course—he was obviously anxious to keep the focus off himself—but we were glad to have his eagerness about family therapy.

Not Carolyn. It was painful for her to come, and one sensed she would have liked to leave almost immediately upon arrival. Some difficult, barely submerged turmoil was stirring inside her. She was alternately furiously angry—especially when confronting Claudia—and devastated. Those defeated expressions crossed her face only when no one was watching her or talking to her. We would be following a dialogue between Claudia and her father, and I would steal a glance at Carolyn and see that she was wrapped in sadness. Devastated is the right word. Carl and I were puzzled.

It also concerned us that Carolyn held back from participating in the therapy. The mother is so central a person in the family that we couldn't afford to have her pulling against us. After the first few critical sessions in which they worry about being left out completely, fathers often settle down to being willing, if peripheral, participants in family therapy. But if mothers lack interest in the process, it will founder. They are truly the key to the family's psychological life and the gate through which any intruder must enter. Did Carolyn blame herself for Claudia's troubles? Was she afraid we were going to accuse her? What the hell was going on inside her? We didn't know, but it was clear that before the couple could stand the stress of looking at their marriage, Carolyn needed to be more committed to the process of therapy.

Don started that day's session with his usual half-engaging, half-annoying smirk. "I know what we should talk about today, yuk yuk. We should talk about Claudia's room for a change."

And as usual, Carl returned the quip. "Naaaaah. Let's talk about *your* room. I'm sure you must keep scorpions and snakes in it. And I'm sure it's your mother's favorite place to be."

Carolyn smiled a little. "How did you guess?" Her voice had a tremor, although she was trying to be cheerful. "Except instead of snakes and scorpions, he has all those wires and things—what do you call them? Strobe lights. I just try to stay out of there."

David, owlish and benign through his thick glasses, explained to Carl, "Don has a hi-fi in his room, and he has connected these lights so that they flash in synchrony with the music. It's bad enough, but it could be worse. He wanted to paint the room black to heighten the effect, but we drew the line there—at black. So he has a white room with strange lights." He was quietly proud of Don.

Carl spoke to Don, tamping his pipe in preparation for lighting it. "It's a shame you lost that one. That black room would have been a great place to get depressed in or go crazy in. You could have let the whole family use it when they needed to." It was one of those insidious statements of Carl's that shifts the entire tone of a conversation. Suddenly we weren't talking about a room and strobe lights, but, symbolically, about depression and going crazy. The session had definitely begun.

Claudia responded almost immediately, her voice harsh as she bore down on her mother. "That's something I want to talk about—

Don's room. You're always on my back when my room gets messy, but you leave him alone to mess his up. Why don't you bug him the way you do me? Why me?"

Carolyn sighed, as if resigned to another round with Claudia. "Because when I ask him to clean his room up, he will *eventually* do it. But you won't. I could beg you to clean yours up and you wouldn't do it."

"So instead you hound me like a goddamn shrew, a fucking nag." Claudia was certainly out to pick a fight with her mother.

But Carolyn was so defeated that it was not clear that she would even fight. She tried, but her voice was frail. "Claudia, I cannot tolerate that kind of language from you." Thoroughly unconvincing. Claudia glared, and Carolyn looked ready to cry. She turned to David, more anger crowding into her voice as she spoke to him, as if it were somehow his fault. "Do you hear this? Are you going to let her talk to me like that?"

David smiled weakly, turning toward us from his chair. "I'm staying out of this one, just as they've been implying I should." Carl and I were silent. They needed courage at this point, not interpretation. The daughter was challenging the mother, and the mother appeared to be giving up. It was frightening to see.

"Well, don't you? Do you ever let up from pressuring me? Claudia, do this! Claudia, do that! Claudia! Claudia!" She mimicked her mother's whiny voice.

"You're trying to make me fight with you, aren't you?" Carolyn said, regaining some composure and sharpening her voice to a steely tone. Her eyes narrowed; her mouth became a thin, bitter line. "Well, I'm not going to fight on your childish terms."

Claudia was not to be contained. "What are you going to do? Restrict me? To my goddamn room again? To that house? Go ahead! Do it! See if I care! I'll do what I want to anyway."

As a rule I had a lot of sympathy for Claudia; I had heard the incessant, nagging criticism that she was subjected to from her mother, and I saw her triangulated between her parents. But not today. I sat there thinking, "What a brat. Why does Carolyn take it?" Then I looked at Claudia again. Today she wore jeans with embroidered knee patches and a tie-dyed shirt she had done herself, and done well. Her hair was straight, clean, shining. Her shirt was unbuttoned partway down the front, and she was obviously not wearing a bra. I caught myself looking furtively at her well-formed breasts, then looked away guiltily. Though the features and the body structure of the two women were very similar, at that moment they appeared in stark contrast. Claudia was vigorous, young, and angrily aggressive; her mother was tired, older, discouraged, wrinkles beginning to show on her face.

Something strange and disturbing was going on between mother and daughter. The more apathetic and discouraged Carolyn grew, the more enraged Claudia became. As Carolyn pleaded with Claudia to calm down, Claudia kept daring her mother to fight. Then I saw the tight lines of fear around Claudia's eyes as she glowered at her mother and realized what was going on. The daughter was afraid her mother was going to give up!

I spoke to Claudia. "Hey, Claudia, can I stop you? This is not going anywhere." Claudia looked relieved. She broke off her harangue in midsentence, as if it weren't important. "OK," she said a little flippantly, "I'm stopped."

"Why are you insulting your mother? What are you trying to do?" I asked.

Claudia looked down. "I don't know. She makes me mad. I don't know why. Why does she hound *me?* Tell me the answer to *that!*"

"I'm not interested in your mother right now. Let's talk about you." I didn't like her effort to focus the discussion on her mother.

"All right, so you tell me. You're the doctor." I was beginning to see more and more of Carolyn's problem, and I started to get angry.

"Listen," I said, darting an irate glance at her, "you can talk to her that way if she lets you, but not me." I was really angry now. For a moment I wondered if I should go on. I visualized Claudia getting up and fleeing the room, leaving me openmouthed as she had left her parents. I modulated my voice, carefully balancing my anger with a quiet but considerate curtness. "I'm not your mother."

Claudia was silent; the room was silent. Laura stopped rocking. Don paused in the drawing he was making on Carl's clipboard. Strange—I hadn't meant to get into anything like this with Claudia, and I wondered what to do with the awkward silence. So I did nothing. More silence. Finally I spoke, rather softly, with a faint trace of my anger still in my voice. "What I was going to say was that you looked scared by your mother's resignation. As if you had to fight with her to keep her from giving up. Did that ever scare you, the thought that she might give up?"

Claudia recovered her irony. "No. She would never do that." She was lying, but I was temporarily at a standstill. Just what I get for asking a teenager so direct a question. Sometimes teenagers are blunt, at other times evasive.

Carl's turn now. He didn't even shift in his chair, only cleared his throat ever so softly, and as if on cue, Carolyn turned to him. Carl spoke to her. "I was wondering about your part in this. Do you have any sense about how you let things get to the point where your daughter could degrade you and you couldn't do anything about it?" The question was an exquisitely gentle scolding and a dare in its own right. It flustered her, and she thought for a moment before answering.

"I really don't know," she said finally. "Claudia and I had a pretty good relationship until a few years ago. *I* felt we were sometimes really close." She paused, remembering. "Then everything seemed to blow up. Some of it was this group of young people that she met at school, kids that I really don't approve of. I tried to talk her into staying away from them, and she refused. And that disagreement seemed to rupture whatever trust or liking there was between us. After that we fought over one thing after another." Carolyn had an absent look—musing, puzzled, sad. She caught herself, smiled, and reached her hand toward Laura. The little girl smiled back and took her mother's hand.

Carl wanted to move things along. "But that's pretty standard for adolescence in this world. The adolescent picks something that the parents don't approve of, and the parents agree to disapprove, and the war that follows helps both sides develop a generation gap. The gap's usually needed, though having a war is a pretty painful way of getting it."

"I can see that," Carolyn said quietly, "but it doesn't make it any easier to take. We try to give Claudia freedom, but she doesn't seem able to handle it. She seems to insist that we supervise her. She won't act responsibly when we give her responsibility."

The conversation went on like this for a while—low-key and rational, Carolyn's depression still evident. Throughout, Carl joked gently about the process being a dance in which everybody had to participate: Claudia demanding freedom and then scared when she had it and seducing her parents into breathing down her neck so she could feel comfortable again. Claudia protested that it didn't feel comfortable, and Carl retorted that it was at least better than being all alone in the world and responsible for herself. "You wouldn't want that—it's very scary, being grown-up like that."

"I'd like to try it," she said ironically.

"Maybe you'll get a chance," Carl told her and returned to Carolyn. Nothing really appeared to have touched her. "How about your husband's supporting Claudia against you? Is that still happening? Is that part of what defeats you?"

Carolyn looked up. "Yes . . . no . . . well, it has in the past. But I think that's changing."

Carl: "He *did* stay out of it today." A pause. "You think that's why you're depressed? If he stays out of it and it's just between Claudia and you, you feel that you'll lose?"

"It seems that I will," she said.

I had been listening attentively to this meandering conversation in which Carl was implicitly comforting Carolyn, and I was puzzled. Her despair had a private and inaccessible quality, as if the war with Claudia were only one example of her sense that life itself was defeating her. What was this sadness really about? How had Carolyn developed this bleak view? Did she feel defeated by her husband? What in the hell had gone on in her family of origin? So I asked the obvious question. "Is all this related to the battle between you and your mother? Was it like this in your own family?" Carl and I had been down this road before, and I had a pretty good idea of what Carolyn would say.

The question startled and flustered her. "My mother and I?" Then she smiled a sort of crooked, private smile. "No, not quite like this."

"Can you say what it *was* like?"

"My mother was a very—well, how to say it—controversial woman in our home. Nobody really dared cross her, especially not my father. She had a temper, oh, did she ever have a temper! And she could be very critical." Then Carolyn paused and looked crossly at Carl, as if she were feeling betrayed by getting into this topic. "Why are we talking about my mother? She's not involved in this thing with Claudia!" She was irritated.

"Of course she is," Carl said firmly. "She is the only model you have for being a mother, and we're talking about your being a mother to your daughter."

Carolyn, still cross: "But I'm not like my mother at *all*. I don't think my mother has anything to do with this."

David stirred, as if trying to decide whether or not to say something. He dared. "Carolyn, you bristle if anybody says *anything* about your mother. I think after all these years you're *still* trying to please her."

Carl turned toward David, smiling broadly. "Listen, you psychiatrist you, I'll be the therapist here. You stay out of this!" He said it so genially that David couldn't help smiling, though he was a little embarrassed at being caught analyzing his wife again. It would indeed be a serious problem if David got into the middle of this dialogue because we knew that he was angry about his wife's involvement with her mother, and part of the reason that Carolyn was resisting talking about her mother was that David had pressured her so much about it. We were now inheriting some of her anger at David as we asked about this area of her life.

Carl was not to be deterred. "So your mother was critical of everybody? What was she so angry about?"

This was Carolyn's day to feel intimidated. If it wasn't her daughter, it was this damned therapist. But she acquiesced. "I don't really know. I know that my mother worked awfully hard all her life—she was a teacher and a very strong person. My father, on the other hand, had a 'back injury,' or so the story went, and he spent a lot of time reading and doing odd jobs and supposedly looking for work. And he did work for a while from time to time. But Mother supported the family mostly, and she never let Dad forget it."

Carl: "So Mom was furious that Dad was sitting on his ass and mad at herself for letting him get away with it."

Carolyn, softly, as if to herself: "I suppose so. But she really took it out on him. He paid plenty. And so did the rest of us."

"You too?" I asked.

"Me too." That devastated look again as she remembered.

"How was it between you and your mother?" I wanted to know.

Carolyn turned toward me, looking very much afraid of the question. Still, she was apparently willing to answer it. She crossed her legs and reached into her pocketbook for a cigarette, lighting it carefully and slowly as she began to speak. I hadn't known that she smoked.

"I have always been afraid of my mother, I suppose," Carolyn said, exhaling the smoke rigidly, "and as my husband says, I probably still try to please her." A pause. "She can be very critical of me, just devastating at times, and it always tears me up."

I was startled to hear her use the word "devastating"—we obviously agreed about how she felt. As she talked more about her mother, her body tensed perceptibly. We were pushing her, true, but gently and slowly, and we were well aware of her pain.

"What does she criticize?" I asked.

"Oh, it doesn't really matter," Carolyn said angrily. "Everything I do displeases her—the way I handle the kids, where I live, the way I dress. When she's cross, it doesn't matter what she's mad at." Then she seemed to shift mood, smiling slightly. "But don't get the wrong idea. There are a lot of good things about her, too—and a lot of good things between us."

"Any sense of what's behind the attack on you?" Carl asked. "You aren't your father's favorite or something like that, are you?"

Carolyn blushed. "Well, yes, I suppose I am. My father and I have always been quite close, though I'm not sure my mother would *know* that. I think she would say that she and I were quite close. And in some respects she would be right. It's really very confusing to me."

Carl: "So you're really pretty deeply connected with both your parents."

"More involved than either my brother or my sister, I think," Carolyn said matter-of-factly.

I asked if her siblings were both younger than she. They were. I had one more question, though I thought I knew the answer to it before I asked. "Did you ever fight with your mother? Ever push back when she pushed you?"

Carolyn shook her head slowly. "No. As I said, I think I've always been afraid of her."

"Still?" I asked, smiling. "Even at age . . . ?"

"She's sixty-eight." Carolyn thought for a minute. "Well, maybe I'm not still afraid of her anger. But I'd be afraid to fight with her now for fear of hurting her."

I wondered silently to myself about the mother, trying to visualize this older woman who had felt so powerful and so hurtful to her daughter, and about her being still older now and perhaps frail, and then about the father who was weak, yet who could make his wife so angry. These were hazy, unclear images, full of contradictions. My picture of where Carolyn fitted in their lives was blurred, too, though some patterns seemed very clear.

Carl, obviously thinking about some of the parallels: "Can I push you to take this a step further?"

Carolyn said yes rather tentatively, not knowing what Carl was up to.

Carl: "Does what happens between you and Claudia make any sense now, when you think about what has gone on with you and your mother?"

Carolyn: "No. It seems very, very different. I would *never* talk to my mother the way Claudia talks to me. Not in a thousand years!" She was indignant at the very idea of any parallels between the two relationships.

Carl smiled slightly. "That's what I mean. It's so different. It's as if you've somehow arranged it so that Claudia defies you and degrades you in the way you never dared do to your mother."

"So?" Carolyn said, a little scornfully.

"So you've become your mother in this dance, and Claudia's become like the part of you that wanted to stand up to Mother and didn't dare to." Carl was still smiling.

Carolyn did rebel at Carl's deceptively bland comment. She flared in anger. "But I don't *arrange* for Claudia to defy me. She does it without my permission and over my strenuous objection. It makes me *furious* when she defies me!"

"Sorry," Carl said shortly. What he meant and what was communicated was "you're wrong." Then, in a tough, even voice: "What you get credit for is what *happens,* not what you say you *want* to happen." Then he added, lightening his tone a bit and glancing at David, "Of course, your husband has to take a lot of the credit, too. I don't mean to scapegoat you." Another pause. "But it would be a mistake to avoid looking at your part in the way this thing goes."

Carolyn was still indignant. "I can't see it. I will not believe that any part of me would want my daughter to talk to me this way."

Carl, not relenting: "But it's what *happens.*"

Carolyn: "But not what I *want* to happen!"

Carl is a skillful fighter, so he shifted position. "It may be even more complicated than your having a vicarious rebellion through your daughter. It may be that when Claudia starts degrading you, in your head she becomes your mother—you know, running you down, criticizing you. And you feel the way you did when you were a kid —defeated." Carl turned to Claudia, taking the pipe out of his mouth and placing his hands on his knees, leaning forward in his chair. "You didn't know you could be your own grandmother, did you? Your own mother's mother."

Claudia tittered nervously, then grew serious. "But she is always criticizing *me*, nagging me!"

Carl just couldn't stop grinning. "Well, at those times she's just imitating her mother. You guys take *turns* imitating her mother. How about that?"

Claudia shook her head in disbelief, waving Carl off. "I think you're crazy, Dr. Whitaker."

Carl: "Well, you know, that's an occupational hazard."

Carolyn was having a difficult time maintaining her anger in the face of Carl's good humor, but she kept trying. "I don't see why my mother has to be a part of this. I'd rather leave her out of it."

Carl: "Great! I'm all for that." Carolyn looked puzzled as Carl continued. "But one way of getting her out is to admit that she's involved in this war."

"I just don't see it," Carolyn insisted.

I had been following the battle between Carolyn and Carl closely, and I wanted to get into it. "I don't see why you're so defensive. It might be a good plan. You might learn how to fight by fighting with Claudia!"

Carl followed at once. "That's right. You could learn to stand up to Claudia in a way that really meant business. It would help her, and you might then even be able to stand up to your mother, not to mention your husband."

Carolyn completely ignored the reference to David. "But I *yell* at Claudia; I scream and stamp my feet. It does no good!"

Carl was suddenly very sober. "It's not a matter of noise and volume. It's a much more serious problem than that. It's a problem of how you can *experience yourself differently*—feel yourself worthy of respect, demanding it, and feeling more confidence in yourself as a person. But especially important to you, I think, is being able to feel yourself in the older generation with regard to Claudia." Carl's voice grew gentler, and Carolyn softened visibly under the conciliatory tone. "It seems to me that your mother's power—or attack, because I'm not sure she *felt* powerful—was so painful to you that you resolved somewhere, at some time, not to be assertive or powerful. And part of that decision is truly a charitable wish—not to hurt your children the way you were hurt. But you also don't like being run over, nor should you." Carl paused as he looked at Carolyn's face, also somber and composed. He considered her dilemma, as if looking for a move she might make to solve it. He concluded: "Maybe you could find some way of being assertive where you wouldn't feel that you were being cruel or mean."

"That sounds nice, I suppose," Carolyn said, disarmed by Carl's gentleness, "but how do you do it? I feel just terrible when I scream at Claudia."

I too felt a quiet sympathy for Carolyn; I could see her sadness about her mother and her pain about the conflict with Claudia. She sat motionless in the chair beside her husband, and he watched her with some concern. There are moments like this when you want to go over and take someone into your arms and hug him or her, and maybe Carl or I should have done it. But we couldn't or didn't, and the moment hung there between us. I thought about how quickly the mood had changed—how a few moments before Carl had been aggressively and humorously pushing Carolyn. She had been angry then, guarded, keeping us at a distance as we pushed to break through.

These moments when the therapist is pushing a person in the family may seem abrasive and unpleasant, but they serve a purpose. The patient is usually approaching a confrontation with some part of his or her own suppressed pain and fighting off the moment. The therapist's persistence is an act of persuasion, of forceful caring about the outcome. The moment finally comes when the individual's grief and frustration burst into open admission. Then, and only then, can the therapist approach the long-denied agony directly.

It is a difficult problem for the therapist—you can't only be warm and benign with people, because it isn't honest and it isn't respected. They will think of you as ingratiating and powerless. You must push them, sometimes very hard indeed. But you can't only push—you have to be caring, too. Carl had pushed Carolyn, and now we were much gentler with her as she lowered her guard, letting us see and have some access to her vulnerability.

When we don't dare cuddle someone physically, I suspect that we cuddle them with our voices. That was what I felt as I said to her, "Sounds like you took your mother's attack pretty seriously." Carolyn looked up at me. "And now you attack yourself, or get Claudia to attack you." I waited. "Are you very tough on yourself?"

"Yes," she said emphatically.

"Maybe that's the first battle you have to fight," I said, borrowing Carl's cryptic mode.

"What do you mean?" she said.

"Against the part of you that is so hard on you." I spoke caringly. It was as if I were also saying, "Please cheer up a little."

I felt peaceful; the room felt peaceful. Nothing dramatic had happened, far from it. But a tension had eased as Carolyn admitted that she was troubled, that she was discouraged, and that she might now let us come near her pain. She was neither defensive nor angry as we talked quietly with her, and her willingness to let us approach was a great relief.

Carl had been outside the conversation for a while, a good vantage point for seeing something different, some new angle that the therapist who is more actively involved doesn't perceive. "What happened to your parents' war? Did they resolve it?" he asked.

Carolyn flinched visibly. Then she looked straight at Carl and said, evenly but with a sorrowful undertone, "No, it's very bitter between them. It's very sad to see people approach the end of life like that."

Then she stared through the window at the afternoon sky. I watched her profile, the glare from the window catching the bright surface of tears streaming down her face. She didn't make a single sound.

"I guess your sadness makes a lot more sense to me now," Carl said gently.

CHAPTER 8

Toward Marriage

There was a new quality in the next session. Carolyn was there—really there—not just sitting miserably, wishing the hour would end. She settled in her chair in a new way, giving the impression of wanting to stay for a while. She had risked showing a fraction of her pain, and we had responded with ordinary human concern. Nothing dramatic. But for Carolyn, it was not a small thing.

If you assume that psychotherapists are at least symbolically (and probably at heart) mothers, then originally Carolyn had to feel about us some of the things she felt about her own mother: it was dangerous to come near. If she revealed her real feelings to us, she might be hurt, as she often was by her mother. So she had stayed hidden.

Good old transference. Even though we know about it intellectually, we therapists keep being stupid about it, flattering ourselves that the patient is really reacting in the beginning to *us*—as real, individual human beings. To some extent that does occur, but we are deluding ourselves if we think that the patient isn't also struggling with subtle and largely invisible ghosts and images out of the past. The importance of what happened with Carolyn is that she expected us to respond like her mother—with criticism and blame. When we didn't, she was relieved and more than a little surprised. Suddenly we were a little safer, and she decided to risk getting involved. We were delighted on a number of counts, one of which was our greater freedom to move.

So we began to ask direct questions like "What's wrong with the marriage?" and waited to see what happened. At first, not much.

Husband and wife sat there and simply tried to answer.

Carolyn was, as we knew, quietly furious with David because he worked all the time. Even when he was at home, he was constantly on the telephone or at his desk. The desk was in the bedroom, and Carl didn't waste any time making a joke about *that*. "At least you could insist that he keep a sofa bed at the office if he's going to have his desk in the bedroom!" Everyone laughed, but it wasn't really funny. This was a painful issue for David and Carolyn.

You might assume it isn't possible in family therapy to talk honestly about sex with children present. Actually, it's not only possible, but fun, once you get past the first awkward moments. You have to be a little bold, and you have to take lightly the out-of-fashion but still prevalent notion that children don't know anything about sex and don't need to know anything. One of the principal reasons that the Brice household was so tense was that Carolyn and David didn't have a very good sexual life. In fact, at the time of the family crisis, fifteen-year-old Claudia was probably having a good deal more sexual experience than her parents. And that, of course, is part of why Carolyn was so angry with her.

We didn't learn much about Claudia's sexual experience until much later in therapy, but we knew at this time what the parents knew—that Claudia was sleeping with several boys, frequently. It didn't appear to be a very healthy experience: it was casual, compulsive, and largely unloving. This kind of early sexual abandon in adolescents is a complex subject in its own right.

We assume that part of the agenda in Claudia's sexual life—a mostly hidden, unconscious agenda—was the search for that quality of tenderness and support which people usually call mothering, though it actually involves both parents. Claudia was, or had been, very dependent on her parents. When she and her parents began their war, she needed to transfer her dependency elsewhere. So she disguised it as sexuality, seeking in a series of apparently casual encounters a delicate mixture of freedom and cuddling which her life lacked. She needed to feel close, but she was frightened of real closeness lest it be constricting and enveloping. Her "promiscuous" approach to sex evolved as a possible compromise solution to her need for freedom and closeness.

Claudia was also responding to the family's anxiety and guilt about sex. Carolyn and David scolded Claudia indirectly about her affairs, but in the scolding there was a hint of intangible, covert encouragement. They said "don't" in a way that came out sounding like "do." The message which Claudia listened to was the one that urged her on.

David and Carolyn had every reason to encourage their daughter surreptitiously to have an active sexual life. After all, they couldn't talk about sex themselves, and at least Claudia confronted them with the subject. Just how children pick up hidden anxieties and needs in their parents and act them out is a fairly mysterious matter, but we have no doubt that it happens. Claudia's problems with sex were her *parents'* problems with sex. She was simply following her parents' subtle instructions that she "get herself into trouble."

If Claudia could simply have enjoyed herself, perhaps it wouldn't have been so bad. Her parents might have learned something, and this might have helped their repressed, anxious lives. But she was stuck with the same sense of guilt and inhibition as her parents, and her sexual life proved to be unfulfilling and self-destructive. Because her parents hadn't helped her grow up with healthy attitudes, she couldn't really help them with *their* attitudes. Still, she kept trying, and at least she generated some anxiety in the family. Anxiety is always helpful in therapy because it is often what motivates change.

So we didn't ask Claudia about her sexual problems. She felt hounded enough already, and we knew that her real problem was her parents. But because we guessed that they couldn't talk about sex, we asked Claudia about her *parents'* sexual problems. It was a tense moment.

Carl was smiling, as almost always, when he turned toward Claudia. "How about sex and your parents? You think they have a good time sexually?" Carolyn blanched, and David took a deep breath.

Claudia smiled wryly. "I don't know, but I don't think they do very much. At least Mom always looks frustrated to me." She surprised us by the ease with which she spoke, as if she had been waiting for a long time to address the subject. She may also have liked the sense of being one-up at being able to talk at all about the Great Taboo.

"What about Dad? Think he's frustrated, too?" Carl asked, always wanting to keep things equal.

Claudia was amused. "Well, he must do all that work for *some* reason."

David attempted a feeble joke. "Think I *enjoy* my work a little too much?" In spite of David's good humor, there was no doubt the couple was quietly horrified by Carl's intrusion, via their *children*, into the bedroom.

Carl turned to Don. "How about it? You think your parents enjoy sex enough? Or don't they tell you?"

"They don't tell me," Don said, deadpan.

"And you don't ask? I should tell you about the culture in the South Pacific where it's the duty of the children every morning to ask their parents about their sexual experience the night before. You know, to make sure everything went all right." Carl beamed. "We're just very backward here, with all this guilt and everything." Then he half winked at Don. "Just think of how helpful it would be for your parents if you guys could do that!" Don laughed anxiously.

Though Carl was experiencing no great success in opening up the subject, he wasn't about to give up. He looked slyly at Laura, who was trying to avoid looking at him. "What do you know about sex?" Carl asked.

"Nothing!" Laura said in a coy pout.

"Oh, don't tell me that!" Carl said. "You're just trying to pretend that you're an old-fashioned girl. I know about you modern girls." Then, more seriously: "Can you ask questions of your parents about sex?"

"I can ask Mommy," Laura said, looking at her mother. The two of them looked very warmly at each other.

"Very good," Carl said, "but you shouldn't leave your daddy out. How's he ever going to learn anything about sex if you don't ask him questions?"

"He knows," said Laura shyly, looking down at the floor.

Carl: "I know he knows facts and dull stuff like that, but he may not know some other things, like that sex is not bad, the way his parents told him it was. And if you ask him lots of questions, he may discover that sex is just part of being human. Grown-ups have a very difficult time with that, you know." Carl was talking to Laura, but he was also talking *through* her, and her loving and trusting naïveté, to David. In this way he was able to speak with a warmth and spontaneity that he couldn't achieve as yet with David or Carolyn.

Having disarmed the children with his banter, Carl could now turn to the parents. But I beat him to it. "Is sex a difficult area in your marriage?" I asked Carolyn. She looked a little as if she'd been asked to strip and perform a sexual act in front of the children, but she mustered her courage and managed to speak.

"Yes, I suppose it is. It certainly isn't satisfactory." Carolyn glanced shyly at her husband. "But I think it's more serious than that. The issue is more that we don't have much life together anymore. The lack of sex is just part of a general lack in our lives."

"Think you're both having an affair?" Carl asked in his cryptic manner.

By now Carolyn had learned to be tougher and more sophisticated in dealing with Carl. She arched one eyebrow slightly. "Not that I am aware of."

Carl laughed. "Well, the usual pattern is for the husband to have an affair with his work and for the wife to have the affair with the children. And each feels that the other is being unfaithful."

Carolyn was torn; she was enjoying Carl's levity, but she felt angry about some of the issues he was raising. She tried to smile, but only bitterness emerged. "Well, I certainly feel about his work as one might feel about another woman. As if I'm constantly being cheated on."

David had been looking a little sheepish, since his work was ostensibly the villain, but now he grew angry. "Well, I'm certainly aware of your 'affair' with the children, and, I might add, with your mother!" They were moving rapidly toward a confrontation.

The talk about sex hadn't lasted very long—partly because they were embarrassed by it and partly because Carolyn was right. The real issues were larger and more diffuse than sex. Before long, the familiar anger was back in charge, and it was to remain there for some time. It had been worth trying to try to talk about sex for a while, if for no other reason than to let the family know that we weren't afraid of the subject. And sex provided one way we could tell the family that it was all right—in our eyes—to talk about subjects that society says are taboo. "Go ahead," we were saying implicitly, "talk about it." Of course, once we became aware of it, we had to respect the fact that at this point they really *couldn't* talk about sex as a family. But the time would come.

The reader should not be put off by our teasing, intrusive, sometimes meddling approach. As we have said, the therapists have to push a little in order to get the family to break through the "everything is all right" facade that families feel they have to maintain in the beginning. But we also try very hard to respect their initiative in choosing their own subjects and proceeding at their own pace. We try to keep the right balance of "pushing" and "waiting," and sometimes we err in one direction or the other.

And the humor. Does it seem insensitive? I hope not, because it's often very useful. Families in difficult situations are likely to become very grim, morbidly dedicated to their issues and positions. Arguments that might sound ludicrous to an outsider become life-and-death dramas, each person holding on implacably to his or her interpretation of the facts. Nobody can give in because this would mean defeat, loss of face. Humor is one means the therapists can use to try to break this grim mood, hoping to wake the family out of their hypnotic trance where all is desperation and struggle. We can encourage them to change their mood by getting them to begin to laugh at themselves—just a little, anyway. Our jokes also help keep *us* sane through hour after hour of seeing tense, angry, often desperate families.

David and Carolyn managed to have something of a fight. For a number of sessions David had hung back from participating in the therapy, and now that he finally reentered he was quite exercised.

"I really think it's unfair to hang all your unhappiness on my working. I work for a living, for God's sake!" David paused, searching for words. "It's like your quarrel with Claudia; once you start in on something, that thing is what's responsible for all your problems. Well, I think you have problems of your own."

"Like what," Carolyn asked, "since you're so informed about my problems?"

"Like your relationship with your mother, for one. I feel she lives in our goddamn house, you're on the phone to her so much. And like your feeling that you don't *do* anything. You do what a *lot* of women do, but it isn't enough somehow. And it's *my fault*, apparently, that you aren't satisfied being a housewife and a mother!" For somebody who hadn't said anything for a while, he was doing fairly well, and Carolyn was taken aback by his anger.

She searched for a means to retaliate. "You talk about my mother so much, but how about your parents? Why did we have to move here? To get away from your father's pressure on you and to keep your mother from coming to you all the time with her problems with him." She wasn't doing too badly. "Also, I think that one reason you work so much is to please your big daddy. You have to live up to his standards and make a million dollars! Well, I'm not going to be as saintly and patient as your mother. I'm not willing to be married to some man's career!"

David lunged at her angrily. "But you wouldn't want to *do* anything about it, like find yourself a job or something to occupy you besides Susan Walters and her incessant troubles!"

Carolyn recoiled from David's anger. "Wouldn't that be wonderful! I could get as busy as you are, and then we'd *never* see each other."

David sounded bitter. "Well, maybe then you'd see some of my troubles, feel what it's like to be financially responsible for the family."

Carolyn: "But you would never try to understand my problems of this big house and three children. It would be *beneath* you to try to understand petty problems like that!"

Each had been injecting a little more anger at each step, and the argument built in intensity. Now they sat glaring at each other, wondering whether to escalate further. Then David blew up.

"So what the hell do you expect me to *do* about your problems? Beat my breast? Fast? Quit my job? What the hell do you want? I'm just *one human being!*" The fury in his tone, rather than the words he spoke, seemed to push Carolyn back into her chair, as if by an invisible hand. She had been defending herself until then, but David's outburst brought a dramatic change in her. Suddenly she was crying, again silently, tears streaming down her face. Her side of the argument collapsed in an instant. We heard a quiet, whimpering sound, a valiant effort to avoid breaking down into uncontrollable sobs. David stared in horror at what he had done, obviously feeling dreadful and wondering what he could do about it. The argument, barely begun, was over.

As I sat there wondering myself what to do, I felt a strong need to comfort Carolyn. Her hair drooped over one side of her face, and she looked sad and helpless, though strangely soft and appealing, too. I am an inveterate sucker for tears, especially women's tears. This time, though, I was suspicious of my response, perhaps because the crying itself seemed mysterious. One minute Carolyn was furious, and the next she had collapsed in tears. The transition was too abrupt. I thought to myself, "She looks like a little girl who has had a spanking." Nor was this a passing idea. I was beginning to see in Carolyn, a woman nearly ten years older than I was, a child who was crying because she had been spanked verbally. And I was feeling very parental. Still thinking to myself, I went a step further: Little girl. Spanking. Who did the spanking? David? Father? Mother? That was it!

I spoke to Carolyn. "Can I share a fantasy with you?"

Carolyn had stopped whimpering, and she looked up, her eye makeup streaked on her cheeks. "Sure," she said.

"I had the very clear fantasy that when David yelled at you, he suddenly became your critical, scolding mother." I waited a few seconds before resuming. "One moment he was your angry husband, and you were his angry wife. Then he became angrier, and it was like turning a switch. He became Mother, and you became a little girl." I was caught up in conveying the idea. Carolyn, you see, was responding to David as a transference figure, as a symbolic person. Transference occurs in every marriage, but when there is significant trauma or difficulty in the family of origin, seeing the partner as parent can seriously interfere with the marriage. It had certainly stopped the fight between this couple.

Carolyn looked straight at me, her eyes swimming, her face somber. She dabbed at the tears with a tissue. "That's interesting," she said reflectively. "I suddenly felt very frightened. I don't know why."

I wanted to make it very clear. "I think that at that *moment* you were remembering, and afraid of, the mother you had when you were a little girl. Suddenly David wasn't David to you any more. He was Punishment, Criticism, Blame. And it's very scary when that sort of thing happens." I was sounding a little parental myself. Then I asked, "Does this happen at home? Do you get to feeling intimidated like this when the two of you argue?"

"Yes, I think so," she said, mulling over the infrequent arguments at home.

"I'll tell you what you can do," I said, looking forward to giving some advice. "You can say to yourself when that happens, 'He's not my mother, and I'm not a little girl.' Then you can go right ahead with the argument."

"I suppose I can try," Carolyn said unconvincingly.

Carl had been silent for some time. It was not until he spoke that I realized I had been focusing entirely on Carolyn's part of the argument. "That might be very helpful. Because it seemed to me that both of you got scared that the argument was heating up and cooperated in bringing it to a halt. David agreed to raise his voice in a way he knew you couldn't take, Carolyn, and you agreed to break down. And David agreed to let your tears throw him. So the whole argument collapsed." Carl kept it nicely bilateral.

David was feeling accused. "I had no intention of making Carolyn cry."

Carl, firmer: "You're not hearing me. *You* didn't do it. Both of you seemed to get scared. It took both of you to stop the fight." Then Carl smiled faintly. "And that's a shame. You might have gotten some of these issues out on the table if you hadn't gotten scared."

David sighed, turning to face Carl. "On the table, maybe. But solved? I don't know about that."

Carl shuffled among the stacks of letters for his pipe cleaners, speaking to David as he searched. "I'm like Gus—I can give you some advice about that."

David was obviously eager to hear Carl's words. "I can always use more advice. Whether I follow it or not."

Carl turned back to the group, fiddling with his pipe, beginning to clean it. "Oh, it's really advice to both of you." A pause. "What you can do is to stop this psychotherapy game you play with each other."

"What do you mean?" David asked.

"What I mean," Carl said in a benevolent and deliberate voice, "is this process of your trying to be psychotherapists to each other."

"I'm not trying to play psychotherapist to Carolyn," David said a little crossly.

"Of course you are," Carl answered immediately. "You talk about Carolyn's problems with her mother and her problems in finding herself a new role now that the kids are growing up, and you sound like a worried mother yourself." He waited, smiling. "But don't just blame yourself. She does the same to you, trying to help you with your compulsive work pattern and with *your* parents." Carl stopped, letting David absorb what he had said, and David did think back over the argument for perhaps a half minute. Then he ventured another defense.

"It's hard to see that Carolyn is trying to help me, certainly."

"What else would you call it?" Carl asked.

David, after hesitating: "Blaming."

Carl: "Oh, I would agree with that. And it's not really that helpful on either side. But the problem is, you are aware of, and talking about, *her* problems, and she is talking about *yours*. And you're obviously not helping each other, though you keep trying."

Carolyn had grown more and more perturbed as Carl talked, and finally, she intruded. "Well, what is marriage *about* anyway if it isn't helping each other?"

I couldn't resist jumping in. "It's about a lot more than that," I said, and we were off, into a fairly lengthy debate about marriage and helping.

Our view is that marriage usually begins with the dream that our partner can be that idealized figure—parent, therapist, lover, friend, co-worker—who will help us fill all the hungers and needs which each of us brings to marriage. We especially hope that our partner will help us complete the difficult and unfinished business of growing up. And helping certainly *is* in the air of contemporary courtship; just listen to the popular songs full of lyrics like "Help me," "I need you," and "You have so much to give."

The confusing factor is that marriage *is* therapeutic. Married people live longer than single people, on the average, probably because they have someone with whom to share the work and stress of living. And marriage helps people change: to grow more sensitive, more caring, more responsible, more aware of the needs of other people. It *is* helpful to come home from work discouraged and have your spouse say a few comforting words and to give you a sympathetic hug. It *is* helpful to talk with someone else about your problems. But—and it is a big qualification—the very process of sharing the hurts and discouragements and pain of life with your spouse can sometimes lead to trouble.

If both partners are pretty secure people, reasonably independent and strong, with a basic sense of self-confidence and self-reliance, then they aren't likely to ask really *major* help from each other. They accept life's pain, its aloneness, and its stress as something they must handle—when the chips are down—themselves. They are aware that life can be more pleasant if they share *some* of the stress with someone else, but they don't usually try to escape the basic demands of living by making that someone else feel responsible for them as people.

But if they begin marriage like most of us—and Carl and I are likely to admit to couples that our marriages started out with some of the same unrealistic expectations as everyone else's—they feel dependent and scared and then look for help in major ways from their spouse. Each of us hopes that our spouse will provide us with that magic totem, security. Of course, we want excitement and companionship and practical help, too, and a lot of other things. *We bring too many needs to marriage.*

If one of the partners were very grown up and independent and mature and the other were mildly disturbed and immature, the helping process might work better. The mature one could help the immature one, and then they could go along as equals. In our experience this rarely happens. Some mysterious chemistry usually links partners who are virtually psychological twins. They are truly mates. The partners may *look* very different psychologically. The alcoholic's wife, for example, may appear to be very mature in comparison with the childish dependency and impulsiveness of her husband. But scratch the surface, and chances are she will reveal herself to be just as insecure a person as he is; she, however, is someone who gets her feeling of security by taking care of someone else. She has carefully concealed her insecurity by playing the *role* of helper.

We believe that married people are exquisitely well matched in a number of ways—in their general maturity, in their capacity for intimacy, in their tolerance for anger, in their sexual "temperature," in their capacity for being vulgar, or spontaneous, or honest, or a host of other psychological dimensions. And—very important—they are matched in the seriousness of the problems that they bring to marriage.

What usually happens is that they begin by making minor demands on each other.

Husband: "Gee, I feel lousy tonight. The boss was on my back all day."

Wife: "I'm awfully sorry, darling. Here, sit down, let me get you a cup of coffee and we can talk about it." It is all very innocent, and sure enough, husband feels better when he unburdens himself to his wife. And she may do the same thing the next day, complaining to him about the boredom of housework, or a nosy neighbor, or the impossible children. But the fact that it helps is one of the big problems. If a little help is good, why not a lot? So they begin asking more and more of each other, until soon they are bringing really major stresses to the marriage: "Help me with my relationship with my parents," or "Help me with my indecision about what to do in my career," or "Help me with my bad feelings about myself." Often the requests aren't stated directly, but the plea for help is there.

And matters quickly get complicated. Both partners begin to be afraid that they can't meet the other's needs. "How can I help my wife with her feelings about herself when I have the same feeling about *myself?*" the husband asks himself silently. And he begins to feel panicky. "How can I help my husband with his unhappiness with his career when I am not happy with what I am doing?" the wife asks herself. She too feels panicky. And each pulls away from the other because of the stress of the demands. There simply doesn't seem to be enough help to go around.

Then they both become alarmed about the retreat. Each turns toward the other, implying in various ways, "Please don't let me down like that! That's what my parents did, and I can't stand it." But the distance persists, and pleading soon gives way to angry demands and to pressure. Each says implicitly, "If I can't persuade you to meet my demands, I'll *force* you to! I'll show you!" They each turn to some "substitute" interest—his work, her kids, her mother, his drinking buddies, his affair, her affair. They are really trying to make each other jealous, each trying to show the other that someone or something else is supplying an element of support or involvement that they *really* want from each other—but are by now too proud to ask for directly. The interactions become angry and convoluted, a jungle of pressures, indirect demands and bitterness about unmet needs. Beneath the developing storm of anger and blaming are two cowering, wounded, lonely, tearful children, posing as adults. Though each knows about the needy child in the other, they both are afraid to admit its existence. Each would like to break down and cry and admit how scared and lonely he or she feels, but neither one dares.

One of the complications in this "help me" process is that during the long struggle each partner comes to see the other as a parent figure. Spouses don't ask for this symbolic process to occur, and many times they aren't consciously aware that it happens. But the experience of appealing to each other for help begins to "cue" powerful associations out of childhood. Carolyn, for example, had first to feel dependent on David; then, when he began to be angry and critical, she started to reexperience the trauma of being criticized by her mother. If she had never put David in a "parent" role in her life, she might have been able to see his anger as no more than the ordinary irritation of a husband who was her equal. Instead, his anger felt much more threatening and dangerous than that. It plunged her back to the time when she was a little girl looking up at the towering figure of an angry mother. The same symbolic process was happening to David, too, though we weren't as clear about the ways in which Carolyn was a parent to him until later in the therapy.

This reawakening of the associations of the "old family" is one of the things that happens to sex in a troubled marriage. It falls prey to the security needs of the couple. Out of their insecurity, they begin to see each other as parent figures, and soon sex feels as taboo and anxious a part of their lives as it was in the homes in which they grew up. In fact, sex between legally married adults may begin to have overtones of incest because this "parenting" process in the marriage is so powerful. It's very difficult to be both lover and parent to someone at the same time.

Is our interchangeable use of "parent" and "mother" and "therapist" confusing? We are indeed accusing the couple of playing all three roles with each other. Where are fathers in all this? If Carolyn is going to see her husband, David, as a symbolic person in her life, shouldn't she see him as father? Actually, we project so many symbolic images onto our spouses that we do see him or her alternately as mother, father, brother, sister, even grandparent. We re-create a variety of different family relationships in the marriage in order to try to solve some of the problem areas out of our past. And we don't stop with the marriage; our children too are soon involved in our incessant attempt to re-create our family of origin.

But because the mother-child relationship is the primary model for intimacy in our lives, it forms the basis for the deepest levels of intimacy in marriage. It is this early relationship that appears to set the tone in our lives for profound issues like the degree to which we trust and care about the Other and trust and care about Self and the degree to which we distinguish between Self and Other as separate, yet related entities. Fathers are certainly important in many ways in the early lives of their children, but this influence is expressed most crucially in the kind of participation they have in the marriage. If the relationship between husband and wife is good, the relationship between mother and child is likely to be good. But whatever the situation in the family world, this world is most intimately communicated to the child by the mother. It is the mother-child relationship that is later *transferred* most powerfully to the marriage. The warmth, the caring, the sense of belonging that develop in a marriage are first modeled in infancy between mother and child, and psychological disturbance between mother and child comes to bear heavily—much later—on the child's eventual marriage. When the partners turn to each other and ask, "Help me!" they are asking for completion of the mothering process. Thus, whatever the biological sex of the participants, helping and mothering seem to be synonymous. Of course, "mothering" is also probably the central model for psychotherapy.

In our culture the father's traditional role (and admittedly, all is in flux at the moment) is that of mediator between the intimacy in the family and the stress and competitiveness of the outside world. The toughness and objectivity that are traditionally associated with father are also valuable traits in the therapy process. For much that is wrong in the mother-child relationship consists of *too much mothering*, a symbiotic overinvolvement that becomes very frightening when it is later transferred to marriage. Thus, the therapist must really be psychologically "bisexual"—able to be intimate like the traditional mother, but able, too, like the traditional father, to teach separation and weaning and facing the fears of the "out there" world beyond the family's borders.

Both Carolyn and David had more stress than they felt they could handle, and they each were acutely aware that their partner was asking for help which they couldn't give. Still, they managed—unhappily and just barely, but they managed. Then one year David got a substantial promotion in the law firm and was suddenly in charge of its major division. Laura went to school for the first time that same year, leaving Carolyn alone at home, at loose ends, almost unemployed. Simultaneously, Claudia began to pull away from Carolyn even more strongly. Thus, at the very time when David felt additional stress from his job, Carolyn felt the stress of feeling unneeded and unnecessary. She tried pulling on David for more attention and more help with her depression, but he had his own problems. Claudia, sensing the deep and escalating tensions within her parents and between them, agreed to help out by becoming the focus of the family's mounting stress.

During this session Carl and I talked for some time about this marital "helping" process, and the problems we saw in it. It was a low-key, reasonable discussion. But the longer we talked, the more worried we saw the couple become, as if we were undermining basic tenets in their life. Finally, David asked the obvious question. "What are we to *do* if we don't help each other? Should we *hurt* each other?"

This one was Carl's, and he took their concern very seriously. "Of course not. But you can assume that for now each of you has failed as a therapist. So give up trying to help. You can even go a step further—feel free to *turn each other down* if you get asked for help."

"But why?" Carolyn asked.

"So that you can begin to use *us* for therapists," Carl said emphatically, "and loosen some of this stranglehold you have on each other. If we can be your therapists, you should begin to be free to be each other's *peers;* you know—lovers, friends, antagonists, mates. And stop this older-generation game with each other."

David was interested, but still skeptical. "But if we stop trying to get help from each other, where does that leave us when you guys aren't around? Would we keep this up forever?"

"No," I said, "I don't think so. What we hope for is that each of you, and the rest of the family, get enough out of therapy to be your *own* therapists when it's necessary. Not to need each other so much, not to feel so dependent on each other. Once you each become sure that you can handle life's basic stresses on your own, helping has a whole different meaning. Then it's *sharing* life, the good and the bad, rather than feeling frustrated that someone in the family isn't protecting you enough or feeling guilty that you aren't protecting them."

"That's right," Carl said, in synchrony with what I was saying. We agreed so completely about this that we could argue almost as one person. "Helping each other after therapy is over should be much more fun, much more casual, less binding, and less threatening. But to reach that point you may have to exaggerate your separateness for a time, to get over having exaggerated your togetherness in the past."

Don had been listening, and he chimed in cheerfully. "I like that, my old man and old lady being lovers. Imagine that! Just like on *Star Trek!*"

Carl turned toward Don, "You like that stuff, eh?"

Don: "Well, it's really pretty disgusting, but it would be a change, you know."

Then I glanced at Claudia, who had been silent the whole hour. She looked meditative and troubled, as if for the first time she had given serious, conscious consideration to her parents' marriage and found herself wondering about her place in it. She was unprepared for the thought that she might no longer be needed.

CHAPTER 9

A Partial Resolution

We assumed—rather naïvely, it turned out—that since Carolyn was feeling more cooperative and since she and David had begun to talk about their marriage, we might proceed to a straightforward resolution of the marriage problems. If this happened, the easing of the marriage binds would free Claudia from her complex entanglement in her parents' affairs, and she could go unfettered about the business of growing up. So much for our assumptions!

Carl got a call from David Brice about six o'clock on a warm, humid Wednesday evening in August. Carl and Muriel were about to go sailing, and the call was an unwelcome intrusion. Carl talked with David for a few minutes, then called me. I had had a late appointment, and as I walked in the door and was being greeted by the usual hugs and cheers of Mark and Sarah and Julia, Margaret said, greeting me warmly, "Welcome home, darling." Then she gestured toward the telephone which lay with its receiver on the table—"You've just had a call." I made a wry face as I went to the phone.

"Hello, old man," Carl said cheerfully. "Sorry to interrupt your homecoming, but how would you like to see a family tonight?"

"Tonight?" I said, feeling as if I had just stumbled into a hole. Margaret and I had been looking forward to taking a long bicycle ride with the children after dinner.

"Who is it?" I asked, trying to guess which of the several families we were working with at the time was in trouble.

"The Brices," Carl said, sounding weary, too. "I got a call from David saying there was a round-robin fight going on between Carolyn and Claudia, and he sounded worried." He paused. "I have a nine o'clock free in the morning, but I said I would check with you, and if you weren't free then, maybe we could meet with them tonight, much as I hate to. It didn't sound as if it could wait until next week."

"I don't have that time free," I said mournfully, watching my mint chocolate ice-cream cone melt before my eyes, just out of reach. It was hard to know who was unhappier about it, Carl or I. "All right. My office or yours?"

"Why don't we meet at yours?" Carl said. "It's closer to every-body."

As I was leaving the house an hour later, it was still light, but cooler, a gentle breeze moving easily off the lake and through the late-day trees. Sarah and Mark were climbing on their bicycles and Margaret was hauling Julia into the child's seat fastened to hers as I waved to them rather sadly and got into my old Volkswagen.

When I pulled up at the trim brown-brick office building where I practice, the birches that had originally attracted me to the building were bone-white and luminous in the hazy light, all that remained of dusk. The Brices were there already, piling out of their big station wagon. Don skipped toward the office, and Laura held Carolyn's hand as they crossed the parking lot. Claudia was ensconced in the shadowy recesses of the back seat, and David was leaning over the front seat, apparently trying to talk her into coming into the office.

I moved quickly toward the building, wondering, Why Carolyn and Claudia? I had thought they had quieted down. What the hell is going on? An awkward fumbling as I unlocked the outside door in the dark, the family watching me, and then the ritual of other doors and lights and the coffeepot. Carolyn sat down with the younger two children in the waiting room, looking tired and worried. Still no Claudia and no Carl. I opened a window in the stuffy office, and the swish of a passing car moved past like a long wave, the sound hanging in the air after the car's lights disappeared. Then only the quiet sound of evening crickets outside. I sat down and stared around at the empty office, thinking of Margaret and the children. I could hear faint voices in the hallway; it was Carl, arriving with Claudia and David.

The family moved into the office very quickly as if glad to be there, except for Claudia, who was the last to enter and came in with her head down. The parents sat together on my large brown sofa, and the children assembled in the smaller chairs around the room. Carl and I sat together, as usual. Claudia hunched down in one of the soft leather chairs facing us, her face still averted. When she finally looked up, I exclaimed, "Ye gods, what happened to you?" Her right eye was puffy and rapidly turning black, and her whole face was swollen from crying.

It was David who answered. "She and her mother have been in quite a fight—and still are." He was smiling faintly, as though he were proud either of the fight or that he had been the mediator. Then the smile disappeared, and a somber mood settled over him.

Carl and I looked simultaneously at Carolyn. She too bore the evidence of struggle; her collar button had been ripped off, leaving a tear in the fabric of the tailored flower-print blouse, and her hair was slightly disheveled. Her jaws were clenched and her eyes narrowed in what was obviously a continuing fury.

"What happened?" I asked Carolyn.

And again David answered, "They were getting ready for dinner, and Carolyn was trying to get everybody to help her set the table and so forth—"

Carl stopped him. "How about letting them talk about it? They were in it. Or were you in it, too?"

"No, for once I didn't seem to be. I deliberately tried to stay outside this one anyway."

Carl: "You mean aside from being the narrator." David was having a difficult time with Carl. There was indeed something faintly smug about David's approach to the conflict, and I didn't like it either.

I asked Carolyn again, "So what happened?"

"I don't know if I can talk about it," she said, tightening her lips still further and then exhaling in a rush, as if literally releasing pent-up pressure. Claudia glanced down momentarily, thought better of it, and raised her head to look directly and angrily at her mother.

"Here we go," I thought, wondering just where we were going. Carolyn hesitated at the edge of reopening the conflict with Claudia, then turned to me, though she obviously had to struggle hard to resist a further encounter with her daughter.

"I was making what I thought was an especially good dinner," she began, "or at least it was a very difficult recipe. A French dish with four separate stages. I was very tired—I hadn't been able to sleep very well, had gotten up early, and had run a lot of errands during the day." She thought back to what had happened. "And suddenly it occurred to me that everybody else in the family was doing what *they* wanted to do, and there I was in that hot kitchen trying to do something for them." Another pause. "Don and David were in the family room in the basement, having a chess game or something. Laura was upstairs with her dolls, and Claudia was playing the piano in the dining room, right next to the kitchen. Well, I got fed up and went out in the hall and shouted that I wanted some help straightening up and setting the table."

Don spoke up, a little fearful, complaining. "And I didn't hear you, Mom. Honest. If I did, God, I would have come!"

David volunteered, "That's true, Carolyn; neither of us heard you."

"And I didn't either," Laura said plaintively. "I was listening to my record player."

"Well, anyway," Carolyn said, "Claudia heard me—she was about ten feet from me—and she didn't come either!"

"I did so come!" Claudia muttered.

"Not until I shouted at you!" Carolyn said, now sure of her ground and not about to back down. Then she calmed herself and turned to me again. "Claudia finally stopped playing the piano and came in, sulking as though I had beaten her. She set the table very sloppily and reluctantly. But there was a lot else to be done—the salad had to be made, the kitchen floor needed sweeping, the living room needed straightening up, the dining-room chairs were still in the living room from the bridge party the night before. There was a lot else. But she only did what I asked her to do and pouted the whole time and then left. I was very angry, and I still am! So I yelled into the other room and asked if that was all she was going to do, and"— she paused, wondering what words to choose—"she said something back to me that was just vile. I can't repeat it. But I just saw red suddenly. I was not going to let my daughter talk to me that way."

Claudia glowered out of her chair in the corner, looking trapped.

David cleared his throat to get our attention. "Can I say something?"

"Sure," I said.

"Well, I was coming up the stairs at that point, and I arrived just in time to hear Claudia say it, and I don't blame Carolyn for being angry."

Carl dropped a cryptic remark. "Isn't it amazing how beautifully timed these things are?" He was referring to the fact that David appeared at the very instant that Claudia had said whatever it was that made Carolyn so angry. The old triangle was so much a part of the family that David almost inevitably walked into the developing storm. But the remark was lost on everyone but me. I was eager to find out what had detonated Carolyn's temper, turning to Carolyn with my question.

"Well, what *did* she say, for God's sake?"

Carolyn looked thoroughly embarrassed, and Claudia rescued her by blurting out angrily to me, "I said for her to do it her fucking self, that's all. Nothing terrible."

Carolyn flared. "Nothing terrible? What do you call terrible? I don't intend for my daughter to talk to me like that. I just won't tolerate it!"

I didn't want them to start fighting again, so I kept prodding Carolyn. "Then what happened?" With some relief she went on to describe the rest of the fight.

"I just completely lost my temper. I started screaming at her at the top of my lungs that she had to get out of the house, that I would not have her living in the house with me if she was going to talk like that. And she said something else, which I don't even remember, and suddenly I hit her. I didn't mean to hit her very hard, but I did."

Claudia muttered toward the floor, "I said that I wouldn't leave, that's all."

"Funny," I thought to myself, "instead of Carolyn's trying to keep Claudia from running away, she's now trying to throw her out, and Claudia is refusing to go!" The war stays the same, but the people shift positions without even realizing they are doing it.

Carolyn darted a glance at us, then at Claudia. She raised her voice slightly. "Well, it was the final straw; it was just as defiant as you could get. It felt like she was saying that she would tell *me* what to do and I had to take it! Well, I'm not *going* to take it!" She and Claudia, at the brink of going at each other again, looked at Carl and me as a safe reference point that enabled them to restrain themselves.

It was a difficult moment, in which we were expected to supply a cue to what the family should do next. Should they continue their fight as before? Should they talk to us about it, each trying to justify his or her position? Should they search their past for some clue that would help them understand the origins of the anger? Actually, they had already answered the question by calling us in the midst of their fight. The process of encounter was in motion; they just wanted us as chaperons so that it didn't get too dangerous. It is very tempting for the therapist at this flash point to become anxious about the potential for violence in the family and to say to them in various implicit ways, "Now, now, let's be reasonable about this." Behind this message from the therapist there lurks the therapist's fear of anger. "Keep it cool, please, because I'm scared of your anger."

But Carl, I suppose because he had been at this spot so many times before, didn't hesitate about what was appropriate. "Can you say that to Claudia?" he advised Carolyn, who was starting her complaint about her daughter again. Carolyn realized that this was the cue which the two of them had been asking for and that it meant they were to continue their confrontation. There was some fear in her face as she turned to her daughter, and we heard the strength drain from her voice as she tried to speak to her.

"Claudia, I just can't accept this kind of behavior from you."

Claudia raised her head and challenged her mother. "And I can't take being hit by you."

But I didn't share Carl's confidence about handling the situation this way. I found myself looking at the sharp edges of the heavy glass ashtray on the table beside Claudia. Then I saw the easily grasped contours of the small stone sculpture which Margaret had given me and which stood within inches of Carolyn. What a fine blunt instrument it would make, hurtling across the room! I grasped the arms of my swivel chair tightly. I had a strangely tangential thought, finding myself wondering how I could get blood out of my off-white carpet.

Then, out of somewhere in my own head, I began to hear the distant tones of a reassuring voice. "Now wait a minute! You're getting too excited." As soon as I said the words to myself, I realized what had happened. Suddenly I saw the family that I had grown up in; we were sitting around the dinner table, talking quietly, pleasantly enough, and all the while silently angry with each other about a thousand little things which we didn't dare mention. We were not even *aware* of the anger most of the time; years later I realized how carefully we muffled any anger and aggression in our family. What was happening in this interview had happened to me before: the "patient" family began to break one of my family's implicit rules,

"Thou shalt not express anger directly!" And like my parents, I tended to equate the verbal expression of anger with dangerous physical violence. When the "patient" broke *my* family's rules, I got anxious! After all these years, after all my own therapy, after all my training, after the creation of my own family with very different rules (Margaret and I do have fights), you'd think that I would know better. This is simply one of the hazards of being a family therapist, however; the family is so powerful and so "involving" that it sets off reverberations that go deep into the therapist's own life. The family you are treating suddenly becomes a version of the family you grew up in, and you become a "patient," struggling with your own feelings. Another reason to have a co-therapist—it usually doesn't happen to both therapists simultaneously!

So while Carl calmly told the family to "go ahead" with their fight and while Carolyn and Claudia tried to address each other, I tried to relax. From time to time, however, I glanced at the statue so near to Carolyn's fidgety, angry hands, and at the darkening, puffy cloud around Claudia's eye, and at that damned ashtray poised like an armed missile on the teak tabletop.

Carolyn calmed down considerably once she began talking directly to her daughter, as though Carl had called her bluff when he gave her permission to see the conflict through. "Claudia, what makes me so angry is not what you said—I've heard all those words before. It's your *attitude* that infuriates me. It's degrading and mocking and generally disrespectful. And I don't know why it's taken so long for me to get here or just what's happened, but suddenly I can't take it anymore." She waited a moment, and when she began again, her voice had a kind of settled integrity, not its usual trembling quality. She seemed really to mean what she said. "Oh, I suppose I could take it indefinitely. But I won't. We've come to the point where something *has* to change. You have to change your attitude, or you have to get out." Then another thought occurred to her, and she almost smiled as she spoke, a quizzical, speculative tone to her voice. "Or *I* have to get out. I suppose that's possible, too." And she turned to David. "If you feel that she's right in this and I'm wrong, then maybe I should leave and you should deal with her." She grew calmer and calmer, and David looked alarmed.

He stammered, "I—I don't know whether to say something here or not. I thought I was trying to stay out of this one."

"Say what you feel," I said, curious about what was going on in him.

David spoke to Carolyn. "I think I am with you. I think her attitude is lousy. I'm not sure you needed to hit her, but I am sure that she should show you more respect, deference, whatever you want to call it." Now he sounded more forceful, and Carolyn heard the emphasis in his voice. She remained silent as she realized that her husband was supporting her.

I glanced at Claudia, who was obviously furious.

"Well, I think she could show me more respect, too, like by not hitting me in the face! Is that respect? How can I be expected to respect somebody who hits me for just talking back? All I did was to refuse to do anything else—Christ, I had already done what she asked me to!"

Carolyn flared back. "Claudia, we are not equal in this house. I am your mother, and I refuse to let you talk to me in certain ways." Her voice eased a bit, took on a note of compassion. "I am sorry I hit you. I really didn't mean to, or at least I didn't plan to. And most of the time I am—or I try to be—pretty considerate of your feelings. I don't degrade you, and I won't stand for your degrading me."

Claudia was at the end of her short patience. *"That is not so! You criticize every damn thing that I do!"* she screamed.

Carolyn was startled. At first she reacted with that supercool detachment that was her usual response to Claudia's outbursts. Then there was a change. She turned toward her daughter, her eyes flashing in anger. Her voice was strong and assertive. "Claudia, I don't criticize you. I nag you. I prod you. I push you to do things."

Claudia yelled again, *"You damn sure do! All the time!"*

Carolyn winced, then raised her own voice to a shout, not as loud as Claudia's, but angrier. *"And the reason I do is that you force me to! When I ask you to do something, you do it grudgingly, or you just refuse to do it."* Her voice dropped, though her forcefulness did not diminish. She was very direct, aiming the words. "And I don't really *care* if it's reasonable or not at the moment. But I want you to *follow what I ask of you,* not because you agree with it, but because I *ask* you to!" Now her voice swelled and pushed against us all. *"Or I want you to get out of the house! I don't know if you understand this or not, but you have to choose between obeying me or leaving! It's that simple!"*

It was Claudia's turn to be shocked. For a moment she lost her poise. Both women were sitting on the edge of their chairs, straining toward each other, then recoiling, caught in a magnetic storm of force and counterforce. Quickly Claudia regained her position and resumed yelling. *"What do you think I am? A six-year-old? Like everything you say is right and I should do it just because Mommy says so? Well, maybe I don't think it is right! I'm not six years old!"*

Carolyn, still loud but not shouting: "That's *not* the point! I'm perfectly willing to give you more responsibility when you demonstrate that you can handle it. But the point is that I am *not* going to stay in the same house with a daughter who disobeys me!"

The other people in the room sat white-faced and rigid. Laura, frightened, shrank back into the sofa. David was pale, glancing back and forth between the two antagonists. Don stared wide-eyed, his mouth open. And Carl and I sat, not helpless but inactive, following the course of events and realizing that we were like referees in a hotly contested game, on the edge of the action but important.

There had been an inhibited quality to all the other fights we had witnessed in the Brice family. The anger would be muffled and bitchy or else one-sided, flaring out from one person and not answered or reciprocated by the other. Or it would be cut off when one participant refused to go any further or left the room. But this fight leaped hot and strong from both sides, neither person relenting, giving ground, or holding back. A tight cord had held other fights together, binding the antagonists to each other, as if there could only be one "person" in each argument. But now Carolyn and Claudia had risked breaking whatever bonds tied them together. They were two separate, sovereign, and very angry people. However painful, however tumultuous, this fight was an accomplishment. If there had been a symbiotic link between mother and daughter that had previously dictated the incessant compromise of their anger, it seemed now to be vanishing in a fire storm.

As the argument continued, rising and falling in intensity, Carolyn's strength became more and more evident. She was *immovable* in her insistence that Claudia either acknowledge her authority or leave. At first I found the fight exciting: the birth of Carolyn's assertiveness, of her greater sureness about being a parent, and Claudia's forceful exposure of her sense of the injustice of her situation. It seemed a necessary and therapeutic catharsis, a crisis that might enable them to reach each other.

But as the argument continued, Claudia grew more and more

worried. She sensed her mother's insistence on being the "adult" in their relationship, and she was not willing to capitulate. She regained that old suspicious look, as if, in losing the battle, she were forced to look for some devious way to maintain her position. As I saw the panic grow in her, I started to worry once more about what she might do.

Claudia began to have trouble thinking of what to say in response to her mother. As she groped for words, she suddenly struck me as very young and very vulnerable. Before, I had always seen her anger, her rebellion. Now I saw a scared girl who was considering what it might be like to be forced out of her home. I thought about this, too —the court hearings, her being moved to a foster home, the social worker who would be assigned, and the problems of trying to work with this pretty and troubled girl if she were moved out of the home. Claudia looked confused, betrayed, and cornered.

I myself began to feel somewhat confused. I was now not certain whether the interview was constructive or another disaster in the making. As it progressed, the disaster theory gained ground. Claudia simply couldn't manage to make concessions to her mother, even if allowed to yell at the top of her lungs about her position. I could see what I thought was coming: Claudia would defend herself, raising her voice or her tactics to meet her mother's increased strength, and the mother would respond in kind. The escalation would continue until one or the other broke—and what a damaging and costly breaking this might be!

The most immediate problem was what Claudia had in mind at the moment. She glanced anxiously at the door, and I wondered if she were thinking of walking out again. A lot depended on this very delicate moment. Claudia appeared so defeated and so trapped by her mother's new strength, and so demoralized by the fact that David had sided firmly with Carolyn, that she apparently had no defense against complete capitulation—except flight, of course. I sat there thinking to myself, "Claudia needs some support," but I didn't know what to do. Carl shifted in his chair as if he too were trying to find some way of helping.

Then suddenly it happened. Claudia stood up, took the three long strides to reach the door, and blurted out tearily and very angrily, "Well, you can have the whole damn mess! I can't stand it anymore!"

As before, everyone was so startled that no one moved. David and Carolyn sat blankly as she passed in front of them, and Carl and I watched her walk by us. She had to squeeze through a narrow space between my knee and the sofa to reach the door, and I was tempted to block her path. But keeping Claudia in the family wasn't my job. If somebody stopped her, it should be her parents, and they were apparently not able to. So I did nothing, and Carl did nothing, and in the long agony of one or two seconds, all the disasters replayed themselves in my mind: the court hearings; the foster home; the bitterness all around.

Then Claudia reached her hand out, grasped the doorknob, and wrenched it. Loud as a shot the stunned onlookers heard the unmistakable "clunk" of a locked door that refuses to open. The door was immovable. On my way in I must have unwittingly relocked it when I took the key out, and it is one of those unusual doors that remain locked on both sides.

Claudia turned around and looked at me, her mouth hanging open in amazement. Horrors of horrors!—trapped with your parents and family in a therapist's office! "What the hell!" she said. At my right Carl laughed suddenly, a gentle but contagious laugh that punctured the seriousness of the entire situation. Everyone fell, like proverbial dominoes, before a laugh that summed up our anxiety and relief and sheer delight at the ultimate absurdity. Here we were, poised at the edge of a tragic drama, enacting a script in which the hurt and enraged daughter storms off into the dangers of the world —only to be foiled by a faulty stage prop.

"What the hell!" Claudia repeated, trying not to smile and failing. An embarrassed grin crept across her face in spite of herself and persisted right through her faltering protest. "I want to get out of here!"

"I'm very sorry," I said, smiling, "my unconscious must not have wanted you to leave."

And that made Claudia angry again. "Dammit, I want *out* of here!"

"I wish you'd stay," I said softly, admitting in the way I said it that I knew I really didn't have the power to keep her, that it was only a request. "I think you ought to try to struggle some of this stuff out with your mother."

The room was very silent again as Claudia glowered at me, then at her mother. I made a motion to get the keys out of my pocket. Just as I pulled the keys into view, Carolyn spoke. Her voice held a note of considerateness and apology, a softening. "Claudia, sit down, and let's talk about it." A pause. "Please." This too a request, not an order. It was as if she had realized that Claudia could leave, really leave, and that she too was acknowledging this by the way she asked her to stay.

Claudia sighed, captured by the softness in her mother's voice. Real caring, when it happens, is absolutely irresistible. She returned to her seat and slouched in it with more than a little relief. And while she sat down, as if offering a gesture of confidence, I unlocked the door.

For a moment nothing happened. Claudia was still not able to talk to her mother. When the pause began to seem awkward, Carl intervened, speaking to Claudia. "Can you try to put into words what you were expressing by walking out? Or talk about the feelings that pushed you so hard?" He was very serious and delicate with her. The laughter had been a marvelous relief for everyone, exposing the absurd understructure of the situation, but as valuable as it had been, it was important now to avoid laughing at Claudia or having her think we were laughing at her.

But Claudia was still not ready to talk, and Carl was concerned. I thought I saw the problem; she felt herself so scapegoated that she wasn't willing to become the focus of anybody's questioning, however gentle. So I turned to Carolyn. "You think part of your anger doesn't belong to Claudia, and maybe that's some of why she was so resentful?"

"What do you mean?" Carolyn asked.

"This started," I said calmly, "when you were mad at everyone for not helping with dinner. But Claudia is the one who inherited all the anger. I don't blame you for being angry at Claudia's degrading you—I'm just trying to get at other aspects of this struggle. Do you feel the whole family doesn't help you enough, that they all presume on you?"

"Yes, I guess I do," Carolyn answered finally. Another pause. "It's true that everybody assumes that I will keep everything picked up and organized and supply the meals and the clothes and everything. And I get tired of it." Her anger began to grow again. "Don has never hung up a piece of clothing in his life, almost. He's supposed to take out the garbage, but I get tired of nagging him and do it myself. Laura, maybe she's too young, but she's supposed to set the table."

"How about your husband?" I asked, smiling slightly. "You haven't introduced him to the fact that dishes fit his hands as well as they do yours?"

"Him?" Carolyn said, glancing at David, her voice a mixture of pique and amazement. The idea that David could help with the household chores struck her as incongruous. "He'd never stoop so low." She was bitter. It was surprising how quickly we moved away from the argument between Carolyn and Claudia into this less explosive but important issue. Claudia felt scapegoated by her mother, but Carolyn felt used by the whole family.

Carl picked up. "It would have been interesting to see what happened if you had opened the door and thrown the dinner out in the backyard. Maybe they would have heard you the next time." Then he turned toward Claudia, who was looking both relieved and a little lost at seeing the focus move away from her. "Where are you in all this? Still angry?"

I expected Claudia to rise up again, vindictive and blaming, but instead she began, gradually and softly, to cry. The tears merged with her words. "Whenever something like this happens, it's always like this. I'm always the one blamed, like it's all my fault."

"Well, clearly it isn't," Carl said to her gently. "Did you really believe that it was all your fault?"

Claudia answered, catching her breath in the midst of several short sobs, "I can't help it when she yells at me like this." Her voice grew higher-pitched, as if she were suffering again under the pain of her mother's attack. "It begins to seem like it *is* me, that everything that goes wrong *is* my fault."

"Well, that for sure is not so," Carl said emphatically and reassuringly, "and I hope that everybody can sort out and own up to their own part of the blame." He spoke gently to Claudia again. "It's sure good to hear you admit that you get hurt and scared as well as angry. It makes you seem very human to me."

In the midst of her quiet sobs Claudia took two startled breaths, pulling herself out of the crying to look warmly at Carl. Then, embarrassed, she looked away. For the briefest moment, however, the two of them exchanged a kind and loving glance.

That silence again, the people in the room respecting a significant moment. Hearing someone admit she was in pain was such a relief after all the attack. The meditative silence continued. Carolyn looked calmer now, and melancholy, as she sat across from Claudia. "Where are you?" Carl asked Carolyn.

"Oh," she said, awakened from her musing. "A little embarrassed, I guess. As I listen to Claudia, my anger seems overdone, out of proportion. I don't know why I got so angry."

"Oh, that's clear enough," Carl said. "I was thinking during the silence about our first meeting and how we had to keep the two of you from fighting then. This anger built up in both of you over a long period, and you had to get it out of your system. I think this fight had been planned for a long time."

Carolyn was worried. "But does it *have* to be like this? Isn't there some better way for us to resolve our differences?"

"I certainly hope so," Carl said. "This is pretty brutal for everybody." He paused, a note of discouragement in his silence. "Maybe now that the two of you have gotten some of this fury out, you can move on to warmer things."

"But how?" Carolyn wondered.

"I don't know exactly how," Carl admitted. "If I had a formula for it, I'd tell you." A reflective pause. "There are so many things going on at once in the family. You are validly trying to establish some authority with your daughter at the same time that she is validly attempting to find more freedom and independence. The fight you had tonight should have been resolved ten years ago. You and David are also trying to get together after years of being apart, and you are trying to reorganize the family so that everybody takes more responsibility. It's a tangled-up mess, and it's going to take some time to sort itself out."

"It certainly is a mess," Carolyn said, discouraged.

"The hope," Carl said, his voice brightening, "is in this new tone of voice that I hear now. It's a lot more considerate and a lot more personal. I think the real solution is to get beyond this question of who's going to be in charge and to develop a better person-to-person relationship." As he continued to speak, Carl sounded encouraged. "I don't think any parents ought to let themselves be degraded by their child, but with all this complexity to cope with, I also don't believe parents can be always in *control*. There's too much to control. A family has to operate with a kind of intuitive synchrony, like a team that wants to win. You play well together because you want to, not because somebody makes you."

"Wow," Carolyn said. "We're such a long way from that." She glanced quickly at Claudia, and the girl met her mother's eyes briefly, then looked away.

"That look you gave each other was a start," Carl said. "You want to take it further? Are there things you want to say to each other?"

"I'm sorry I lost my temper," Carolyn said contritely to Claudia.

Claudia, still hurt and angry, answered moodily, "Me too." She deliberately left it unclear whether she was apologizing or blaming her mother further. The encounter was forced.

"You characters," Carl chided them. "You're not sorry—even if you're not quite as *angry* as you were a few minutes ago. Don't make believe you didn't mean what you said. That's when we really do mean what we say, when we're angry. So you blew up! So what? Let's go ahead."

The session was almost over. Everyone looked very tired now that the tension had eased. I had liked Carl's discussion with Carolyn, but I had a sense of uneasiness, as though the fight were still essentially a mystery to me. The question which I had at the beginning of the hour still bothered me: why, after we had finally got down to work on David and Carolyn's marriage, had this sudden explosion occurred? Suddenly the image of Claudia's unhappy face at the end of the previous session flashed before me, and I saw the connection.

"Claudia," I said. "Can I share a thought with you?"

"Sure," she said, but hesitantly.

"I think I figured out why this fight happened. Remember last session? Your mom and dad were getting down to work on their relationship?"

"Yeah?" Claudia said, a questioning note entering the word.

"Well, I think it scared them, scared you, scared everybody. So the family unconsciously agreed to go back to yours and Carolyn's war to rescue your mom and dad from the hot seat. That way they didn't have to face each other, and you didn't have to lose your role in their relationship."

"I never thought of that." A gradual smile of confirmation spread across Claudia's face.

"Except the family really may have goofed this time," I added, smiling.

"How's that?"

"It may not have been the same old fight after all. You and your mother may have gotten somewhere this time."

"Thanks to that weird door of yours," Carl said. And with the laugh, an end.

CHAPTER 10

Releasing

For a few days after the encounter between Carolyn and Claudia, both Carl and I felt uneasy about the family. We were worried, of course, that there would be more confrontations between the two women. We also had some concern about how the interview in my office had gone. One of the cardinal rules for the therapists is that we should not allow one member of the family to be badly scapegoated if we can prevent it, and by permitting the fight to escalate to the point where Claudia felt overwhelmed, Carl and I had violated that rule. We had simply made an error. Decisions in the heat of battle are difficult to make, but we should have come to Claudia's rescue before she got so desperate that she had to walk out.

Normally, David would have taken Claudia's side, but this time he had left the job of mediation to us. Perhaps Carl and I were so impressed when Carolyn emerged from her aura of defeat that we underestimated the effect her anger was having on Claudia. At least part of the reason for David's incessant intrusion into the women's disagreements was clear now: when Carolyn came out of her depression and began to fight, there was a lot of power in her pent-up anger. Perhaps Claudia did need protection at times.

Our worry about continuing explosions was apparently unwarranted. There were no calls, no further emergencies. At the regular meeting the following week the family came into the office talking animatedly to one another. Claudia was cheerful and rested, smiling benignly as Don cavorted around, attracting attention. Only the slightest discoloration remained under her eye. She and her mother

sat on the same couch, though Laura was carefully positioned between them. Still, it looked almost friendly. My suspicions were
confirmed when Claudia and her mother glanced at each other with
mock pique and shared amusement at Don, who was emitting high-
pitched squeaks as part of his monkey imitation.

"Guess what, Whitaker?" Don blurted out when everyone was
seated and he had their full attention.

"*Dr.* Whitaker, please," Carl retorted, smiling. "Won't you ever
learn?"

"Oh, I forgot," Don apologized. "*Dr.* Whitaker!"

"That's better," Carl said.

"As I was saying before I was rudely interrupted by this impudent
doctor," Don continued, "something veddy inter-esting has happened. Mother and daughter now speak to each other. Are even
friendly at times! It's true. Household is definitely quieter."

As the story unfolded, it became apparent that Don was right.
Following the explosion, Claudia and Carolyn had made some tentative moves toward each other. Their "talks" had begun one night
while they did the dinner dishes together, and this particular conversation continued for nearly an hour afterward. The content wasn't
momentous; the fact that they were talking was what mattered. The
real breakthrough had apparently come when Carolyn started out on
her regular early Sunday morning walk to a nearby park and asked
spontaneously that Claudia come along. And Claudia agreed.

"I don't remember what we talked about," Claudia recounted,
"but it just felt good to share something with Mother." Everyone was
a bit mystified by the peace, as well they might be after the crisis of
the previous week.

I ventured an opinion. "Maybe what was important were the
overtones in your voices. Maybe you each heard the other's caring."

"I think maybe you're right," Carolyn said, though she still
sounded a little perplexed by the change.

The remainder of the interview was taken up with a discussion,
initiated by the family, about how they might avoid such angry confrontation in the future. Carl and I said that the best way to avoid big
explosions was to have more fights and to have them sooner. Little
disagreements, promptly aired, avoid a dangerous buildup of anger.

We also talked about the family's need to develop a new language
system, something we frequently reiterate in our work. The mem-

bers of the family had to learn to talk about themselves and their own feelings rather than to engage in a critical attack on someone else. Instead of saying to Claudia, "You are a no-good shirker," Carolyn should have said, "I feel harried and unappreciated here in the kitchen. Would you help me?" The family listened attentively while we talked about this new language. They certainly understood on an intellectual plane what we were talking about, but putting it into practice would remain difficult. Old habits change slowly.

They also needed to democratize their system of conflict, we told them. All the fights seemed to take place between Carolyn and Claudia. Why didn't Carolyn fight with David? Were Don and Laura always spared criticism? It was a simple point, but an important one. One relationship could not be expected to bear all the stress of a family, and the more the family could deal with conflict *as a group*, the more productive we felt they were likely to be.

The major topic, however, was how the family could become "a better team." Both Carl and I like the metaphor of the team, since it vividly conveys the need of a group to function in synchrony, though each member obviously has an individual role. We felt that Carolyn worried too much about not being in control of her children, particularly Claudia. The various chores that revolved about the dinner hour were a good example. How could they shift from a system in which the parents—chiefly Carolyn—had all the responsibility and all the control to one in which the family shared the sense of both responsibility and control? How could they begin to feel differently about helping one another with the many practical chores that needed to be done? How could they develop more enthusiasm for their activities as a group?

We were careful to say that we did not approve of adults' allowing their children of any age to degrade them or push them around. It was important that Carolyn had been more forceful with Claudia. But we shared their belief that strength and force in adults need not be expressed by screaming at top volume. It could be a humane, sensitive use of power. And if they worked hard enough, perhaps the power in the family could also be democratized, with the children assuming more responsibility as they became able to shoulder it.

This point should also be clear to the reader: we do not advocate the high noon scream-out as a solution to family problems. When families have accumulated a great deal of anger over a long period of time, they often need an arena in which some of that anger can surface, and they need to learn safe ways of releasing it. Despite our occasional errors, the fights that take place in the therapeutic interviews are under pretty careful supervision and much more likely to be productive than the same conflicts carried out at home. Neither Carl nor I encourage families to plunge naïvely into "letting it all hang out," especially if the family is not working with experienced therapists. There is too much at stake, and the issues are too complex, to assume that a simple formula that says "express yourself" can be anything but another disappointment—and perhaps a hazard—in the long pull.

The family was relaxed at the end of the session, stimulated by the discussion but with few subjects of their own to talk about. The next interview was also rather benign, with a good bit of joking and casual talk. Claudia and Carolyn continued their "making up." Having asserted herself, Carolyn was now able to loosen some of her controls on Claudia, and Claudia responded to the freedom by staying home more. Paradoxically, Claudia gave in to what her mother wanted only as Carolyn both demonstrated her power and lessened her demands.

The family also held several conferences about chores around the house and reached an agreement that all, including David, would help more. He agreed to supervise and help the children in the after-dinner cleanup of the kitchen and family room, and Carolyn was delighted. So far the system seemed to be working.

The next interview was much the same—by now almost boring in its lack of conflict. I felt a little uneasy about the "social" quality of our conversation, chitchat about the weather or current news topics, punctuated by labored discussions of minor family problems. Carl revealed no outward sign of being perturbed by the sessions. He held Laura on his lap and helped her draw pictures of monsters, whom she affectionately named Mommy and Daddy. He quipped with Don about his diffidence, saying that he would have to let us work on it for him since we needed a problem to focus on. He talked with David about the business world and politics. Carolyn talked about her parents, who were coming for a visit.

I thought I knew what was happening, and it was time to talk about it. "You know," I ventured finally, "this doesn't feel like therapy to me. I don't think we're accomplishing much." Silence in the room.

"I've been thinking the same thing," Carl said quietly, with a puff on his pipe. "I've been wondering if maybe we're through."

Carolyn, who had been so reluctant about therapy in the beginning, blanched. Obviously the thought of quitting was threatening to her, but she didn't utter a word. Don, on the other hand, said, "Yippee!" Then added, "Can we go now? Or even sooner?"

"Patience, shrimp," Carl said to him, "or you'll become the next scapegoat if you're not careful." He paused, adding, "Then we'll *really* help you!"

"What do you mean, I'll become the scapegoat?" Don asked, a little anger in his voice, and a trace of fear.

"Well, you never know," Carl said enigmatically. "Sometimes a family elects three or four scapegoats before it resolves the stress. But you can never be sure. You might just get off with being a brat."

Don stuck his tongue out at Carl. Carl's statement was said in fun, but there was a note of seriousness.

David spoke up. "You know I've been thinking, too, that we might be through, but I thought maybe you guys knew something that I didn't know."

"It may be the other way around," I said, "that the family is the only one that can know when it's time to quit. We could go on forever once we get to know a family. You really can't trust us to tell you when to stop."

The talk about ending therapy continued for a few minutes. Clearly there was a lot of indecision. In the process of working, we had established a pattern, a rhythm of meeting and struggling with problems that had become a reassuring part of the family's life, though therapy also had its threatening aspects. The prospect of discontinuing brought the family up short, making them realize that they had become dependent on the hour each week, the neutral ground, and the therapists.

The family was not of one mind, however. Carolyn and Claudia seemed worried about the possibility of quitting, perhaps fearing a resumption of their warfare. David was indecisive, weighing and measuring alternatives in his compulsive manner. Don continued to press for stopping, and Laura didn't care either way. The hour wore away as the family sought some definitive basis for making a choice. They didn't find it.

Carl had his appointment book out, and I reached for mine. We sat there looking at the family while they looked at us. It was time.

"Well," Carl said blandly, "what should we do?"

"I don't know," David answered, his brow in its familiar furrow. The question of the next appointment had become strangely important.

After a roaring thirty-second silence Carl made the move I expected. "Maybe we should quit for a week or so, and you should see how things go. If they go well, great. If they don't, then all you have to do is pick up the telephone."

"Sounds fine to me," David said warmly.

Carolyn still hadn't spoken, and we needed to hear from her. Everyone turned toward her.

"Well, all right," she said, looking worried. Then she managed a brief smile. "But only if we can come back if we need to."

"Of course," we answered in unison.

And so they left, the younger kids looking a little as if school were out for the summer, the adults cheerful and cordial but not relieved. Claudia's worried, furtive glance caught my eye as she left the room.

After they had gone, Carl and I talked for a while, drifting back over what had happened, musing about the family's future.

The explosion between Claudia and Carolyn still puzzled us. It seemed to serve quite well to get the focus away from the marriage, for we may indeed have pressed too quickly into that sensitive and troubled realm. The family under stress is a delicately balanced ecosystem, dependent on the very structure which provides it with so much pain. By suddenly shifting our inquiry into the marriage, we left Claudia without her usual role, and we raised the level of anxiety in the couple precipitously. With a "wham," the family restructured itself along its old lines.

But the fight was not quite the usual one. At least on the surface, it was a dyadic conflict this time, since David did not intervene, a circumstance which may have left Claudia in very panicky territory. Again, dependence on the familiar. This fight was also a lot more intense and continuous than usual, since even Claudia's habitual agreement to terminate the struggle by fleeing was thwarted. The temperature setting on the family thermostat went *way* up.

The fight also seemed to dispel the implicit fear in the family that verbal confrontation was analogous to murder. The anger poured out, and nobody died. In fact, the "binding," "symbiotic" quality between Carolyn and Claudia seemed to be broken by the fight.

With two people so turned on, it had to be clear to them that they were two people, not one person. And they badly needed this sense of separation. With the separation came some of the appropriate generation gap which had been lacking, as well as a warmer relationship.

Perhaps the most valuable part of the fight was the intimacy of making up. It is strange that people sometimes can't admit their caring until they have done some very painful things to one another, and someone finally cries out in agony. The process of attack and reconciliation is a mysterious one, but very powerful and ancient in human affairs. When the history of accumulated aggravation seems to dictate such confrontation, it is very frightening for those involved since reconciliation is never guaranteed. Confrontation can lead to disaster in relationships, as well as to renewed caring, with so much of the balance held by the unconscious intent of the people involved.

In fact, the Brice family's *will* to work out their problems seemed their strongest asset and an absolutely essential ingredient in psychotherapy. As we looked back over their progress, we saw a family struggling to get somewhere and in the process of struggle creating their own therapeutic "happenings." The family didn't deliberately keep Don at home at the first interview, or send Claudia crying from the room, or decide to back away from the marriage and reconfront the mother-daughter relationship. The collective—and creative—unconscious life of the family did all this, and this intuitive-unconscious group process, in collaboration finally with the therapists, is the real curative agent in family therapy. The most powerful moments in therapy are when the family's unconscious process mingles with the therapists' unconscious thoughts, as when Claudia's troubled image suddenly appeared to me at the end of the confrontation hour, allowing me to see something new in the family. These are the moments we hope for but can never achieve deliberately. They must happen.

The family's latest creation—the good humor and relaxed talk—raised some interesting questions. While it was possible that they were really finished with therapy, their major problems solved, we certainly doubted it. This development was almost certainly what we term a "flight into health," in which the family is threatened by the process of rapid change and "invents" a pseudo-goodwill which allows them an excuse to escape the therapists. Thus, they cope with their anxiety about change by agreeing as a family to be "cured." It is a bit like the youngster who sees the image of the hypodermic needle before him and suddenly reassures his parents that he is "all better now."

There is another aspect of early termination: it often represents a pledge of solidarity within the family, a growing consensus that "we can do it ourselves." Even if the family later decides to continue treatment, they have been through a rehearsal for the independence that is essential to normal living. By deciding to stop therapy, the family can also assert control over the pace and depth of therapy, demonstrating to themselves and to us that they can always drop out if the going gets too uncomfortable.

It was important to support the Brices' sense of well-being and independence; like parents watching their children go bravely off to school, we didn't want to undermine their initiative and self-reliance. We felt that they had much more work to do, but we assumed that they would return if they wanted to do it. If they did return, it should be with a new sense of freedom to plunge deeply into therapy, convinced of the safety of instant escape if things got too difficult. Perhaps then the agenda would be different: to change the basic organization of the family, not only to resolve a crisis.

Carl and I were finished with our discussion, ready to go home. There were dirty coffee cups beside the coffeemaker; the chairs were slightly askew. The aura of the family was still there, however—the anxious laughter, the furtive fond glances, the moments of tension and fatigue. They were still a single presence all around us, a murmuring of voices that spoke of their caring and their will and their anger. I thought then of Claudia, sitting alone with the individual therapist some months before, and once more of the family, connected so intimately and so forcefully with one another.

"Can you imagine trying to work with any of these people alone," I said to Carl as we rose to leave, "now that we've seen how involved with each other they are?"

Carl smiled a peculiar smile while he locked his office door: "Not only can I imagine it, but I did it for fifteen years." Then his voice became more somber, revealing the fatigue which we both felt. "It's so much easier to see where you are after you've left."

CHAPTER 11

The Underlying Crisis

Fortunately, not all couples are as fearful as the Brices of facing their marital problems. They recognize the conflicts, realize that both contribute to them, and go to a therapist together to do something about them. Especially if they go early, before the history of "injustices" has mounted to an ominous level or before the children have become deeply involved, these couples constitute the easiest, the most hopeful, and the most exciting work that we do. Young married couples can make rapid and dramatic changes in their newly formed "world," and helping them make these changes can be deeply satisfying.

There are probably many more couples and families like the Brices, however. The marriage crisis remains hidden, almost invisible, even though serious. The couple simply don't see the problems, though sometimes they have to work hard to avoid seeing them. The reason they don't want to look is obvious enough to the outsider: they are so dependent on each other and so afraid of any disruption of their relationship that they cannot admit the true magnitude of the problems. They have developed a technique of temporizing over the years: they walk away when they are angry, pretend affection when they don't feel it, and hope that time and effort will change their attitudes. They become timidly and anxiously estranged, living through their days with suppressed yearnings and muffled screams, exchanging the contentious and exhausting pressure of their inner lives for an uneasy peace.

They also develop a myth of catastrophe. As tensions build, images of threat begin to invade their consciousness, fleeting day-dreams that foretell of disaster and ruin. The images vary, depending on the family's particular tensions and vulnerabilities. For some, affection itself has a dangerous quality, threatening to entrap them ever deeper in the coils of marriage. For others, the fear of separation or divorce is the imagined disaster. Some imagine losing their pride and crying like children. But for almost all, anger is the omnipresent enemy, lurking under all the hours of their lives and all their words, the part of themselves that they wish would go away, the force that promises to rend the very frame of their lives.

The partners accumulate so much: needs for affection; desires for freedom; intense anger; sexual cravings; an aching sense of alone-ness; bitterness at broken promises; multiple disappointments and humiliations. Their postponed hunger for life becomes more and more demanding as time passes, yet anything that might uncover these needs and frustrations becomes a threat in itself. *So frightening are these tensions that the couple often cannot allow themselves to be consciously aware of them.* All the drama of conflict takes place quietly, implicitly, so that even the participants at times question the reality of their experience. "Am I imagining this?" "Did he really say that?" "Is my feeling valid?" The conflict surfaces for a time, fright-ening the couple, who then relegate it to a vague "tomorrow."

Psychotherapy, particularly marital psychotherapy, threatens to "uncover" the anxious turmoil in the marriage. "If we seek help as a couple," the partners say silently to themselves, "it will all come out." The anger, the bitterness, the hurt, the sense of self-blame that each carries—this will be the harvest of their opening up to each other. "Maybe it will destroy what we have" is their fear. They dread not only losing the stability of the marriage, but damaging their fragile self-images. Rather than risk their painful and tenuous secu-rity, they suppress the possibility of working on their marriage to-gether. "Too dangerous," seems to be the final judgment, although at most this is only a hazily conscious decision.

The evasive "strategy" which the Brices developed to conceal their problems through scapegoating Claudia is not practiced on adolescents alone but can involve children of any age. And there are many different "symptom patterns" which children develop as a result of the burdens they carry. Children who are hyperactive, have persistent sleep problems, are underachievers, wet their beds re-

peatedly, stutter, adamantly refuse to go to school, have violent temper tantrums, refuse to eat—these and other symptomatic children
are probably suffering from the stresses of their parents' marriages.
Therapists of our persuasion are not only aware of these connections,
but immediately involve the family in treatment when they receive
such a referral.

The scapegoat need not be a child. One of the spouses can agree
unconsciously to be "the problem." Either partner might become
depressed, develop tension headaches, become obsessed with his or
her job performance, develop insomnia, begin to drink, develop
stomach ulcers or hypertension, fight with the children or his or her
employer, acquire a phobia. One wife became terrified of leaving
home without her husband, even to go to the grocery store. It was
not until her husband admitted that he had been thinking for some
time of filing for divorce and they went together for therapy that
they found the source of the phobia. The wife had sensed the marital
rift, intuited her husband's intent, and unconsciously created the
symptom to keep him close to her.

Why does only *one* partner usually have the "symptom"? Because
of the couple's need to protect not only the marriage, but the whole
family. At least one spouse has to be able to cope with the reality
world, while the other "specializes" in contact with the disturbed
feelings present in both partners. The "sick" spouse may then go to
an individual therapist, even though the crisis is basically a marital
one. This decision may have grave consequences for the couple,
some of which we will discuss later.

The development of a symptom in a family represents two contra-
dictory trends or unconscious "plans." The stress "belongs to" one
person, and thus for a while the family can avoid facing the real
dilemma in the marriage. But there is a second-order unconscious
plan. The person in crisis may eventually link up with someone
outside the family, thus unbalancing the family system and precipi-
tating an open crisis. Thus scapegoating, the mechanism for maintaining temporary stability, leads to an eventual break in the impasse.

But of all the creative strategies which couples use to avoid facing
their problems, at the same time walking sideways toward them, one
pattern seems to be gaining popularity: the affair. It is a desperate
attempt by the couple to break the marital impasse, one that takes

them to the edge of disaster, and often beyond. A brief look at one couple, typical of so many that we see in our practices. Like the Brices, John and Eleanor Kenderson found the early years of marriage close and satisfying. But that marvelous sense of coming alive through their love for each other did not last. They soon drifted into the kind of purgatory which the Brices experienced: feeling tied to each other, with little enjoyment. They both had been unhappy as children, and the few good years during which they were dating, falling in love, and getting married seemed now to have been a mysterious interlude. Their present lives were a monotonous plain of moderate despair. It did not occur to them that they had re-created in their marriage the same feeling that had existed in the families they had grown up in, but it was true.

The impasse in the Kendersons' marriage was quiet and durable, and sometimes they had to look hard to recognize that there was any difficulty at all. Weren't all marriages like this—a succession of cool, greyish days in which there was much to do but little to savor? Their angers were petty, not deserving the energy they required. Yet largely out of fear, they learned to contain them. When the anger did surface, the storms were brief, bitter, and destructive. No good came of the fights. Caring seemed to have died altogether, replaced by duty.

After a few more years they felt that nothing ever would change. They both were afraid to leave each other and their young children, whom they *did* love, but they did not expect what they silently yearned for: a return to those fleeting years when they frolicked in a different land where they felt both warm and free, excited and safe. Had it been a dream? Or was that merely all one was allowed of life? Silently (and few of all these hopes and doubts had been spoken), they began to wonder if perhaps they were dying. When that suspicion surged, an insidious panic began to grow within.

Even later they were not able to understand exactly what had happened to change their expectations for their relationship, but something significant unquestionably occurred. Perhaps it was the week they spent with his college roommate and his wife, getting to see at close range a marriage that seemed happier than theirs. Maybe it was her sister's divorce, and the shock waves it sent through a family that had known few divorces. It may have been a book or a movie that set up reverberations, or a crisis that friends went through. However "it" arrived and on whatever level it was received, the couple responded with some hope to the possibility—only vaguely sensed at first—that something in their marriage might change.

On questioning, they were eventually able to recall a specific conversation. They had seen on television a movie in which the husband had an affair. Maybe they should have been suspicious that at eleven-thirty at night their talk was wide-awake, even sprightly. Eleanor had finally said, humorously, of course, "Well, if you ever have an affair, I don't want to know about it."

"Not even a hint?" John joked.

"I don't think I could take it," she said with a laugh. They did not realize that unconsciously or half-consciously, they were working out a plan.

In the next few months John found himself noticing other women in a way he had not felt for some time. He did not say to himself, "I am looking for someone." But it was true. Like an animal coming out of hibernation, he was hungry and hunting. He was not aware that he was looking for someone who was also looking for him, who also felt a certain urgency to do something dangerous and as yet unthought of.

The critical event occurred at an office party which Eleanor could not attend because she was sick. In the interest of occupational duty, but with a secret elation, John went. Perhaps it was just chance that Teresa, a young woman with whom he had exchanged a few interested glances at the office, was there without her usual boyfriend; perhaps it was part of a plan more subtle than most of us would like to admit can exist. However it happened, John and Teresa spent most of the evening talking with each other. They hardly noticed the rest of the party.

Strangely enough, what they had begun talking about were their problems. She was worried that she had not received the usual raise. He was discouraged with some of the problems his children were having at home. She was a little upset that her boyfriend had not come to the party. He was feeling bitter about his wife's tendency to get sick whenever there were important business events. Then they quickly passed on to other issues, finding in talking that they had a lot in common: both liked modern art and movies, and both enjoyed having a dog and taking long walks. It helped that they felt tired and a little blue and that both had a little too much to drink, but something subtly and genuinely exciting stirred in both of them.

He offered to drive her home, and smiling furtively, she accepted. In the car he felt dizzy, excited, and scared. His heart raced wildly. When the young woman nestled her head in the hollow of his shoulder while he drove, he could think of nothing except kissing her. All the way to her apartment they rested in this kind of ecstatic suspension, like statues ready at long last to leap into life, but afraid. "I hope the ride lasts forever," he found himself thinking—and wondering if the thought weren't strange. He did not realize that what he was really seeking was just what he was experiencing on the ride home —the delicious experience of nestling snugly with a mysterious, forbidden person.

For a week the newly met couple remained poised at the edge of what alternately seemed like disaster and paradise. They had lunch together twice, and they were unable to talk—except by implication—about what they were thinking. The event which they anticipated and savored also frightened them. Finally, she invited him to her apartment, and once there, they rushed into each other's arms with a force that was primitive and intense. The lovemaking that followed was, as they said to each other, "the best it had ever been."

The husband, now lover, suffered a good deal of guilt. He was unable to tell his wife, saying to himself that this, after all, was just a temporary arrangement; perhaps, as she had asked, he might never need tell her. It puzzled him that he felt a certain loyalty to his lover; he could no longer enjoy intercourse with Eleanor and found excuses to avoid it. The lovers settled into a routine of meetings they found all too infrequent and rushed, though the very brevity and guilt associated with the meetings helped maintain the intensity of the encounters. These were dreamlike, passionate experiences which left both protagonists puzzled. Both wanted to keep the relationships that preceded their affair, yet they were drawn so powerfully toward each other that it made them question much in their lives. Why did they feel so alive and intense with each other? And why, if they enjoyed each other so, were they reluctant to leave their other partners? The complexity of their situation was in itself appealing. They also wondered, as they mused silently and separately, if they knew each other at all. There was so little time to talk.

Then Eleanor began to suspect. The failure of their sexual relationship, the one area in which John had seemed to retain some enthusiasm for her, made these doubts arise. For months she dodged the questions that appeared like dream fragments in her occasional reveries. Then the questions became vague images: of men and women together, of places, of words and deeds. Usually she avoided imagining the deeds. She wanted to ask. She was afraid to ask. She waited.

Husband and wife became aware that something was about to happen, though they could not know what it was. Like two exhausted birds hovering over an uncertain sea, he guilty, she ridden with self-doubt, they finally settled on a piece of flotsam from the wreckage of events. It was a tiny piece of physical reality: in his pocket, a matchbook cover bearing the name of a motel. All she really had to ask was: "Is it true?"

With relief and dread, John said, "Yes."

What followed was a classic confrontation. If John's affair was a kind of reawakening, so now was this marital encounter, though of a very different sort. Eleanor was enraged, hurt, confused, and racked with a sense of failure. John was guilty, angry, also confused, but not apologetic. The two partners fought and cried, talked and searched, for an entire night. The next evening, more exhausting encounters. Feelings that had been hidden for years emerged; doubts and accusations that they had never expected to admit were articulated. Eleanor had to find out everything, and the more she discovered, the more insatiable her curiosity became. The more she heard, the guiltier her husband became and the angrier she grew, until he finally cried for a halt. It was his cry for mercy that finally led to a temporary reconciliation of the couple. They cried together for the first time either of them could remember.

For a while they were elated; they had achieved a breakthrough in their silent and dreary marriage. They felt alive together for the first time in years. Somewhat mysteriously, they found themselves going to bed together in the midst of a great tangle of emotions—continuing anger, and hurt, and guilt, and this new quality: abandon. The lovemaking was, they were to admit to each other, "the best it had ever been." How could they have moved through hatred into caring so quickly?

They came to rest for a few days. Then the question dawned on both of them: what about the lover? What was to become of that relationship? John was reluctant to promise that he would not see her again, and sensing this, Eleanor panicked. The fighting began once more, this time with a new, urgent sense of impasse. He could or would not give up a situation which she found intolerable. A day later Eleanor, crying as she talked to a sympathetic neighbor, wondered aloud about what to do. The neighbor suggested psychotherapy for the couple.

Thus do a good many young couples come into therapy. The extramarital affair is certainly not confined to young couples, and many young couples go into therapy without the spur of an affair. But this situation does provide us with a model for looking at family therapy in which the "identified patient" is a young couple.

First, some dynamics. If one overhears gossip about an affair or even listens carefully to how one thinks about such an event, the logic is fairly simple: "John was unfaithful to Eleanor." Thus, he did something *to* her, and it was a bad thing. While there is a sense in which a surreptitious affair is a "dirty trick" perpetrated by one individual on another, this essentially moralistic explanation grossly distorts what is often a very complex event.

In our view, the affair, like many major marital events, is intuitively "arranged" by the couple. It is unconsciously agreed on in advance, and the "innocent" party actually aids and abets the "crime"—though the use of the word "unconscious" is perhaps a bit misleading. If Eleanor and John had listened carefully to their joking conversation about the possibility of John's having an affair, they could have realized that they were "toying" with the idea and that Eleanor was giving her implicit consent. She was in effect endorsing him as the "chosen one" and giving instructions about how he should behave: he should not tell her. Later Eleanor may also have made the affair easier by turning off sexually, by ignoring John's attempts to talk about their problems, and by overlooking the early evidence that he was looking for a partner. They were following an unspoken prearranged script in which she agreed to be especially innocent and naïve, and he agreed to be covert and "wicked." Just as the couple plan the affair together, so do they seem to plan its duration and even the process of "discovery." There seem to be no real secrets in marriage, only the deliberate failure to verbalize what each partner senses intuitively is happening.

But just as the forces that lead to an affair do not originate within one person, so they also are not confined to the marriage or even to the unholy triangle. There are, at least symbolically, many people in the adulterous bed. The affair can be seen as one political event in a network of relationship struggles that can extend in all directions, but most commonly into the family of origin.

When John was ten, his parents were divorced. Their marriage had been stormy from the beginning, and the ostensible reason for the divorce was John's mother's alcoholism and the sexual encounters with other men which her periodic drinking sprees seemed to encourage. John's father had his problems, too; he was a distant, chilly man who could be quietly and subtly sadistic to his wife. John and his sister went to live with their mother, but John bore the brunt of the stress in the years that followed the divorce. When he came home from school in the afternoon, his mother would be waiting for him. She would be drinking, and she would want to talk. Never mind John's homework or his need to see his friends. She had to talk to save herself, and he had to listen. To her rantings about his father. To her sorrows. To her flimsy schemes for success or revenge. Nor was John's task merely to listen. Since he was the new "man of the house," he became in time the object of much of the hostility which she still felt toward his father. John's mother was terribly dependent on him, she loved him with an inappropriate love, and she abused him.

John and his mother began a persistent, quiet conflict. The issue centered on John's freedom: to date particular girls; to leave town on trips with his friends; to make his own decisions about the courses he took in high school. His mother could not say to him, "I'm afraid you will leave me the way your father did," because she did not see the motive behind her attempt to bind John to her.

But while John's mother sought to tie him to her, she was not very loyal to him. Periodically she became reinvolved with her ex-husband, and they would date each other for a while. Then John would feel abandoned and depressed. These "affairs" with John's father never lasted for long, and they were almost invariably followed by drinking sprees and other, more desultory affairs. Then John would become even more depressed, since the roles he was assigned depended on his mother's whim—now her substitute husband, now a mere child.

John suffered quietly, at times aware of being vaguely angry and conscious that his mother was involved in his irritation. At other times it was much worse, an agony in which he felt trapped, suffocated. He would then see his mother drowning and feel himself being pulled down with her. "I have to get out of here," he would say silently. He had had complicated nightmares in which he was being killed in various ways, but suffocation was a frequent theme.

Eventually John did escape, largely through the efforts of his father, who saw some of John's problems with his mother and began to spend more time with him. He helped John begin to think about a career and eventually sent him to college. Once in college, John found that he had a good brain, and he began to do well. For a time achievement became his life's meaning and something of a salvation. He still felt lonely, but as he realized that he could survive in the world of the intellect, his depression and confusion began to lift. He felt alive for the first time in years. It was then, just as he began to be aware of his own strengths, that he met Eleanor.

A pert, intensely energetic blonde, slim and intelligent, Eleanor appealed to him immediately. She had some of his own emerging love of ideas and some of the anxious friendliness which he recognized in himself. They fell in love quickly and with great excitement, spending long afternoons walking in parks, running together along a lake's edge, renting bicycles and finding lonely country roads to explore. They stayed up late going to movies, necked on a bench outside her dormitory, and didn't study. They each failed a course that semester, something unheard of for either of them.

John's father offered to help them financially, and they decided to marry and continue their studies. Their lives rushed together in what felt like great relief to both of them, a close and happy synchrony. There was much to cope with and little incentive to look at their differences. While Eleanor was the more obviously insecure of the two, the relationship they formed was a thoroughly bilateral "adoption" in which each "mothered" the other with ardent devotion. Here at last was someone who really cared, paid attention, and helped.

Like John, Eleanor had grown up in a home with parents who were unhappily married, but her parents had never dared legalize their emotional divorce. Eleanor was haunted throughout her early years with the pain of her parents' estrangement. She wondered if there were anything she could do; she even wondered if it could be her fault. Eleanor's mother made the children her life; after all, she had to have some companionship. Eleanor became very dependent on her mother because her mother trained her to be so, though neither mother nor daughter realized it was happening.

What Eleanor did realize was that for some reason she could not name she could not trust her mother. Somehow, when Eleanor really needed her, her mother was never "there" in a psychological sense. Rather than be genuinely sensitive to Eleanor's needs, some of which were for more independence, her mother used her as a security object. Unconsciously sensing her mother's anger at the self-sacrifice she imposed on herself for her children, Eleanor was always afraid that her mother would leave her.

Thus, John and Eleanor had sharply contrasting "basic" life anxieties. *John feared being smothered, overwhelmed; Eleanor feared loss of support from someone on whom she was dependent.* These were anxieties which they could sense. When Eleanor got too close, John became uneasy. When John was distant, it made Eleanor very uncomfortable, even alarmed. So for a number of years they kept a delicate balance: not too close for John, not too distant for Eleanor. They were graduated from college. With continuing help from John's father, they could afford to have children while John went on to graduate school. Teaching college chemistry was to be his career.

As is so often the case, it was only after they had closely supported each other for several years that the tension finally emerged in their marriage. The couple dare risk a breach in their symbiosis only after they have each gained some life experiences and have benefited from the close supportiveness of the marriage. They cannot expose their problems until they have achieved enough sense of security to think that they may be able to survive going it alone.

John began to resent the small ways—or so they seemed to him —that Eleanor was dependent on him. She had never learned to drive, and he had to take her places and run errands for her. There were other things she "couldn't do" and was afraid of. She was sick a lot. She cried easily. Taken together, these things began to make him feel resentful. He asked her to change. She tried but failed. Gradually his resentment shifted to anger and to a quietly accelerating panic. "These are small things," John would say to himself. "They shouldn't make me so upset." He began to hyperventilate, and suddenly he found himself saying to himself, "I'm suffocating in this marriage. I've got to get out of here!"

What John did not realize was that he had transferred to Eleanor his resentment at his mother's "binding" him in so closely. Eleanor's demands and her dependency on him were indeed irritating, but they did not warrant the fury and panic which they created in him. Feelings which he had suppressed at home with his mother came roaring up in him like a geyser, frightening him with their force. When he said to himself that he had to flee the marriage, it was in part his own feelings which he sought to escape.

John thought of confronting Eleanor and demanding more psychological space in their relationship—more freedom for himself, more breathing room. But he could not do it, as he had not been able to with his mother. Instead, he retreated, a defense he had learned well as an adolescent. When this happened, Eleanor became more anxious, making more demands on him, which in turn provoked further retreat. This period of increasing, but still manageable, anxiety was the time in which the "plan" for the affair was conceived.

The affair represented freedom for which John had long yearned. The marriage had re-created the sense of his adolescent prison, and he invented a symbolic escape. And he did indeed enjoy the wild country into which he fled. But the excitement of the affair was structured in his mind in strict relation to his sense of confinement in the marriage. He needed the marriage for security, the affair for a sense of excitement and freedom. Neither was complete without the other.

When the affair was finally confessed to Eleanor, it became the converse of an escape. Suddenly she was faced with her worst nightmare come true: betrayal, abandonment. She was enraged and terrified by the thought that she might lose John. She had transferred onto him the fear of abandonment that haunted her childhood; so the affair, significant enough in itself, assumed cataclysmic proportions. Eleanor's panic and desperation reactivated John's old fear of engulfment. The more frightened Eleanor became of losing him, the more frightened John became of being imprisoned again. The thought of giving up his lover was like abandoning forever the very idea of freedom. The spiraling stress that drove them to seek a therapist was indeed the stuff of terror, Eleanor clinging frantically to John, even though she knew that she was driving him away, John flailing out at what he realized unconsciously was his mother, at the same time that he was acting *like* his mother. Both of them felt on the very edge of craziness.

Was there some evil spirit that had cast together these two people so much alike in some ways, with such exquisite access to each other's deepest vulnerabilities? Was this, in fact, a relationship designed to drive each of them crazy? Our conviction is that they married each other in part because they sensed, unconsciously, the potential for just such a crisis. This was a relationship which would eventually force them to face their central life fears. In what Freud described as a repetition compulsion, they re-created the central dilemma for each of them in order to work through it and this time to have it come out better. Eleanor would somehow master her fear of betrayal; John, his fear of being smothered and engulfed.

Thus do we see many of the crises of marriage: the partners manage to activate in each other anxieties that plunge them back into the central conflicts in their respective families of origin. They do so not out of perniciousness, but out of a mutual, collusive, and unconscious attempt to grow. If they can face these horrors together, perhaps they can really live at last. Ordinarily, only the person whom we really love, who touches our very roots, has the capacity to drive us crazy, and it may be only this person who has the capacity to help us find our deepest strengths.

John and Eleanor were most afraid of what many couples find the threatening aspect of their marriages: deadness. In this context the affair becomes a search for more energy, more life, more excitement. It represents an effort to counter what the systems theorists call negative entropy, the progressive "running down" of the system toward lower and lower levels of available energy. This trend threatens the growth of the individuals, if not their lives, and the need to find access to their repressed vitality is both mutual and urgent.

The couple's search for more energy and excitement is centered on the sexual relationship, but it is, in fact, a more general quest. John was puzzled that he could feel such passion, such tenderness, such abandon with his lover, someone whom he scarcely knew. He also did not understand why his and Eleanor's sexual relationship had deteriorated so badly. The answer to his confusion lies in the power of the human mind to associate and transfer experience. Because it became their chief source of security in life, John and Eleanor's marriage was easily associated with their families of origin. Marriage began to have the feeling, the aura, of "home." With this association came some of the powerful repressive habits that both had learned in their families. John had intense sexual feelings for Eleanor, but because he had been so overinvolved with his mother, he could not allow himself to feel them, experience them openly. Eleanor possessed for him some of the connotations of "mother," and these vaguely sensed qualities contravened his need for sexual experience. He repressed his sexual feelings for Eleanor in order to avoid these "incestuous" connotations.

When Eleanor asked John to describe his lover, Teresa, to her, John was speechless for a minute or so. Then he said with some amazement, realizing it for the first time, "Well, she's actually a lot like you. I even think you might like her." He had found a lover with whom he could experience openly some of his accumulated, but repressed, sexual feelings for Eleanor. Teresa was a stand-in for Eleanor! All this outpouring of sexuality really "belonged" in an emotional sense to the marriage.

The affair thus becomes a "model" for the kind of freedom and intensity which the couple seek for themselves. Eleanor must ask in detail about John's experiences, for she really wants to know what it is like. After all, she too must overcome some of her inhibitions if they are to have an exciting sexual life. And the sense of fierce competition which she suddenly feels toward this rival for her husband gives her an incentive which she badly needs. John has gone scouting in the jungle of forbidden experience, and he has found a quality of excitement, a breaking of taboos, which the couple then incorporate into their relationship in order to break down some of their own marital taboos. For a while this appears to work; their relationship "heats up" dramatically.

The affair demands that the couple communicate on a more profound level than they have in the past. The initial "explosion" is obviously a message of powerful, if garbled, import, sent from the "adventurer" to the "innocent." John says to Eleanor, by implication, "This is the kind of exciting sex I would like with you." He may also say, "I want more freedom," or "I like it when somebody treats me with tenderness." The implications that he is angry with Eleanor are certainly not hard to miss. Once John's "message" has reverberated somewhat mysteriously throughout their relationship for a while, however, the process of opening up can become more two-sided. Eleanor asks about what is behind John's actions, and he tries to reply, and then she begins to say more about her feelings, her dilemma. The couple start to talk about subjects that they have not dared face before; for instance, just what is it that John is unhappy about in their sexual experience? How does Eleanor feel when John disappears into his studies for weeks at a time? They begin to talk more honestly *because they have to*. Their relationship is in such desperate straits, teetering at the edge of separation or divorce, that they overcome their timidity and face each other. It is now or never!

The search for help is also an element in the creation of the affair. The amateur psychotherapy which the partners have been practicing with each other has failed, and the adventurer is elected to find a psychotherapist for the couple. The fact that John tells their troubles to another amateur, a lover, is probably only a mistake in judgment. The intent behind the search is genuine, and the need real. Both John and Eleanor badly need help, even though the affair is not very adequate assistance once the crisis has been created.

For all the overtones of meaning which an affair has, and for all the people who at least symbolically have a part in its creation, it remains an enormously risky venture. The acts of betrayal are not evil premeditations, but usually ritual reenactments of previous betrayals in the families of origin. John did to Eleanor what his mother did to him. In spite of the potential for growth for all the parties, the affair leaves real wounds in those who feel the sting of disloyalty, and sometimes these wounds heal with difficulty or not at all.

Often the affair represents the beginning of an end of the marriage. The couple understand none of what lies behind their situation, and they become polarized in a terrible duel fought largely over guilt and innocence. The "adventurer" is sanctimoniously cast out by the deeply injured "innocent victim," and while each may secretly cry to be understood and forgiven and taken back, the proud faces they present to each other are stern and unmoving. In frightened self-defense they become progressively more committed to unalterable positions, the breach between them widening and deepening with each acrimonious day. The affair that began as an impulsive decision becomes a seemingly desirable alternative to the bitter marriage, and divorce promises, though it cannot produce, an end to their agony.

The affair puts the entire relationship at grave risk. The couple have strayed from the ordinary path to the edge of a terrible cliff where they stand, balanced precariously. There, even a few words, a few days, a few critical events, may make all the difference. In this atmosphere of desperation, psychotherapy for the couple, or the lack of it, may hold the balance of the rest of their lives.

CHAPTER 12

Return

Two months had passed before we heard from the Brices again. David made the call, and he didn't tell Carl what the immediate problem was. He simply sounded worried.

We had begun therapy with the family at the beginning of summer. By August we had reached the point of early resolution or of plateau—we weren't sure which. Now it was early October and still mostly warm, with a cool shadow moving for a few days over the land, then retreating. Still, one thought of winter. As I drove to the appointment we had set up for the Brices, I wondered about therapy and the season. Were we getting down to work with more seriousness, now that the work year was under way and winter coming?

The family greeted me cordially as I walked into Carl's office. I hesitated at the edge of saying that I was glad to see them again, realizing that they were not glad to have to see us. Indeed, they looked anxious—not the happy group we had said good-bye to in summer. Only Laura seemed her cheerful self.

David was officiating for the family. He spoke to Carl. "I felt that we should schedule an appointment as soon as possible. Something happened with Don that concerned me, and I think it bothered Carolyn and Don, too." His voice was as calm and reasonable as ever, though I realized as he talked that beneath his strained moderation he was upset. If only he could admit it openly!

Carolyn had an irritable air, her quick eyes glancing at me as she moved her chair to face David. She and Don were sitting in the two chairs in the center of the room, and David was alone on the couch to Carl's right. Don sat between his parents. Claudia and Laura seemed miles away on the couch to the left, as though they were separate from the conflict that was emerging before us. As Carolyn began to speak, I noticed that Don looked worried and distracted. He had worn a light jacket to the session, and he showed no inclination to take it off even though the room was warm.

"I certainly *am* upset," Carolyn said to David.

"What if Don tells his view of what happened?" David said, a somewhat scolding quality in his voice. He looked disapprovingly at Carolyn, and I was puzzled about what was happening. The couple were talking about Don, but they seemed to be fighting with each other.

Don's attention grew more focused as the talk was directed at him. He spoke to his mother. "Well, I am still mad about what happened. It was the worst thing that ever was. Well, not the worst, but it really killed me!" His manner had a quality of panic and anguish new for him. This was more than childish anger; it was real pain, truly upsetting and confusing. He concluded, "What really bugged me was that you kept sounding like you were right about everything."

Carolyn was immediately defensive. "I wasn't saying to your father that my way was *right!*"

Until this point Don had managed to avoid looking directly at his mother, but now he turned toward her, glowering, raising his voice suddenly and forcefully, almost yelling, "Yes, you were! You said you were *right!*"

Carolyn was shocked at Don's outburst. She turned to Carl and me as though afraid of pursuing the argument with Don. "There's something I want to get at, and we might as well get at it right now. Because I'm *amazed* at how ready Don has been to attack me for the last few weeks, but especially the last few days." She seemed angry at Carl and me, as though it were somehow our fault.

Don was not to be deflected. He continued to speak loudly, leaning toward his mother, his hands still in his jacket pockets. "Because I'm pretty mad at you! If what you do is destroying me, I get very mad at you for that! This is wrecking me. It kills me. It really makes me feel bad!"

Carolyn flushed and tightened her grip on the chair arms. She looked as though she might burst into tears or scream. At that instant Carl interrupted, signaling everyone with an extended hand to listen to him. "Hey, just a minute." The family looked in his direction, apparently glad to stop the impending explosion. Carl was good-humored but firm. "I'm glad for you guys to fight this thing out, but I'd like to try to help you get somewhere with it." Having gotten their attention, he paused. "I'm very confused. I have no idea what you are fighting about. Can you fill me in?" Then he looked at Don and said, "How about you? Can you tell me what's going on? How did it start?"

Don, who looked as though he too might cry, was immensely relieved when Carl spoke to him. His voice was choked as he began. "Well, I guess it started when I came out of my room."

Carolyn was unable to leave him alone, just as moments before Don had been unable to stop fighting with her. "An *hour* past your bedtime!"

Carl ignored her, continuing to focus on Don. "You were in bed?"

Don relaxed a little. "And I came out and I yelled downstairs to Dad that I wanted to borrow Claudia's bicycle the next morning, and I asked him if he would leave her a note for when she came in from her date."

Carolyn persisted in interrupting Don's story. "No, no, you asked your father to ask her when she came in, and he said it was too much trouble to explain, that you should leave her a *note.*"

I was irritated at her interruptions; they seemed so petty.

The intrusions also confused Don. As he resumed telling his story, still trying to talk to Carl, he had increasing difficulty with his syntax. "Well, so I yelled down to Dad, and Mom yelled from another room that I was supposed to go, to get to bed, because it's just silly. So I yelled to Dad and asked him to come up to my room, and he started to, was coming up. But this time Mom yelled at him not to come up, that it was too silly and that I'm just stalling going to bed."

"And then what happened?" Carl asked.

"Then I asked Dad if I could come downstairs then, and he said yes. So I went downstairs, but by this time I knew Mom was mad, and I was feeling, you know, a little scared. I asked Dad if I could write the note, or he told me to go ahead and write the note. I was worried then if Mom was going to punish me, but I went ahead to find some paper in the study. Then Mom yelled at me that I'd better not do it, that I was supposed to go to bed, or she would punish me. Then I really got scared."

David spoke to Don for the first time in the retelling, and his words seemed sympathetic. "So you came back to me to ask me what to do, and I told you to make your own decision." At David's words I felt my chest tighten. My anger surged as I heard the impossible dilemma in which Don had been placed.

Carolyn interrupted again, her face strained and angry; although she seemed to be disagreeing with David, she spoke to Don. "No, that was later."

Don had been having trouble telling his story coherently, and now he became visibly confused and very anxious, his words tumbling out in a rush. "No. Yeah. No, not yet. And so—yeah. Then you, she yelled to Mom about you'll thwart your decision because she knows you'll thwart your decision because she knows she's right, because she knows you didn't think of any of the reasons." I couldn't make sense of the speech at all. Don even seemed confused about whether he was talking about his mother or his father.

David appeared to be rescuing his son as he took the floor, though there was more than a little condescension in his voice as he summarized. "Anyway, to get to the end, Don went on upstairs to his room. Later I came up, and he was just *sobbing* under the covers. I guess that was the first time I realized what a really difficult spot he was in. I talked to him for a while and said that I would intercede with his mother, that he could go ahead and write the note."

Don seemed pathetic—vague, distracted, completely blocked. I felt the strongest urge to comfort him in some way, to say, "Hey, now, it isn't as bad as all that." But perhaps he was in more difficulty than any of us had realized.

Carl's reaction was very different from mine. "Jesus Christ!" he said, the words quiet, incredulous and irate. Startled, the family looked in his direction. "Did the two of you see what just happened?" He spoke to the parents.

Carolyn's face had been angry for some time, but she softened as she spoke, obviously aware of Don's situation. "Don got confused about the story. I guess it *is* complicated."

Carl was having difficulty containing his anger. "Did you see *why* he was confused?"

"Well, we were all trying to tell it," Carolyn admitted.

Carl: "Did you see the point when he fell apart? When his logic began to break down?"

"Yes." Carolyn was a little apologetic.

"It was when the two of you began fighting over the accuracy of his story. You were both trying to 'help' him tell it, but you disagreed as to just what happened. And when you put him in the middle of your disagreement, he simply collapsed, right here in front of us."

"Sounds just like the other night when they were fighting about Don's writing the note," I added, speaking to Carl.

Carl glanced at me briefly to acknowledge my remark, then proceeded with the family. "That's right, everything that has happened here today is a continuation of the fight you were having at home." He waited, wondering where to go next. "Could we go back to that? Because I think it's pretty important."

"Of course," Carolyn said. Carl's anger was beginning to make her feel defensive.

"Let me see if I have this straight," Carl said, easing his voice at the note in Carolyn's voice and turning slightly to include David in his inquiry. He spoke to David. "You took the decision at first and told him that he could write the note to Claudia."

"That's correct," David said.

Carl looked at Carolyn. "Then you countermanded David's decision and told Don that he couldn't do it, that he had to go to bed."

"Yes."

Carl turned again to David. "And then you told Don that he could choose which one of you he was going to obey. You didn't even *try* to talk this out with Carolyn?"

"No," David admitted apologetically.

Carl was barely managing to contain his exasperation with the parents. "Do you have any *idea* how the two of you worked out a system like this, where you are free to countermand each other? Because I assume it must happen on both sides. This time it seemed to be structured so that you made a decision, David, and then Carolyn overruled the decision. But the scary thing is that she did it without *talking to you* at all. She acted as though you *didn't exist.* She just told Don to do it her way." Now Carl looked at David more pointedly. "You must do the same thing to her at times, and in fact, you did it in this situation. You didn't fight with her to get the decision back, and you didn't give in to her decision either. You turned the decision over to *Don!* You gave him the balance of power, as though he had to decide which one of you to obey." Carl was trying hard to keep the blame equalized between David and Carolyn and making an effort not to offend them too much. "By turning the decision over to Don, you ignored Carolyn in the same way that she ignored you."

I was a captive of my identification with Don in his predicament, and it was an appropriate place to confess it. "And Don couldn't take that kind of dilemma. That's why he fell apart that night—he couldn't decide which of his parents to obey." I continued. "If he takes sides, he becomes the mate of one parent, and the other parent becomes the child."

Don rose from his somnolence, a slight smile on his lips. "He also gets punished." The adults smiled, glad for the note of humor.

Carolyn was still worried, though, as if she were managing in spite of Carl's effort to see the blame as all hers. "I didn't know that I was putting Don in such a difficult position."

Don had taken heart, and now he looked almost gleeful, his energy returning rapidly. "See, see, she admits it!"

Carolyn looked disconsolately at Carl. "But this anger of Don's just throws me. I don't know what to make of it."

Carl smiled as he spoke. "That's pretty obvious to me. I think it's because *David* is still angry at you for the other night, and he subtly signaled Don to express that anger for him. He didn't stand up to you directly, but he took Don's side against you. And Don cooperated by lashing out at you."

Now it was David's turn to show distress. "You mean I used Don to fight my own battle?" He paused, letting the idea settle over him. "Well, now, that's disconcerting." An even more upsetting idea then occurred to him. "Do you think that's also what I did with Claudia?"

Carl, succinctly, with a sense of victory: "Yep."

David managed a smile as he turned toward Carolyn. "No wonder you've been so hostile toward me lately; it's because I've turned the kids against you." Carolyn responded with a weak smile of her own.

I was concerned that we were creating a new scapegoat in the interview, shifting from blaming the child to blaming the parents. I interrupted, speaking to the parents. "I think it would be a mistake to say, 'David did this to Carolyn,' or 'Carolyn did this to Don.' This sort of pattern takes everyone to make it work, even Don. The *family* evolved this situation, and everyone can only take part credit, in my view."

"Sure," Carl said enthusiastically.

"You mean Don could be playing us against each other, as well as our using him in our fights?" David asked.

Before Carl could answer, Don piped up. "Oh-oh. I was afraid this would come out. Now's the time for me to leave."

As we had borne down on them, David and Carolyn had begun to look demoralized. Now, as we shifted the focus to include Don, they took heart. David addressed both Carl and me. "Well, this is a mess, I admit. But what could we have done differently? How could we have worked it out?"

Carl wanted to answer, so I waited as he replied to David. "It really isn't a matter of *doing* something different. The real problem in this situation is that you and Carolyn were not together. There was a rift between you, and this was the situation you chose in which to express that silent disagreement, admittedly with young Donald's cooperation." He glanced at Don, then returned his gaze to David. "You can't be disciplinarians together when you aren't together psychologically." Carl searched for words. "And I suspect that it's a separation that goes further than this situation. I would guess that almost anything you focused on together would bring out this disagreement."

Carolyn asked tentatively, "You mean our marriage is the real problem?"

Carl hesitated, not wanting to heap more blame on the couple, his voice gentle as he answered. "Well, I'm not so sure there are any horrendous skeletons in your marital closet. It feels more like a *fear of conflict* that's the problem, rather than some particular issue you are fighting over. You know, if you and David could have faced each other and had a fight over your disagreement over Don the other night, it might not have gone this way. But something keeps you from facing each other squarely, and I think the real problem is your *inability to be open with each other as a couple*. That makes you vulnerable to bringing the kids in as intermediaries."

I added, "And the scary thing, if I can worry you a little more, is that this is probably the way it began with Claudia. Don is the *second* scapegoat. And the likelihood is that unless you manage somehow to open up your marriage, he'll stay in that position, or you'll shift the stress to Laura or back to Claudia."

Claudia had been silent for most of the interview, observing the interchange with a combination of interest and skepticism. Now she spoke. "You mean Don is just standing in for me in my old role?"

"Yep," Carl said.

Claudia turned toward Don, leaning forward so that she could see him where he sat on the other side of Carolyn. "Listen, old buddy," she said warmly, "I'm not sure it's worth it. Maybe you'd better decline the honor." As she spoke, I was aware of how different she was in looks and bearing from when we had begun therapy with the family. She was wearing a wool skirt and sweater and her hair looked full-bodied and stylish. But the most striking feature was her voice, rich with overtones of humor and irony.

Before Don could answer Claudia, Carolyn interrupted. "You mean we haven't changed at *all*?"

I smiled confidently at her. "Didn't say that. I think the family has changed a lot. Listen to the good humor in Claudia as she just spoke to Don. That's new. And listen to the 'as if,' hypothetical way we can talk about all this. The quality of desperation that used to be in these conflicts is almost gone. The conflict with Don is still minor compared to the one with Claudia, though the *pattern* is similar."

"Then what *are* you saying?" Carolyn was perplexed.

Carl: "That you haven't yet faced your marriage directly. And the fact that you haven't still causes troubles for you." He paused, then added firmly, "And for your children."

The room was quiet, but it was a good quiet. As I thought about what we had said, I realized that the family was accepting it, relieved to hear it, even though it probably meant much more work.

Carolyn sighed, as though for everyone. Then she leveled her gaze at Carl and me. "I guess we have more changes to make." I felt relieved that it was she who said it, since she was the one most likely to feel defensive. The "we" was a welcome word. The silence continued. I looked at Laura, surprised that she had managed to be so placid throughout the hour. She was attentive and involved.

The silence was interrupted by David, speaking to Carolyn. "You shouldn't chew on those beads; some of them might be poisonous." Carolyn was wearing a folk necklace of seeds which she had touched lightly to her lips in the meditative silence.

At David's remark, Carl laughed—a deep, loose, insinuating chuckle.

David guessed immediately that Carl was laughing at the barely concealed hostility in the fantasy, and he added quickly, "And I want to kill you slowly!"

Carolyn looked up at Carl. "You think they might be curare?" She sounded a little worried.

Carl: "You'd be paralyzed. You couldn't talk."

David laughed, saying to Carolyn, "It would never paralyze your mouth, darling."

Carolyn smiled, looking toward Carl and me. "Help me, you doctors. I'm being scapegoated."

CHAPTER 13

Hate

When the family returned for the next interview, Don looked cheerful enough, and the family not as depressed as might be expected at the prospect of reentering therapy.

Don addressed Carl. "Dr. Whitaker, where are those magnets you had around here? Can I play with them?"

"I thought you stole them," Carl said, deadpan.

"Aw, Whitaker," Don said, "why should I do that? Then I'd just have to sit here and be bored."

"Or pay attention," I said, smiling.

Don shifted out of his ironic stance at my remark, addressing the two of us now. "By the way, I must admit that was a good session we had last week. It was the best ever."

"That's because you were the star of it," Claudia said jokingly, warmly, but with a touch of jealousy. She now had some of the complacency of the scapegoat emeritus, basking in parental approval. Then she turned to Carl. "Don has a new weapon, too. All week, he kept saying to anybody who got near him, 'Don't you triangle me!' It's like he was drawing his six-shooter."

"Claudia, you are a *pain*," Don said with sudden irritation, apparently embarrassed by the remark. "I liked the session because for once the great Whitaker wasn't being so sarcastic but was helping me with my problems. Mom and Dad were catching it instead of me."

I asked Don, "You think Carl is too sarcastic with you?"

"Well, a lot of times he is, but he wasn't last week." Don waited, then decided to address Carl. "You are sometimes sarcastic as heck,

Dr. Whitaker. The other thing that I don't like is that I'm not treated as an equal." Don's mood had now changed back to his old petulant, bossy tone.

"But you're not an equal," Claudia interjected. "I'm not either. We're just kids."

Don was emphatic. "I don't want to be a kid."

Claudia had made her peace with this issue and was now full of advice. "But you have to accept your role."

Don, not to be contained, launched into a rather confused and rambling speech. "Well, I know a lot of kids, and a lot of kids *are* kind of stupid. All right, there's a smart guy in the crowd, and he thinks he knows enough to vote. And he's for this man, and this is his reason: 'He's good because he used to play baseball with my father in school.' So those dumb guys spoil it for everybody else. I think they ought to have an IQ test to see if you are smart enough to vote and to do a lot of other things. Kids aren't all *alike,* for God's sake." I found myself becoming irritated at Don. He sounded spoiled, demanding, almost imperious.

Carl asked Don politely, "Are you saying that because you're smart, you ought to be considered adult?"

Don was disconcerted by the question, mumbling in reply something about people not listening to Baby Jesus, even though he was smart.

Carl's tone was solicitous. "I guess I'm concerned about how you might be hated."

Don was startled. "Hated?"

Carl: "Yes, by people."

"By anybody?" Don asked, troubled.

Carl, gently, his words all the more powerful for their understatement: "You see, there are a lot of people out there in the world who are upset about feeling dumb and looked down on because they don't have a way of being sure about themselves. And they are going to sense that you are looking down at them and hate you for it."

Don remained off-balance. "Who said anything about dumb people?" He really hadn't heard himself at all.

Carl, still gentle: "I thought that's what you were talking about— the kids at school who were dumb."

"Oh, them." Silence, while he thought about what Carl had said. "I guess I do look down on them."

"Any feeling for how it got this way?" Carl asked. "How you got the sense of belonging with the adult generation?"

Before Don got a chance to reply, Carolyn interrupted. While she made every attempt to be reasonable, her voice betrayed her indignation, the irritability of the "wronged" party. "I don't know if this is quite on the point, but I am still concerned about Don. We have *so* much difficulty with him." She said "concerned," but she really meant "angry." She crossed her legs and leaned forward, her hands gesturing as she explained. "It's one thing after another. He couldn't get middle C to work on the piano the other day, and he threw an enormous tantrum. He yells at Laura and fights with her constantly. He belches loudly and laughs this awful, raucous laugh when he does. And he fights with *me* all this time. And that's the part I don't understand. We'll be getting along fine, he'll even help me in the kitchen, and then, boom, he's furious with me and yelling at the top of his lungs. I'm *amazed* that he can be so angry at me, because other times he is so nice and helpful."

"I've noticed something about the pattern," David interposed, "if I could say it." The whole process was beginning to bother me now. First Don, petulant and upset, then Carolyn, quietly indignant, and now David, ingratiating his way into the debate about Don. The process had all the earmarks of their usual triangulation. Still, both Carl and I waited and listened. "It seems like the times when things are going smoothly between me and Carolyn are the times when our relationship with Don deteriorates. We've been getting along all right for the last week, and Don's been terrible." A pause as he thought. "What I try to do is to find something Don and I can do, you know, as two men. We go down into the basement to do something in the workshop or some other activity. But it doesn't seem to help. Don stays angry."

Carolyn slipped in a quiet remark, to Carl. "Would you believe Don belittles the way his father saws a board or anything like that? He's sarcastic about everything!"

As he listened, Don's anger grew. Now he startled everyone with his outburst. "Well, if you weren't such a know-it-all, Mother, and so sarcastic yourself, I wouldn't know how to *be* sarcastic. You taught me how, you and Dr. Whitaker!"

"This is what throws me," Carolyn said to Carl and me, with a gesture of resignation.

I was about to speak to Carolyn and to raise again the issue of their triangulation of Don. But I was stopped by my awareness that I would be repeating what we had said in the last interview. "Where is Don in all this?" I found myself wondering. Then I realized that *his* portion of the triangle was what we had not dealt with. His ideas, his feelings, his fantasies. I didn't know any immediate way to gain access to Don, but as I spoke to the questions raised by Carolyn and David, I noted to myself that we somehow *had* to reach him. "It looks to me as if the two of you have already explained some of his anger, at least from the outsider's point of view. I thought you said it, David, when you referred to yourself and Don as two *men*. It may be that he, like Claudia, has gotten to be in a sort of peer relationship with you and Carolyn. As nice as it is at times, it may be a problem if the two of you and Don try to relate as peers. Part of why Don belittles you, David, may be because you try to be his chum rather than stay his father. Maybe you can't stand the distance of being in the older generation, and you try to bridge the chasm between you by becoming his buddy."

David looked hurt. "But there was so *much* distance between me and my father. Maybe I don't want that to happen to me and Don."

"I understand that," I said gently, "but Don can't feel closer to the older generation if you're not *in* it. It sounds almost as if you reverse generations—he scolds *you* for the way you saw a board. I'm not sure that helps either of you."

While David was trying to grapple with my comments, Carolyn broke in, impatient. "I still don't see how that explains Don's outbursts at me. His anger is just—well, it's out of proportion to the situation."

There was growing tension in the room, but as Carl spoke in response to Carolyn, his voice stayed relaxed. He sounded as though he were discussing a theoretical issue in a very leisurely way. "The conflict for Don and the source of his anger may be related to David and his being the two men. Because when you and David *aren't* together, you may have a tendency to turn to the 'other man,' Don, for support—or whatever. It's as though you and Don have an implicit closeness that David and Don have tried to get but haven't really achieved. You know, when you are 'amazed' that Don can be angry at you, it is because your sense of your basic rapport with him is ruptured."

Though confused by what Carl was saying, Carolyn was definitely interested. "I still don't see what that has to do with Don's getting so angry!" When I glanced at Don then, I saw that he looked very uneasy.

Carl explained. "It's the sudden shift he has to go through. You and Don are close for a while, and he begins to count on it. Then you and David get back together, and Don feels displaced. All of a sudden he's just one of the kids again. And he gets very upset about whether he's a kid or an adult, or whether you love him or don't, or just what kind of relationship he has with you." Carl spoke with sympathy for Don, saying explicitly that he saw the boy's difficulty, yet also managing to avoid blaming the parents.

I summarized for them all, speaking mainly to Carolyn. "This is the corollary of David's turning to Claudia for support, though your closeness to Don may have been a more subtle process."

As Carl and I talked about him, Don had grown progressively more unsettled, shifting in his chair, making occasional noises of irritation or unrest. Now he blurted out at Carl and me, "I think all this is nonsense. It's all made-up therapy crap." He spoke to his mother then. "The reason I fight with you is that you're such a know-it-all and are so *sarcastic* with me." His voice was loud and angry, but there was an undertone of pleading.

Carolyn returned his anger, straightening in her chair to meet Don's challenge. "Well, I for one don't *like* the way you speak to me, and I'm not going to tolerate it."

Carl laughed softly, distracting mother and son from their fight. "You two sound like a couple of old married people fighting. You sure don't sound like mother and son."

Don blazed at Carl. "Well, what's *wrong* with it? What's *wrong* with my fighting with her? She and Dad do it!"

Carl's voice toughened abruptly as he met Don's challenge. "If you listen to your voice, I'll *tell* you what's wrong with it!"

The sharpness in Carl's voice had become a precipice, some dangerous edge toward which everyone had been moving. Don looked as though he saw disaster before him, a plunge to the death, in Carl's challenge. He rose suddenly from his chair with that unmistakable expression on his face—"Let me out of here!" My immediate fantasy was that he was going to leap right over Carl and me since we blocked his passage toward the door.

Indeed, he began moving, and as he extended his leg to take the first step, he tripped over Carl's outstretched legs. Working to keep his balance, Don struck out—in rage, in panic—at Carl. His fist grazed Carl's head, sending his eyeglasses flying. I heard a loud clack as the glasses hit the floor under Carl's desk, the sound simultaneous with a clash of blurred movements so sudden that I could only follow them helplessly. I felt strangely calm, as though my eyes were encountering a situation which I had no time to have any feelings about.

As Don had struck out in panic and anger at Carl, Carl had tackled him, and the two of them went down onto the Oriental carpet, a tangle of limbs. "Oh, my God!" Claudia said in horror as she saw what was happening.

Don's slim frame was no match for Carl's muscular heft. As Carl emerged sitting on his chest, the boy emitted a shriek at once enraged, terrified, and surprised, *EEEaaaaahhhhhhh!* Then he became more articulate as anger dominated. "You bastard! Let me up, you son of a bitch!" His voice was high and intense, but short of a scream. Then he began to kick furiously and to lash out with his one free hand. Carl grabbed the hand and shifted his weight so that Don's legs were immobilized. Feeling himself thoroughly pinned, Don began to yell again, arching his body with all his might. He twisted under Carl, managing to break one of the handholds and to turn onto his side. Then he lunged at the strong arm that still held his other hand to the floor, as though to bite it.

"Oh, no!" Carl said, forcing Don over on his chest. Then he grabbed both arms again and pinned them, far away from Don's head.

"You . . . you. . . ." Don struggled on, all the while trying to find a suitable word for Carl, finally settling disgustedly on "bum!"

Claudia was still white-faced with the shock of the fight, and she pleaded with Carl. "Dr. Whitaker, please! Let him up!"

Carl was breathing hard as he resisted Don's efforts to escape, but he had heard Claudia and tried to answer her. "He's all right. He just got panicked."

With the words, Don fought harder, his voice rising again, "I am *not* panicked. I am just damn mad at *you!*"

"Well, I'm not so sure the anger is all at me, but I'm glad to have you practice on me," Carl said. He was still puffing. "But I don't react like your parents. I'm not about to let somebody climb over me and knock off my glasses." He turned tougher as he concluded, "I'm not the one who got you so upset."

As Carl and Don began to talk, Don's efforts to escape eased. He seemed interested in the conversation. "Well, I didn't mean to knock your glasses off," he pleaded, "so will you let me up? I give up."

"As soon as you calm down," Carl said gently, remaining on top of Don. Then, gradually, Carl relaxed his grip on Don's hands. As soon as Don felt the grip lessen, he struck out again, still fighting. "I thought you were giving up," Carl said.

Don said nothing, grunting and straining as he tried to break free. The tussle continued, but the two protagonists were developing a somewhat better humor about each other. "I'll get a lawyer," Don said with bravura.

"Great," Carl said enthusiastically. "I know a good one to refer you to."

"Why the hell are you doing this?" Don strained to ask.

"What do you mean, why am I doing this?" Carl said, puffing. "You and I have been mad at each other for a long time!"

David finally commented, his voice good-humored, "I see you're not used to this either."

"I'm doing all right," Carl retorted.

As the wrestling persisted, Laura went over to the two protagonists and silently grabbed Carl's collar. His shirt tightened around his neck, and he said, "Hey, no fair! You're choking me!"

"Don't hurt Don!" Laura said plaintively.

Carl looked disconcerted by this development, and he answered, also a little plaintively, "He's all right, honey. I'm not going to hurt him."

"Get up!" Laura ordered.

"We will," Carl said, the shirt still tight around his neck. "Hey, let up, will you? You're hurting my neck." Laura released her hold on Carl's shirt and went to sit with her mother. The family watched with varying reactions as the tussle continued. By now the feeling between Don and Carl was clearly much friendlier, a physical contest which Don could not win, but one in which he could not allow himself to be defeated. He pitched all his effort into the battle, and Carl countered every move. Don was wiry and tough, and for Carl, at sixty, sustaining the effort was plainly a challenge. But Don was wearing down, too, his attempts to break free becoming more sporadic. Finally, he quit struggling. Carl still didn't get up. Remaining sitting on Don, he began giving him a massage.

"What are you doing?" Don asked incredulously.

"Helping you relax," Carl said warmly.

"Hmmmmm," Don said, wondering if he should enjoy the experience or fight some more.

Finally, Carl seemed to have enough. "I'm ready to quit," he said. "How about you?"

Don was quiet. I wondered if he would leap into action again. Then he said, "I give up."

Carl rose with a groan, and after a moment's pause so did Don. Carl sank slowly into his chair, sighing with relief. Don collapsed more demonstratively onto the sofa, beside his father. It was only then that I noticed that David, his body tense and composed, was crying. It was incongruous, this controlled and rational man with a sheet of tears shining down his face.

"Why are you crying?" I asked.

He shook his head several times, saying, "I don't know. Something just happened in me."

At the beginning Claudia had been horrified by the fight, and she remained skeptical, even after its relatively relaxed conclusion. "Why did you do that, Dr. Whitaker?" she asked, a quality of hurt and disillusionment in her voice.

Carl's answer was gentle. "As I said before, we were just mad at each other, Don and I. This has been building up in both of us for a long time."

Don said nothing at all. He didn't look bitter—just very tired.

David moved to schedule the next interview, and his voice was hazy with emotion as he exchanged the few necessary words with us.

The next interview had a quality of freedom and excitement that seemed to be largely a product of the drama of the fight. During the intervening week Don had asked David to wrestle with him, and David had agreed. Don was excited as he told about it. "And you know what, Whitaker, he's stronger than I thought. He beat me! I didn't know he could beat me!"

David was as startled by Don's revelation as we were. "You mean you thought you could beat me?" David asked incredulously. Though far from athletic, David weighed perhaps a hundred and eighty pounds. Don couldn't have weighed more than a hundred and thirty! We talked for a while about Don's "delusion" about his strength. In his effort to be a buddy, David had never really challenged Don, and the boy had grown up with a misperception of his own power.

At Don's request, the wrestling matches between him and David continued for several weeks. He enjoyed the contact with his father's strength, relishing it enough to keep coming back again and again for the reassurance that his father really could beat him. The matches were friendly and casual, but they remained real contests. And David kept winning.

The fight stimulated a flood of feelings in David about his own father. He realized how distant from each other they had been. When David recounted it for us, he had to work to keep from crying again. "My father was always the man of power and influence, but he was such a distant person in my life. I looked up to him, admired him for all his accomplishments, but I never felt close to him." David spoke with the most difficulty when he said, "I can remember only a few occasions when we touched each other." So that was why David had been crying—seeing Carl getting so involved that he actually wrestled with Don. David: "It meant a great deal to me, Carl, that you cared enough about us, and Don, to get that involved. It was certainly above and beyond the call of duty."

Carl's fight with Don was certainly unplanned, and on many levels it was unprofessional. It was a primitive event, precipitated jointly by Carl and the family, and Carl's response to the situation was basically personal. Don's arrogant quality did more than irritate Carl; it troubled him. For Don was indeed the victim of a family process which created in him the fantasy that he was older, smarter, and stronger than he actually was. Without meaning to, his parents had trained him in a kind of subtle delusional thinking about himself, one that implied that he could best his father in a contest of strength and that he could be his mother's substitute mate. Don's quasi-omnipotence was not obvious at first, but when Carl finally became aware of it, it bothered him more and more.

A showdown of some sort between Carl and Don had seemed inevitable from the beginning of therapy. When it finally came, it was physical—unusual for our style of therapy. Yet disturbing as the fight was initially for the family, the effects were positive. Don's "brattiness" disappeared almost immediately. His sarcasm remained, of course, but it had a different quality. As he found his place among the generations, Don seemed to become more secure and more loving. And he warmed visibly to Carl. He was later to say, "I got all my hate out then. I feel much better about Dr. Whitaker now."

CHAPTER 14

The Therapeutic Moment

"What can we do?" the family asks impatiently.

"There isn't anything you can do," the therapist answers firmly, "nor is there anything we can do." A silence laden with doubt. "What to *do* isn't the right question. The question is how to *feel* different, how to *be* different." Another heavy silence. "And I wish there were a formula for getting there. About all we can offer you is help in that struggle."

The dialogue is typical for this phase of treatment. The newness of working with the whole family begins to fade, and the therapist starts to run out of interesting ideas. The question of what *is* going to make the difference is a valid one. The family hopes the therapist will offer them a formula, a technique, a bit of magic. Is there something practical they can *do* that will make life different—and will someone tell them what it is? Should they change jobs, or mates, move to another city, lose weight, take up meditation? Perhaps the therapist can help them rephrase their sentences so that someone will understand them. Maybe there is an insight that will finally make their befuddlement clear. Carl and I honestly confess that we wish we knew the "answer" for which the family searches.

Yet we all know that there are decisive moments when lives change direction. Tides of change usually move slowly in human life, but sometimes a few moments, even a few words, can be very significant. We search and wait for this important therapeutic moment. The therapeutic moment does not have its origin "in" the therapists or in the family but is the product of extraordinarily complex forces in the entire group. If this moment is to have real power, it cannot be planned. It has to happen. So when we attempt to disillusion the family in their search for an "easy" solution and refuse to plan or schematize the process of therapy, we are actually trying to raise the stakes. We are waiting for the kind of dramatic, pivotal moment that occurred between Don and Carl.

When the Brices returned to therapy after a two-month absence, they had largely resolved the original crisis with Claudia, but they were now in the process of reorganizing their triangular conflict around Don. He was becoming the second scapegoat. When Carl saw the familiar pattern, he moved fast, chastising the parents forcefully for what they were doing to Don. The toughness in Carl's voice signaled the end of diplomacy. In response to the Brices' raising the stakes by returning to therapy, this time with the implicit goal of reorganizing the family structure, Carl also raised the intensity of his response. "Cut out the games," he said. "Grow up!" He was indignant, therapeutically indignant. Surely Carolyn didn't need to meddle in David's struggle with Don the way she did. Surely David could have done something to prevent Carolyn from invalidating and ignoring him. Why hadn't the couple turned to each other and argued out their obvious disagreement instead of putting Don in a bind? A thoroughly parental scolding, well deserved.

Something changed. Perhaps David and Carolyn felt genuinely ashamed. Don appeared at the next interview feeling liberated from the parental triangle, ready to fight. When Carl came to his defense, it gave his anger new license. First he attacked his mother, and she registered her week-long amazement at his ready irritability. Then, seemingly out of nowhere, he turned toward Carl, lashing out. Something unexpected happened in Carl, too, and he fought back. Before the astounded group the two of them tumbled into a physical fight.

The moment did not come out of nowhere. Don and Carl had irritated each other for some time. Don didn't like Carl's "sarcasm," and Carl often had to bite his tongue to keep from confronting Don's arrogant attitude. "It's really not my business if his parents let him talk to them like that," Carl said to himself. Inwardly, Don and Carl had scheduled a confrontation. When it came, the fight was part of everyone's need to raise the stakes of the therapy.

There is a maxim among family therapists: *the family will try to do to us what they do to each other.* In order to neutralize the threat of the professional intruder, they unwittingly attempt to pull us into their system, induce us into their world. There is another maxim: *the therapist will project his own family system onto the family he is treating.* For the therapist who allows himself to become involved on more than an intellectual basis, the chemistry of the family's "pull" added to his own "push" can develop a sometimes alarming intensity. The element of danger, however, is also an element of excitement. We are all self-interested, and if something in the family "catches" the therapist's personal interest and involvement, the therapy will gain real emotional power. Without the therapist's involvement, it stays a technical exercise, something that informs but does not really touch the family. If, on the other hand, the therapist becomes *too* involved, he loses his professional status and is rendered impotent.

Families have any number of intuitive maneuvers for getting the therapist overinvolved. Unconsciously they can arrange a scenario in which one member is so obvious a villain and another so obvious a victim that the therapist is plunged helplessly into taking sides. The family may present a maddeningly superficial and pleasant front at the same time that they are asking for help. Caught in the midst of conflicting messages and intuiting the family's submerged anger, the therapist may become first impatient, then furious. Someone in the family may invite attack by the therapist or flatter him inappropriately, and if he is not aware that these are transference reactions, he may be "seduced" into taking a particular role in the family. Families can confuse the ablest of therapists by changing the topic with dizzying rapidity. They can look beseechingly at the therapist for help, while taking almost no responsibility for or initiative in solving their own problems.

In the beginning phases the therapist must hold fast to his technical skills to avoid becoming entrapped in the family system. He must relate to the group: defining the problems as family dilemmas; establishing rules and procedures for working; encouraging the family's initiative; watching the way the members communicate; looking for new alternatives to suggest to them. He must insist on being the *family's* therapist, drawing his major strength from his status as a professional "outsider." The time comes, however, when his function as rule maker, mediator, and commentator is not enough. The family listens and tries to change, but even though they may behave somewhat differently, say different words, they *feel* the same. The therapist does not "get through" on a fundamental level. The contact remains superficial.

Why, in spite of a genuine desire to change, does the family hang back, persisting in their hobbled dance? If a family has tried repeatedly to change and has met only with pain and failure, making still another attempt can have frightening overtones. Having mustered all their courage to enter therapy, what if they really *try*—and fail again? What then is left except utter despair? The family cringes in fear; they fight against the change which they know they must attempt.

The family also wonders who has the power to produce fundamental change. Just as most suicides require a minimum of two "parties" (someone who wants to die and someone who wants him or her dead), therapeutic growth takes collaboration. The family must *want* to change, and the therapist must *want* them to change. While a model for this mutual effort has been created in the initial, technical stage of therapy, it lacks real guts. Some primitive force is needed that will precipitate a new and more profound level of involvement.

It is not enough for the therapist to be reasonable, benevolent, and mature. Only a strongly personal power can make the almost surgical incision through the family's layers of denial and avoidance, exposing the profundity of their pain and the immensity of their power. This must be a special kind of force, one guided by a caring intent. How can the family come to be so important to the therapist that he is willing to make such an effort?

First, the family must take risks. Most families are constantly exposing filaments of hope in the form of numerous unconscious acts. The Brices were taking such risks when they "scheduled" Don to be absent at the first session, and the same process was occurring when he struck out at Carl. They were challenging, daring, pulling on the therapist for involvement.

The therapist must allow himself to become involved. His emotional investment in the family accumulates slowly, and often he is not aware of the depth of his involvement until some event brings these feelings to the surface. After all, he has been trying hard to be professional and fair. Carl was suddenly *upset* when he saw Don caught in the middle of the parental conflict, and his reprimand to the parents was more than an objective commentary. He was even more troubled by Don's arrogance in the next session. His growing concern about the family led him past their psychological border, toward the volatile interior.

When Don finally hit out at Carl, an alarm sounded in him. He had strayed "into" the midst of the Brice family, and the process of their living now threatened him. A definitive, urgent statement rose in Carl: "No! I don't tolerate that sort of defiance from a child!" And the fight was on.

It was a complex moment. On one level, Carl usurped a parental role in the Brice family. Don had defied Carl in the way that he defied his own parents, and Carl took over for the parents. For a while Don became *his* child, he Don's father, and the model he presented to the family was direct, forceful, yet humane. In being so forceful, Carl was perhaps kinder than David and Carolyn, for while neither of them was able to stand up against Don very well, they could be sadistic to him in numerous subtle ways. Carl was showing the family something new about being forceful, and the model was not lost on them. David and Don picked it up and repeated it in the days that followed in the wrestling matches between son and father. During these bouts Don made the shocking discovery that his father was more powerful than he was!

Carl responded to Don's arrogance with more than parental force. He also *identified* with Don, seeing something of himself in the boy. Carl has often said that one doesn't become a physician without some measure of omnipotence, since the physician must assume life-and-death control in certain situations. Perhaps it was his own need to be omnipotent that he saw in Don and fought against. Whatever the content, the important point is that the therapist sees an aspect of himself in the individual and becomes deeply involved through this sense of identification. We all feel that in some ways our own parents were inadequate, that they failed us. What the therapist does in this critical moment is to see his "child self" in the "patient" and to provide the parental response that he *wishes he had received*. Through his investment in the individual family member, the therapist parents a part of himself. In doing so, he both helps the individual and provides the family with a new model for intimacy.

When Don struck at him, Carl felt a good deal of urgency, for the omnipotence the boy betrayed can be very troublesome. He had seen too many schizophrenic patients wandering around muttering, "I am God," implacably convinced of this delusion. The schizophrenic has had long schooling in his delusion system, and in many instances no one in his family has ever taught him his "size" in the way Carl taught Don. Carl's fight with Don may have reversed some very destructive trends in the boy's life.

The reader may be somewhat perplexed by our alternating references to the "family" and the "individual." It is important to remember that family therapy always takes place on two levels: the *intra*-personal, within the individual, and the *inter*personal, between the individuals. Don is "elected" by the family to have an intense encounter with the therapist, but he is also struggling with his own personal, internal problems. The therapist must "invade" the individual in order to reach the intrapersonal conflict of that person, but in doing so, he provides the family with an interpersonal model for intimacy.

While the family as a whole changes in significant ways during therapy, the most intense moments are often one-to-one encounters between various individuals in the family and the therapists. In successful therapy every member of the family should have a "crisis" and receive his or her share of focused attention from the therapists. The "scheduling" and management of these serial crises, however, are complicated. Carl and I identified immediately with Claudia, for example, though our way of helping her was to move the focus *away* from her. Then Carolyn became "the patient," and we had several low-key but highly significant moments with her. We suggested that the marriage be the next "patient"; but the family chose Don's crisis instead, and perhaps this crisis represented a way in which the family elected to test whether Carl and I had the strength to deal with the marital problems. Once it starts moving, family therapy is somewhat like a stew that is bubbling rapidly. The process is so intricate that you are never sure what is going to rise to the surface, and you never know just how high it is going to boil.

The therapeutic moment is highly variable, and it is difficult to generalize about, except that the therapist finds something extremely significant in what is happening in the family, and he reacts strongly and *personally*. The moment may be loving, humorous, or angry, but it is always deeply felt. The therapist's contribution comes primarily out of his own person, not out of his professional skill. If the therapist is fighting with the family, it is because what is happening in that family has become very important to him. He is pushing for change.

The fact that the therapist becomes personally involved sometimes places his professional role in jeopardy. I was very tense one day because a young mother in a family I was working with was in the hospital after having made a serious suicide attempt. She was a deeply troubled person, and I was not sure that she would survive. When the young mother in another family I was seeing began to complain in a whiny, petulant tone about some problems that seemed minor by comparison with those of my hospitalized patient, I exploded. I yelled at her, telling her how spoiled and childish she was. She left the interview feeling devastated. My attack was all the more difficult for her because she had a painfully distant relationship with her father. My insults were like her worst nightmare come true. When the family returned for the next interview, she and her husband were extremely angry, and it seemed likely the interview would be their last.

I had realized the source of my anger, and I offered the woman a complete apology. I told her the cause of my worry and anxiety and asked her to try to make allowance for the human side of her therapist. "We make mistakes, too," I said. My apology allowed her to see me as indeed human, and it was so unlike anything her father would have done that it marked the turning point in our previously strained relationship. She even admitted that she had been petulant and whiny. We developed a long and good "friendship," and the family's therapy was successful.

When the therapist risks becoming personally involved with the family, it is not an unmitigated benefit. Sometimes our involvement takes us to the edge of therapeutic disaster. While the stresses that push us into overinvolvement with the client family can stem from our current reality problems, even more powerful forces exist in our own family histories. If I had an authoritarian father, for example, and am working with a family with an authoritarian father, I had best be on guard against an inappropriate involvement with this family. When the family with whom we are working reveals a relationship *pattern* that is similar to our own, the danger that we will lose our professional perspective is even greater.

However caught up in the family the therapist feels, he should always be less involved in the therapeutic process than is the family. Even when Carl was fighting with Don, part of him remained very much the professional—monitoring the fight, making casual comments, interpreting. We have several allies in maintaining this vital professional distance, of which the balancing and tempering influence of the co-therapy relationship is the most important. When Carl first challenged Don, he seemed lost in the moment. Then he regained his composure, partly by making eye contact with me. I was his link to the professional world, and our relationship formed a "safety zone" from which he had ventured and to which he could return. Launching into a deeply personal encounter with the family seems possible, in fact, only because of the stability which the co-therapy relationship provides.

Typically, we work in an intuitive rhythm which the reader has probably noted. One therapist becomes involved with the family, engaging their struggle. The other therapist waits silently, observing, ready to help his partner if needed, but remaining less involved and more objective than the active therapist. Eventually, the active therapist gets tired or confused, often because he has become overinvolved. As he retreats to the co-therapy relationship, the other therapist takes the initiative. The pattern may vary, but the dual "in-and-out" movement is virtually essential to both therapists' being able to remain both personal and professional.

Carl and I work with many other co-therapists, and often our partner is a trainee. We bring the inexperienced therapist into the treatment of a family partly as a teaching technique and partly to provide the family with a co-therapist for whom they don't have to pay a double fee. In the beginning we must bear much of the load, but most trainees learn rapidly and begin to participate actively in the process. We may work with some trainees for several years, and toward the end of this time they are usually functioning as competent professionals. It takes time and a great deal of work to develop a successful team, but it is worth it; in many instances we find that the rapport which we achieve with the family is strongly influenced by the rapport which we have with our co-therapist.

The "twoness" of the co-therapy team also has symbolic meaning for the family. We are "parents," a team that may function more successfully than any relationship within the family. We are highly visible. If we degrade or undercut each other, they can see it. If we allow each other freedom and give support when it is needed, they see that, too. When we disagree, they watch carefully the way in which we handle the argument. Whatever we *say* about relationships, the one we *live* before them is the one from which they learn the most.

We therapists must have another kind of protection against overinvolvement, however. We must know a good deal about our own families, particularly the points where we are vulnerable. As we teach family therapy, both Carl and I suggest that trainees work together in small groups in order to help sensitize themselves to their family stresses. The trainee draws a diagram of his family structure on the blackboard, and the group helps him examine points of conflict and stress in an effort to anticipate "blind spots" with the client family. Although these are not therapeutic groups for the therapist, they usually induce a climate of supportiveness and healthy inquiry.

The really well-prepared family therapist will have had therapy himself. While most training programs do not require a personal therapy experience, a good many young therapists are entering treatment with their families the better to prepare themselves for their work. These therapists will have an added protection against the hazards of overinvolvement as they work with families.

Even when the therapist is well prepared and has the support of a partner, there will be many moments when his experience fails him. Something in the family's situation challenges him. He must make a response now. At this decisive moment, when the therapist is searching for something to offer the family, he may need to *invent* a response, synthesizing his own family experience, his own therapy, his current attempt to grow, his imagination, his hope for the future. The *will to grow* is perhaps the most essential ingredient in determining whether the therapist finds something of himself to give.

Whatever the advantages to the patient of an approach that makes the therapist's personal investment, creativity, and growth critical elements in the therapy, these advantages are necessarily complicated by the uncertainties of any attempt to be a person. Therapists inevitably have some bad days, agonizing months, and dull years. We falter, and our patients falter with us. But our professional training and experience usually sustain us through these periods, until we regain a sense of excitement about our lives and can bring this enthusiasm back to our work.

Although we believe that this approach benefits the patient, its benefit to the therapist may be just as important. If the therapist forces himself by the nature of his work to concentrate on his own growth, he is much more likely to stay professionally and personally alive. If Carl had deadened himself to his anger at Don, it would have been easier to deaden or betray himself the next time he had an "unprofessional" but thoroughly natural response. By making room in his work for his somewhat unpredictable personhood, the therapist at least keeps his work interesting.

As Carl and I look around us at the "new world" of psychotherapy, we see much that is interesting and exciting. But we also see trends that cause us to despair. Whether it is behavior therapy, bioenergetics, transactional analysis, Rolfing, Arica, Silva Mind Control, Transcendental Meditation, or a host of other therapeutic newcomers, we see an increasing dependence on technique. The "expert" has an approach to his clients that is schematized and planned, and he essentially teaches it to them. A technical approach can be helpful, adding a useful or enjoyable facet to a client's life, but it can eventually be fatal to a therapist. We have seen many therapists who have married their careers to a "formula" approach and, after five years or so, are emotionally dead to their work. Like the assembly-line worker, whose repetitive pattern forms a metaphor for many modern careers, they tire of their technique. Rather than evolve with their work, they become static, tied to an entity that has ceased to be their own. Although Carl and I use techniques, we certainly fear becoming dependent on them.

We are also distressed by the emphasis on the solitary individual and on the narcissism inherent in many of these "therapies." Although focus on the self and its cravings for happiness is a useful counterpoint to our society's past emphasis on self-denial, we doubt that lasting satisfaction can be had in single-minded pursuit of the self. What is needed is a balanced sense of Self *and* Others in some meaningful relation. To achieve that sense of balance, we believe that people must struggle together—lover with lover, husband with wife, parent with child, child with child. We don't expect that anyone will ever discover a formula that can encompass the incredible complexity of the human relationship, especially in the family.

CHAPTER 15

Collision Course

It was February, the sky an inscrutable gray, predicting neither the relief of more snow nor the promise of clearing. Outside, the old snow draped the landscape like a dirty, tattered sheet. Week after week the Brice family continued in therapy. They had obviously made progress. The children were no longer scapegoated by the parents, and their freedom from this invidious process made participation in therapy seem a little irrelevant to them. They were bored.

On the other hand, David and Carolyn were unable to make much headway with their relationship. While Carl and I prodded them to take more risks, at least to confront their problems directly, they hesitated. David would occasionally become critical of Carolyn, or she of him. Invariably the person being criticized failed to defend himself or herself with force or conviction, yet also refused to yield ground. The conflict that smoldered between them refused to burst into a clean, clear flame. In that cold month Carl and I would have been glad for the warmth of real affection or the heat of direct and honest anger. Neither happened. Nothing could bring this soggy midwinter scene to life.

As we persisted through the frustrating sessions, Carl and I became aware of a slowly growing tension. We realized that part of the discomfort was related to the couple's barely contained anger at us for not "doing something." But Carolyn and David were also becoming increasingly uncomfortable with their marriage. There were awkward silences in which they could think of nothing to say to each other. At times they seemed unable to look directly at each other.

Though remaining muffled and unresolved, their arguments circled more tightly around certain key issues. We began to feel that something was finally going to happen, but the depressed quality in their relationship gave us no assurance that it would be positive. Yet whatever the outcome, movement in any direction was preferable to interminable stasis and boredom. We waited. March arrived, and our first appointment in that bleak month fell on a Wednesday.

After everyone had settled into his or her chair, muttering complaints about the nuisance of getting out of winter coats and boots, Carolyn Brice began the session. Even then, she waited through the silence of several very awkward moments before she spoke. Her voice betrayed her depression. "I guess I'll be the one to start today because I'm unhappy about something that happened last night. I feel strange about saying it because it's something we have talked about before, and by now I don't have much hope that talking about it will make much difference."

With this kind of prediction, I said to myself, she was certainly not going to succeed.

Carolyn continued drearily. "Well, you know this thing we've argued about before every time I wanted something done around the house. We've been talking for some time about getting our bedroom painted—it's an awful pink—or maybe doing it ourselves. It isn't a question of money at all; we could afford to have the whole house redone. But I feel that I can't get David to pay much attention to a project like this one or to anything in our home that I think is significant."

"You mean he won't agree to have it done?" I asked.

Carolyn looked discouraged, sounded discouraged. "It isn't that. He would be glad to pay for it if I would arrange everything. He just won't take any interest in anything except what *he* thinks is important." She sighed. "And that never seems to coincide with what *I* find important."

"Well, what happened last night?" Carl asked, a touch impatient.

Carolyn: "Well, I had the notion that for once I didn't want to do it the usual way—badger David for a decision, then do all the hiring and arranging, then feel cheated because he didn't appreciate it and complained about paying for it. I decided to paint the room myself and surprise him. So I hired a kid to help me move the furniture, and I painted all day to get done by the time he came home."

"Great!" Carl said enthusiastically.

Carolyn smiled painfully, but her face dropped back immediately into its depressed lethargy. "Wait, before you get too excited. You can probably see what's coming." She glanced at David, who was beginning to look uncomfortable. "He came home, late, of course, and before dinner I took him up to see the room. He said nice things about it—it wasn't that. But I could see that it didn't really matter to him. After all my effort I got a few polite, unemotional words that it was pretty. And I just felt so defeated." She looked at Carl and me, fighting back an impulse to cry. "What do I have to do to get him to see me and what I do as important?"

David looked embarrassed and defensive. "But I thought I did appreciate what you did. I was a little surprised and maybe a little puzzled that we hadn't talked about it before you did it, but I *liked* it. I really did."

Carolyn edged toward bitterness. "It isn't that, David. It's the lack of feeling in you. We have this fight about so many different subjects, but it's always the same fight. When you come home from work and we've both had a difficult day, I really *listen* to your complaints and troubles. I take them seriously. But if I've had a frustrating day, felt lonely, worn myself out doing drudgery, had a fight with the kids, it's as though you can only mumble a few words and brush it off. *You never really listen to me.*" Her voice underlined the words, then trailed off in discouragement. "It's as though you don't find me important."

"Carolyn, I think you're wrong," David replied firmly. "I think you magnify my failure to be a good listener and make too much of the whole issue."

"You're doing it *now!*" Carolyn flared. "You are brushing off the issue I'm trying to raise right now!"

As David felt increasingly frustrated, his defensive stance began to erode. His voice tightened perceptibly; his face narrowed in anger. "I'm not brushing it off, Carolyn. I just *see* it differently. I don't undervalue what you feel and what you are interested in. I just don't happen to say words of praise or reassurance in the precise way you want me to."

Carolyn too was angrier. "It's not *words* we're talking about. You know I don't want you to mouth pretty phrases at me. It's feeling in you that I'm missing. You get excited about your damned legal cases

—*they* are important to you—but you don't feel very much about me or about what I do. It's all insignificant to you."

David sat stiffly in his chair, his words delivered with an arching inflection that bent like a drawn bow. "You are telling me what I am feeling, and I don't like it a damn bit."

"Then you tell me what you *are* feeling, if anything," Carolyn said bitterly. She alternated between anger and despair, now attacking David and now mocking him and daring him to attack her, but despite her quiescent fury, a quality of hopelessness pervaded her words.

"I am damn angry at you," said David. "That's what I feel."

Carolyn continued to retreat from her anger. "I wish I could feel hopeful enough to get very angry," she said mournfully.

David hesitated, falling silent. Carl and I saw the argument about to fail as so many of theirs did, flaring forth briefly, only to become snarled in a series of guilty recriminations, ending in muted despair. "Why give up and get depressed?" I asked the two of them. "If you keep going, maybe you'll get somewhere."

David took heart and uttered the sentence which he had apparently suppressed: "Well, Carolyn, what is it you want anyway? I really don't know what I can do." His tone was that of an adult speaking to a child whose demands were becoming annoying.

The condescension was not lost on Carolyn. "You can go straight to hell!" she shouted, enraged. She hesitated, her eyes brimming with tears, fighting to keep from crying. Then anger won over grief. "I sit here and ask you to pay a little more meaningful attention to me, as if it weren't hard enough to ask your own husband to help you feel better about yourself and the insignificant problems you have in a day, and you ask what you can *do?*" Now the tears crowded forward again. "Are you blind? Deaf? Have you no feelings at all about me?" These were difficult, difficult words, wrenched from her with great pain.

David retreated in the face of her hurt. "Carolyn, that isn't the issue at all. My caring about you isn't a question in my mind." His cool reasonableness was brutal in contrast with her open pain. "The question is whether I can meet some of your demands. And I don't think some of the demands are *appropriate.*"

Carolyn's reply was almost a snarl, and she mocked David with a tone reminiscent of some of Claudia's former maneuvers. "Oh, you don't think they are *appropriate*, do you?" She was trying to provoke him into open anger. As we saw the conflict between them mount, Carl and I glanced at each other, at once relieved that they were risking more directness than usual and concerned about where the fight was leading. The children all looked worried and helpless, separate from the conflict.

Carolyn was succeeding. A muscle bulged at the base of David's jaw as he clenched his teeth. Then he began, his voice expanding with anger as he spoke. "Well, dammit, Carolyn, I think you demand too much attention and reassurance from me. Sometimes you act like a scared little girl who wants her hand held." The accusation registered visibly, and Carolyn flinched at the words. David hesitated, then proceeded. "There are ways that you don't meet *my* needs either, and I don't think I have to mention what they are!" Another flinch in Carolyn, a deeper wound. The charge that she was not an adequate sexual partner was obviously extremely painful for her.

Determined not to break down and cry, Carolyn gripped the arms of her chair and glared at her husband. "And I *refuse* to accept sole responsibility for our sexual problems. Your approach to me is often *so* mechanical and *so* unfeeling that I would have to degrade all my sensibilities about what makes a loving relationship to have sex with you at a time like that. I think I have a *right* to expect some feeling from the person I share my body with! I just can't disconnect what I feel from what I do! But you, for God's sake, you could make love in the midst of a furious fight. It's all you think about."

A note of viciousness crept into the argument. "And *that's* a manipulation, I think," David said scornfully. "If I jump through the hoop and say all the right things, you *might* consider my application to go to bed!"

Carolyn, fast on the heels of David's reply: "And you don't think you manipulate *me?* If I work my ass off around the house and make your life comfortable for you and jump into bed at the slightest hint from you, you might, just *might*, condescend to pay attention to me or at least listen to my words, if not the feelings behind them!"

"Oh, Carolyn!"

"Oh, David!" She mocked him again. The couple clashed, two boulders colliding and grinding in place, only the surfaces abrading, making no progress. The longer the argument went on, the more frustrated each became, and the stronger the intensity of the collisions. Although this argument resembled many of their others, there was a real difference. This time neither partner was willing to be defeated. Both held their ground with a tenacity that allowed the argument to go further than usual, though it was discouraging because it produced so total an impasse. At least now the long war had been officially declared.

David flared. "If you mock me once more like that, I'm going to walk straight out of that door and you can solve this damn thing by yourself." I felt my chest tighten as he made the threat. There was little question where Claudia had learned her technique of mocking her mother or where she learned to walk away from an argument.

Carolyn wasn't impressed. "You might as well be out now, for all the commitment you have to our marriage." Still, she stopped short of daring him to leave.

David had had all he could take, and finally he was shouting. *"Carolyn, that is not true!* You have no *right* to tell me how committed I am to my own marriage. You are not a mind reader!"

Carolyn's voice was full of anguish, pain. *"I have a right to tell you how lonely and unhappy and unloved I feel in this marriage!"*

They glared at each other, tears streaming down Carolyn's face, David's face red with anger, poised at the edge of violence, or uncontrollable grief. I had the distinct fantasy that Carolyn was going to fly at David's face with her fingernails or that he was going to grasp her neck and strangle her. The moment was one of suspended agony, the couple trembling in the midst of the mysterious and powerful forces that coursed between them.

Finally, at what seemed to me the brink of an irrevocable act, I had to demand that they stop. "Where is this getting you?" Such awkward words, so ridiculously matter-of-fact in the midst of their charged feelings, but all I could think of. Apparently with great relief, they both turned toward me.

"Nowhere" was their almost simultaneous answer. I wasn't so sure myself. It had taken courage to push their argument beyond its usual polite limits, though they clearly needed help if they were going to do more than batter each other. I felt sympathy for both of them when I looked at the tense anguish of their faces. When I spoke to them, I had a sense of their problem *as a couple.* I could see the collective pain; the collusive, interlocked, and entrapping patterns; the overarching stress that engulfed them both. I felt gentle, addressing not so much the individuals as the marriage itself. "I wish you could talk about *yourselves*. Your words are *so* full of accusation and attack. The problem is still the other person." The tone of my voice conveyed an understanding of how difficult it was to change.

We had spent a lot of time working on the process of their dialogue, coaching them to say "I feel" rather than "you are," pushing them to describe their doubts and agonies rather than attack. But their rapport always collapsed when they were under stress. They returned to blaming and attacking each other with depressing regularity. The problem was not that they didn't understand; it was that the psychological foundation of their relationship was still disturbed. They remained symbiotically entangled, their perception of their marriage often violently distorted by their mutual and pervasive insecurities and by the psychological shadows of their separate family histories. When they began as now to yell at each other, it was because each of them actually *felt* that the other person constituted a locked door that excluded them from their own personhood. They still experienced the door to freedom and happiness as being in the Other, not in the Self. Neither had dared cross that definitive threshold which marked entry to the exploration of Self.

The couple were stopped short by my remarks, and for perhaps a minute they were silent, almost guilty. Then Carl broke the silence, sounding not nearly as sympathetic as I. He has sat through many years of such marital flogging. "Yeah," he said dispiritedly, "it seems like such a waste that after all this time you're still fighting about who's to blame. As if you really believed it could be just one of you." The couple looked toward him soberly. "It doesn't seem to me that your anxiety about sex, Carolyn, is any more of a problem than David's fear of intimacy or that your inability to be independent deserves any more credit than David's inability to be giving and supportive." He glanced at David to balance the second half of his criticism, speaking with force but without harshness. "The question is what you are going to do about these two-sided problems. Neither of you has been able to move beyond putting pressure on the other, as though that were somehow going to do some good." The couple winced under Carl's words, finding them painful and true. "If you could look at yourselves, you might learn something. Then maybe you could come back and *ask* for something from each other rather than whine or shout about what the other person is doing wrong."

As Carl spoke, I began to think about their argument, trying to isolate its central components. I didn't agree fully with Carl's criticism of them, and I wanted to rescue some positive element in their struggle. Finally, I decided to say it to Carl. "You know, I wonder if we're giving them credit. We told them to be more direct about their anger, and they did it. At least some of their complaints are pretty clear now. The question is: how can they change it?" My words sounded clinical and impersonal to me, and I wanted somehow to get back in touch with the couple. I could not forget the urgency in Carolyn's angry plea to David for more attentiveness, more approval. I also felt the panic in his defensive cry that he could do no more than he was doing to help her.

I realized as I looked at Carolyn that some of her anger was giving way again to depression. I was afraid that she was about to give up completely, and the urgency of that impression overruled any other direction I was considering. "You feel like giving up?" I asked quietly.

"Yes." The profound passivity with which she spoke frightened me.

"Think you could risk it?" I asked gently, daring her in a way which she did not expect. She looked up, puzzled.

Carl darted a glance sideways at me, and I realized that he was with me. It was a terribly delicate moment. Carl's words were low and powerful. "If you could"—pausing, then changing inflection to signal a shift in thought—"give up trying to change *him* or to get approval from him, it might be the beginning of a whole new world." Carl and Carolyn looked directly at each other for a suspenseful moment. Then Carl said, with a tentative expectancy, "Your world would then have *you* in the center of it, not him."

The timing of the remark, Carolyn's mood, Carl's tone of voice, the couple's poised despair—all met with a precision that produced an almost audible click, as when the tumblers of a difficult lock fall into final combination. One knew that the door would open now and something important would emerge. Whatever was going to happen, its locus was in Carolyn.

At first she merely settled in her chair, as though Carl's words had weakened her terribly. She let her head fall back slightly. Her arm hung limply over the chair arm. Turned vacantly toward the ceiling, her face seemed stark, sad, empty. Then tears began to course silently down her face, the only movement in the still room. Carolyn exhaled audibly, the heavy breath a complete sentence of despair.

I spoke quietly. "I'm really glad you can *feel* the hurt." I had the fantasy that Carl and I had led her through an open door to the edge of a long flight of stairs. The stairs were heavily carpeted, and they stretched downward a long, long distance into total darkness. We had pushed her down the stairs, saying, "Go ahead, fall," and she was tumbling down them, in a blur of motion both instantaneous and interminable. She was falling, falling, and we who had pushed her had to catch her.

Carolyn emitted a single sound, at once cry and moan, the quintessence of pain. Then her voice broke into fragments, like water that moves from a contained stream out into the spread of a waterfall. She began to sob—great bursts of sound that tumbled with her as she fell. She made no effort to contain her sadness, and it seized her entire body. Her chest heaved; her face was shut tight against us all, wet with tears. The pain coursed through in waves, now ebbing, now returning with doubled force. The sobbing grew more and more intense until one wondered how she could survive it. Everyone in the room was paralyzed by the power of her agony, the children gazing in fright, David openmouthed, mute. Carl and I could do nothing but witness.

Carolyn had grasped the small decorative pillow on her chair. She clasped it to her chest as if it contained life itself. Holding it seemed to help, and very gradually her crying lessened. Nothing impeded her grief; it merely spent itself. The sobs lessened in intensity and then in frequency, acquiring a reassuring quality. Like an infant that had almost cried itself to sleep, Carolyn appeared to have moved from a really terrible aloneness to a kind of self-acceptance. She had fallen down a great height into the confines of her own body, and now she seemed lost in its interior, closed and private. Still, she clasped the pillow.

Carl said quietly, "I wish you would hold your own body instead of the pillow."

Without opening her eyes or changing position, Carolyn dropped the pillow, clasping her arms together close to her sides.

"I feel *so* alone," she said faintly.

"But you're not," Carl reassured her. "You have yourself." Carolyn started to speak, but Carl interrupted her, not wanting her to talk yet. "Can you feel your body?" he asked. "Can you let yourself be aware of it?"

Carolyn seemed to understand what was being asked of her, for she relaxed in the chair, her breathing deeper now and more even. Her eyes were still closed; her face was swollen from crying. Carl continued. "Can you feel your breathing? Let yourself breathe deep and long breaths. Just think about breathing." Carolyn fell back limply in the chair as though it were the arms of a mother whom she trusted. Her chest rose and fell rhythmically, her breath barely audible. We all relaxed with her, deeply relieved. She was calm, resting.

Still caught in the hypnotic silence that had fallen over the room, I became aware several minutes later that Laura was standing beside Carolyn's chair. She put her hand on the hand of her mother, who sat up, opening her eyes. "Oh!" Carolyn started. Then she saw the look of acute distress in her daughter's face. "Oh, Laura," she said, clasping the little girl in her arms, smiling. "I'm all right!" Carolyn beamed as she looked at Laura. "I just *needed* to cry." It was the child's turn to sniffle slightly in relief.

Carolyn was different now. Her gaze was clear and direct, her voice hoarse but very calm as she spoke to Carl. "What happened to me?"

I could not forget my fantasy, so I answered. "You fell down a flight of stairs, and you caught yourself." I smiled, and so did she. Both Don and Claudia needed to talk to Carolyn then, and the room reawakened to conversation.

"I never knew you could cry that hard," Don said.

"Neither did I," Carolyn replied.

Only then did Carolyn remember that she had been in a fight with David, and she returned to him. He had remained silent, perceptibly frightened, throughout the entire episode. "Where were we?" Carolyn asked somewhat humorously, as though she and David had some obligation to return to their conflict.

"At each other's throats, I believe," David said, but his remark was serious.

Carolyn responded by growing more serious herself. "Well, I think I can resurrect some of my anger at *you* if you like." It was a warning.

"I wish you wouldn't," Carl said forcefully to her. He was speaking, still in a confidential tone, to Carolyn. "You escaped the marriage for a few minutes. Stay with yourself. Don't sacrifice yourself to this war."

"I can't *help* being so angry at him!" Carolyn said angrily at Carl. I could see the power of the argument about to envelop her again.

"Would it help if you closed your eyes?" I asked. "Think about yourself." Carolyn tried it, closing her eyes while facing David. For a full minute she sat upright, her attention turned inward.

It was in the midst of that suspenseful silence that Carl said a little tentatively, "We've got to stop. We've run overtime."

CHAPTER 16

Carolyn

The interview had been on Wednesday. On Sunday afternoon I received a call from David, who sounded upset. "Carolyn has been crying for two hours," he said. "She can't seem to stop, and I don't know what to do. She's quite hysterical."

"What happened?" I asked, worried. Very dependent individual patients often call their therapists at odd hours, as if they had a child's right to instant access to their "parent." But families don't usually call unless something is really wrong. David explained that he and Carolyn had got into an argument, and he wasn't even sure what he had said that had been so upsetting. She had just collapsed into uncontrollable grief.

"What should I do?" he reiterated, exactly the question I had been posing to myself.

"Do you think she is suicidal?" I asked. I was trying to measure the seriousness of the events that seemed to conspire against my Sunday afternoon.

"I have no idea," David replied. "She isn't terribly coherent." Some sort of decision was squarely on my shoulders. I could not hear Carolyn crying over the telephone, but I could visualize her clearly, slim hands pressed against her face, her body arching under the pressure of its difficult labor, wave after wave of pain sweeping over her, each announced by a sob.

I was going to gamble. "Tell you what," I said hesitantly to David. Then, realizing that my uncertainty would be difficult for him, I became firmer, more confident. "Just stay with her. Don't leave her, but don't try to *do* anything specific." I waited, letting myself admit more feeling in my voice as I continued. "Just be *with* her." Every implication was that he should be sympathetic, but not put any pressure on her to make *him* feel better. "And call me in a couple of hours if she isn't all right." I wasn't sure what "all right" meant, but I assumed that David would err on the side of caution.

"All right," David said, repeating my words as though he needed reassurance himself. I didn't blame him.

I worried for the rest of the afternoon. Carl and I might as well have had an interview with them for all the peace I got. Margaret and the children were separated from me by the glass wall of my apprehensiveness, and there was not much question about who was imprisoned by it. My confinement was broken by the sudden ring of the telephone just as the evening meal, at which I had been present but effectively absent, ended. "Gus?" David queried. I could hear no cue in his voice regarding the state of his wife, though I was glad that he used my first name. "I just thought I would call to let you know that Carolyn is fine." The relief now audible in his voice had the effect of a trickle of warm water down my chest, a quick blessing. David explained. "We took a long ride in the car, something that always seems to help both of us. And she gradually calmed down. She's not sure either what got her so upset, but she's really quite all right now."

"Does she want to speak to me?" I asked. Muffled conversation while David asked her.

"No," David returned. "She just said to say thanks."

I wasn't sure what I was being thanked for, but I was very glad that David had called me back. In spite of my efforts to sound firm, he must have sensed my worry. "Thank you for calling me back, David," I said with obvious gratitude. And the remainder of that evening was really satisfying. I had the sense that something good had happened.

Only at our next meeting did I understand that I had done exactly the right thing. It was Wednesday again, and I expected to see Carolyn still looking drained. Instead, she was radiant, rested, bounding with energy. There was also a kind of closeness between her and David that was tied to the conclusion of Sunday's episode. "I don't know what happened," said Carolyn. "David and I were arguing, and suddenly it felt to me that he was utterly heartless, cruel, unreachable. I couldn't stand it anymore, and I started crying and couldn't stop. I know it was more than what he said, and that it was connected with a lot of other things in my life, but I had very little control."

"How did you finally come out of it?" Carl wanted to know, feeling a little on the outside.

"We were driving around," Carolyn said, "and then we stopped somewhere beside a road. I don't remember David's words, but I do remember his stroking my forehead with his fingers." She looked at him warmly. "It was quite loving." Then she smiled and added, still fondly, "For him."

In our discussion later Carl and I realized that when Carolyn had broken down at our previous session, we had responded to her gently and with considerable caring. Our response had created an imbalance in the marriage. Carolyn had felt some sensitivity in our "touch" that she had long wanted from David. Thus, when they got into another argument a few days later, Carolyn found herself in the very center of the harsh, lonely land that was their desert marriage. Her grief was summative, however, a crying for all the solitude and sadness she had experienced in her life. David was merely the most recent and enduring of her relationship failures.

When they called me, somehow I perceived that I was not really needed in person. What was apparently required from me was a form of permission for David to respond to his wife with caring and sensitivity. Without being aware of what I was doing, I told him how to respond, and he did it. No, that is not quite right. He didn't *do* anything of substance. He *was* loving. Without their knowing what *they* were doing, the couple had intuitively scheduled the crisis at a time when Carl and I were normally unavailable because they already had from us the model for what they wanted. All they needed was a nudge to boost their courage. That is what Carolyn had said "thanks" for—for letting them find their own solution and for whatever cue I gave David that enabled him to be atypically sensitive.

Carolyn's cathartic outpourings of grief and sadness signaled the end of her tolerance for her life as it was. The crisis was related to her unconscious readiness now to grow. She had endured feeling isolated, unloved, and unfulfilled for most of her life, and she was desperate for something better. Only her growing awareness that a more satisfying life was possible allowed her to face the profundity of her despair.

Once she had survived these paroxysms of unhappiness, however, she achieved a kind of peace. The worst had come; she had gone to the edge of craziness and peered inside. An internal decision had been reached and now was past; perhaps it was the decision to live. For so long Carolyn had dodged between the painful thorns of self-doubt and self-contradiction. At last she was ready to look around her, as though these internal doubts were at rest. She had a new awareness of the external world, the present moment. It was as though she were awake for the first time in many years, her eyes moist with curiosity. The momentum begun with her "breakdown" rolled on inexorably; now that she had begun to feel better she would allow nothing to stop her.

The enthusiasm that Carolyn began to feel about herself was not purely an individual matter. She had been "elected" to be the first person in the marriage to "abandon" the search for marital harmony and to pursue instead, and at whatever cost, the search for self. It was a shift of focus which Carl and I supported. Any enduring solution to the couple's marital problems had to be founded on fundamental changes in the way in which the two individuals experienced themselves. *Both* needed to be more independent, more courageous, more confident about themselves. Carolyn was merely the pioneer in the new territory of personhood.

Not all couples "schedule" their growth in this way. Some couples grow together in careful synchrony, never losing contact with each other or with their individuality. In some couples the husband is "chosen" to become unhappy with the status quo and to agitate for change. But in a great many families the pattern follows the Brices': the woman is the pioneer, the person who first becomes aware of the possibilities for a better life and who searches with great desperation for ways of achieving it. So powerful, in fact, are women's needs to expand their experience today that the crucial issue for the therapeutic enterprise becomes not whether women will persist in their efforts, but whether husbands can adapt to the force of their quest. In many marriages the women have an urgent need to grow that their husbands cannot match, at least for the present. And if husbands cannot accommodate and adapt to their wives' newfound initiative, the marriages are in jeopardy.

The Brices' problems were plainly more than "marital," in that they represented also a failure in each individual's relation to the self. Of course, both had learned in their families of origin to repress their feelings, to attack themselves, to doubt their own worth. But these tendencies were now firmly internalized, independent of contact with their parents. The marriage, however, provided them with a way in which they could avoid facing their internal problems. Collusively and unconsciously they had constructed a system of grievances against each other that permitted them to avoid examining and experiencing themselves. Even though the marriage felt like the deepest of prisons, the true confinement was an internal one. Carolyn blamed David for all her unhappiness, yet much of her suffering was self-imposed. Though he was more covert, David practiced the same preposterous alibi: if only Carolyn were different. Each gave the other the power of the primordial parent, the source of all oppression and of final deliverance. It was a hall of mirrors, dream images, phantom figures.

What happened to Carolyn is that she discovered herself, and she did it through a powerful encounter with grief and despair. Her terrible fixity on David had failed her, and she fell, crying, down a great height. What she found at the bottom of that fall was both true aloneness and a certain comfort. Carl and I were there, true. But so was her own body. The sense of reassurance which she gained in experiencing her own body sensations may have allowed her to begin to risk greater independence from David.

Whatever the source of her strength, whether it was the support that Carl and I gave her, or the increased self-esteem that she derived from facing and weathering so much despair, or the excitement of greater awareness of her own feelings, Carolyn began to experiment with a new point of view. Most of the events that seemed like an awakening to her, the crowing of the proverbial morning rooster, occurred outside the interviews. In addition to attempting greater independence from David, Carolyn was risking more separation from the weekly sessions. She did report these "happenings" in due time, however, preceding most recountings by the sentence "Something interesting happened to me this week."

Carolyn: "We, David and I, have this *thing* that has been a problem for years. I often want to go to bed earlier than he does, though admittedly I want to do less when I get there—usually I just want to go to sleep." She was smiling! "The other night I did what I usually do, which is to nag David to come to bed. And he did his part and procrastinated, shuffling around the papers on his desk for some excuse to frustrate me." She paused, as though she had thought of something new. "I suppose that I am just afraid to go to bed alone, but I got—I get—very annoyed. Then it suddenly occurred to me that I could go to bed without him! It may sound ridiculous to you, but it was a radical idea to me. What would I do without my flannel and sandpaper security blanket? It appeared as if in a vision to me, I would go to sleep!" I had never found Carolyn funny before, but her self-mockery was making me edge toward laughter. "Which is exactly what I did." She looked piquantly at David. "And you know what? When he came upstairs a half hour later, he was downright *upset* that I had gone to bed without him. He woke me up, grumbling around."

"Ain't that marriage?" Carl laughed. "Change one step, and you upset the whole damned dance." The exciting thing about this monumental incident is that Carolyn deliberately changed *her* step rather than tried incessantly to muscle David into changing *his*. And she discovered to her amazement that he had been dependent on her behavior. When she stopped nagging him about going to bed and took independent action, he felt betrayed. And he was. Carolyn was less and less caught up with the whole problem of what David felt or what David was doing. Faintly as yet, but definitely, she started to hear the blessed tap-tapping of her own drummer.

Later Carolyn again: "David can't stand to go to parties. I *like* to go to parties!" Her jauntiness had emerged gradually, and Carl and I found it more and more attractive. "The other night we had our habitual scene, which is, of course, my nagging him to hurry. I also like to be on time. Usually, I will stand around in my coat, waiting and fuming. This time I decided to go out to the car and wait, and I felt much better. I was having a fantasy of driving off without him when he hurried out the door."

"I must have guessed," David admitted. Through most of these revelations he maintained his good humor, though he was obviously under some pressure as Carolyn continued to accumulate "interesting experiences" during these weeks.

"But the thing I want to talk about happened *at* the party," Carolyn said, glancing fondly at David. "This party was given by some people who like dancing and who have a lot of money. There was a band, and their very large dining room was set afire by this little group of electronically armed warriors. David and I danced and enjoyed it. Then David got into a long discussion with one of his law cronies, and I felt distinctly adrift. I started dancing again with anybody who would ask me. And I, good old depressed Carolyn, actually enjoyed myself. Conspicuously. I suppose that's why I kept getting asked." David looked in less good humor. "When our marital witching hour arrived, David came and said that he wanted to go home. I didn't want to go, and I said so."

David interposed. "I suggested that she stay and get a ride home with Fay, our neighbor, whose husband was out of town that night."

"But you must not have expected me to accept your offer," Carolyn said, also seriously. "Or else you wouldn't have been so upset when I came home."

"At one-*thirty?*" David asked, troubled parent of a newly adolescent wife.

"Two measly hours!" Carolyn said. "If you knew how many hours I have spent waiting for *you!*"

"Not at that time of night!" David objected. Carolyn smiled broadly, obviously pleased by having made her husband jealous, and the argument continued uneventfully onward. Togetherness, the old glue that has fatally cemented so many individuals into joyless marriages, was failing. And at least on Carolyn's part, a measure of separateness was being achieved and even relished.

Aware that David was becoming increasingly uncomfortable, Carl and I made several efforts to provoke him into the same kind of interest in himself that Carolyn had discovered. But for whatever reason—whether the marriage had decreed that it was Carolyn's "time" or whether David experienced a failure in courage—it didn't happen. David could talk about himself, but it was empty talk. He continued thinking and doing, while his increasingly alive wife was swept into a wave of new experiences which nothing could dissuade her from pursuing.

Still later: "You know, these children of ours are spoiled rotten. They do very little work around the house. And I want to change that situation." A week later Carolyn had organized a schedule of duties for everyone. She had consulted David for his opinion, and she had also put him on the list. He was now head of the after-dinner kitchen cleanup crew, as well as senior partner in a law firm. There seemed to be no stopping her.

The children had become peripheral figures in the therapy,

though they attended occasional sessions. They were appropriately bored with their parents' internal politics, and Carl and I allowed them to come as they felt like it. Claudia came more regularly than Laura and Don, remaining fascinated with the process of therapy itself. She raised occasional issues in her own life, and she witnessed her mother's attempt at growth with real interest. The rigors of marriage, while some years distant, held more immediate relevance for her than they did for the other children. And she was luckier than most of us in being able to witness her parents' struggle to improve their relationship.

Carolyn's journey out of depression was not straight and even. Her path, which she largely improvised, made occasional deep swings downward into her old moods, usually because some obstacle blocked her way. She would come to a session washed out and defeated, ready to blame herself for everything. Because depression is partly a form of self-indulgence—it is actually *easier* at times to attack yourself than to cause someone else discomfort—our response could not always consist of loving reassurance.

I often found myself furious at Carolyn for letting David walk over her so habitually. Angrily, gesturing at her: "If you let David come home an hour late for dinner without even giving you a telephone call, you *deserve* to be depressed. Why should he feel sorry for you? He has a good arrangement. If I could get away with something like that with Margaret, I would probably do the same thing."

I have grossly underrepresented here Carl's talent for creative use of the paradoxical statement, but there was one incident in which his penchant for this tactic was particularly useful. Carolyn had become angry at David one morning just as he was leaving for the office (a favorite and relatively safe time for couples to have a fight) and had stayed angry all day. When he was late coming home, she started the cocktail hour without him, and while rushing into the kitchen to catch a pot that was—appropriately enough—boiling over, she tripped and sprained her ankle badly.

Carl was looking at the taped ankle as he began his remarks at the session following the incident. "You know, that's an idea. Have you thought of becoming an alcoholic? It might be very helpful." While his thread of a smile was definitely present, its meaning was somewhat uncertain.

Carolyn: "I've got enough problems without being an alcoholic."

Carl: "But think about the advantages. Everybody would feel very bad about it. The kids might do more work to help you, and David might have to come home on time to make sure you didn't get hurt. In fact, it might help David to become much more loving if he had to look after an alcoholic."

"Sorry, not interested." Carolyn, puzzled by Carl's tack, began to look less morose.

Carl wouldn't stop. "What's the matter? Aren't you willing to sacrifice to help your family?"

"I sacrifice a lot already," Carolyn replied, beginning to get angry.

"But you may have to sacrifice much more if you are going to help them, especially your husband. Do you know the story of the good Samaritan?"

Carolyn spit out her words now. "Of course I do."

Carl ignored the rapidly developing storm clouds in her face. "Well, he found this robber, see. . . ."

After a few more minutes of coaching on how to be self-sacrificial and helpful, Carolyn was rapidly coming out of her depression and headed straight for Carl. "Listen, you bastard. I have no interest in sacrificing myself any more than I now do!"

However we expressed it, we loved her for her struggle up that ragged, winding road out of the valley. We fought with her to keep going, and when she was really discouraged, we held her in our arms —not literally, of course, though we would have done that, too, if she had asked for it. Carl and I are a little shy, in fact, about physical contact with our patients, but we aren't afraid to care about them.

Carolyn developed an interest in her family of origin, and she made a couple of exploratory trips to visit her aging parents. "I want to see how I behave when I'm with them. Maybe something has changed after all these sessions." She returned with observations and questions and a vague sense that something different was indeed possible in her relationship with her parents. Excerpts from her remarks:

—"You know, it's amazing how deferential and quiet I get when I'm around my mother." A habit she clearly recognized as having been transferred directly to her husband.

—"My father is so infuriatingly *passive*. And he makes these very subtle little digs at my mother. In his own quiet way he really *gets* to her." Seeing the part of her father that was not the simple victim.

—"Do you think I married a man so committed to his career

because my father never did *anything?*" I liked the way she had begun to emphasize words. It was also exciting to see her groping for and finding her own ideas. She had seized the initiative in her own fight and was, in effect, becoming her own therapist.

—"Do you think I sacrifice myself to David to make up for my mother's having been so obnoxiously dominant?" It is always a little strange to see someone experiencing *as her own* an idea which you presented to her many months before. Of course, Carolyn had "heard" our interpretation then, but she hadn't been ready for it. Now it reappeared, rising out of the unconscious like a clear bubble, its time come.

—"I think my mother isn't nearly as bad as my father and I make her out to be. She even has a decent sense of humor."

—"Where is my *brother* in all this business?"

—"I had an idea. When I write, I always say 'Dear Mom and Dad.' But it's always my mother who answers. I wonder if he even gets to read the letters. You think if I wrote directly to him, just to him, he might answer? Or if I telephoned, Mother would let me speak to him without being on the line, too? Why do you suppose he and I aren't allowed to communicate—except through Mother?" Good old Oedipus and his sister Carolyn.

Inevitably, as her path coursed higher, and as Carolyn felt the surge of greater energy, she developed a rather trying double perspective. Although she saw possibilities for herself that she had never dared glimpse before, her life was not very different in its practical particulars. Many things were changing—especially her ability to be assertive with David—but one of the distressing realities that did not change was the routine of her day. It often included time for reading, committee work for a voluntary organization, long chats with friends, yet the day still revolved around cleaning the large house and preparing for the arrival home of husband and children at the appointed hours. When Carolyn finally announced the viewpoint of this situation that she had reached, her remark was preceded by one of her definitive sighs.

"You know, this sounds awfully simplistic, but I think one of my problems is that I'm bored. As much as I love being a housewife—and I really do, usually—I think I need something more." Then she looked askance at me and Carl. "Do you think my family could stand it if I got a part-time job?"

"Naaaah," Carl said. "I wouldn't consider it."

"Why don't you ask them?" I said, forever serious.

For a woman who felt deeply cheated that her mother *had* to work when she was a child, it was not an insignificant moment. She clearly felt guilty for even the thought of not being constantly available to her children and was not far from tears. There was also the complicating factor of a husband whose own mother had never considered any other alternative than being a housewife; David was happy that his wife's domesticity replicated for him a relationship that had been very comfortable. He liked having "mother" Carolyn at home, and he, like his father before him, was even fussy about how his wife did her housekeeping. Criticizing Carolyn's work was merely another exercise for his habitual compulsiveness. When Carolyn turned to the family to pose her question, *she* obviously felt tense, though, of course, everyone (only Laura was absent that day) said it would be fine if she got a job.

Carolyn looked mistrustful of this reassurance, and probably rightly, since such ideas were likely to be more acceptable to the family in theory than in practice. Nevertheless and perhaps aided by additional encouragement from Carl and me, she began to look for a job. The search proved both exciting and depressing.

The job search did not have its roots in an attempt by Carolyn to change her evaluation of herself, but was the result of *already changed* self-evaluation. Admittedly, getting a paying job had appealing attributes, not least of which was its furthering the establishment of a certain kind of parity with David. But she wisely saw it not as supplying personhood, but as confirming and expanding it.

Throughout the several months in which Carolyn's excitement about her own growth occupied most of our time and attention in the therapy hours, David remained in a relatively fixed position. It was as though he were observing Carolyn—now with curiosity, now with envy, often with what appeared to be a benign indifference. Several times I had the fantasy that Carolyn was learning to dance and was practicing within a circle that always included David. She never strayed too far from him and was aware of his response to her movements.

In the main David did not react strongly to anything Carolyn did, though as her interests in the world outside the family became more pronounced, Carl and I thought we detected in him a growing, though still quiescent, displeasure. Carolyn would report that a friend had commented on how much more cheerful and relaxed she seemed, and David would say nothing. He just slumped a little in his chair. Our persisting efforts to involve him more deeply in the therapy process failed. On the surface he remained tolerant and even supportive of Carolyn's efforts, but on a deeper level we sensed that he found them threatening. And he could not acknowledge his anxiety. "No, I'm fine," he insisted. After a while we let him drift, turning our attention to Carolyn.

Then, one day in mid-March, David looked unusually happy at the beginning of the session. "What happened to you?" I asked whimsically. "You look almost cheerful."

"Something very interesting," David said mysteriously. Only then did I notice that Carolyn now looked upset—in fact, morose. David settled in his chair comfortably, preparing to tell his story at some leisure.

"He got a job offer in Boston," Don blurted out. "He's gonna be an executive!" He smiled with the victory of spilling the beans, and his voice betrayed both pride in his father and a certain disdain for him, a divided feeling doubtless influenced by his mother's visible despair and his father's equally evident pleasure.

Momentarily discomfited by his son's disclosure, David proceeded. "I don't know about my being an executive, but I have had a job feeler from a large corporation headquartered in Boston. I'm not so sure how they came to be interested in me, though I did help a local firm arrange a big contract with them about a year ago. The job they would be considering me for would be a major one on their legal staff."

"How do you feel about it?" Carl asked, somewhat atypically. Carl rarely asks how someone feels. He assumes that people should take the initiative for describing their own feelings.

"Excited, flattered," David said, "and a little scared." He glanced at Carolyn. "I'm also not sure any of us want to leave this city. We have a lot of investment here."

"You look very upset, Carolyn," I said.

Carolyn leaned perceptibly toward me, as though eager for support. Her eyes started to fill with tears as she spoke, though she was trying hard not to cry. "I am" was all she said.

"Can you talk some more about it?" I offered.

Carolyn's anger was obviously for David, though spoken to me.

"What is there to *say?* My husband has a job offer! I must wait to know my fate. Isn't that the way it is?"

"I don't know." I smiled, trying to get through the screen of rage and hurt that separated us. "Is that the way it is? Seems to me that 'whither thou goest' is pretty open to question these days. Wouldn't you have any say in a decision like this?"

"Well, would I?" Carolyn turned the anger toward David.

"For God's sake, Carolyn," he replied, "I have a tentative feeler from a company, and already you have me dragging you bodily out of town. All I said is that I ought to *look!* It might be a good opportunity for me, for us. Don't I have a right to *consider* it?" He was defensive and irritated.

Carolyn was a long way from tears now. "You know as well as I do that that isn't the question. You know that *you* expect to make the decision and that I'm expected to go along with it. It's always been that way with us."

Suddenly the argument struck me as amusing, Carolyn furiously accusing her husband of being dominant. "You don't sound all that malleable to me," I ventured. "You sound pretty darn strong."

Carolyn half turned to face me, risking a slight smile as she allowed herself to be distracted from the argument. "Threatened is more like it," she said.

"In what way?" I asked, pretty sure of what she would say.

More anger: "Wouldn't *you* be threatened? For the first time in my life I begin to try to do something meaningful outside my home, and suddenly it looks as though I might have to leave the *only* community I know well, the *only* place where I have contacts and feel at all comfortable. At least here I have friends. And if we move, he will move into a world that is ready-made for him. A job, a secretary, a staff. They'll even manage to get him into a country club. And me? I'll come along as part of the deal. Only I'll have to *remake* my world, start all over again." She again looked furiously at David, unable to avoid fighting with him. "It's not fair. It's just not fair."

David's response combined retreat with anger. "Carolyn, I have a job offer or the possibility of an offer. I think I ought to *look* at it. I don't work just because I enjoy it. I work to support this family, and I think I have a right to consider the circumstances I work under. I like my work now, but there are things about it that I don't like. It doesn't offer me a hell of a lot of challenge, frankly, and I might really *like* this job." A note of coldness had crept into his level tone.

Carolyn had been distracted by Laura for a moment, helping her with a drawing which the child brought over to show her mother. She shifted her attention back to David, jerking her whole body in his direction with an emphasis that freed a torrent of words and feeling. "Of *course,* you should look at it. You'd be dumb not to. But you'll probably like it and take it, and we will move to that damn city and live within a mile of your parents. And you will become the corporation's indispensable darling, and I will see even *less* of you." Her bitterness and hurt and despair fell heavily upon her increasingly frightened husband. "I'll have to compete not only with your job, but with your *family* to get to see a little of you. And I'll be a nobody. A housewife who scrubs a house and waits for her children to come home from school and for ladies' day at the country club. A lot that is to live for!"

"Carolyn!" David was trying to stop her, but it was too late.

"Well, what do we *have,* David, that's worth my moving to Boston and going through all this for? Do we *have* anything in our marriage? Do you think it's worth fighting for? Would it really be any different there? It might even be worse. At least here I have friends, good friends—I have a little bit of a world anyway!"

Carolyn paused momentarily, and David managed to slip in a hurried sentence. "I don't think our marriage is that awful."

Carolyn's reply was a flat, angry, but somewhat discouraged contradiction. "That's because it isn't that *important* to you. Marriage is all right for you if I go to bed with you occasionally and the house looks good and the children don't bother you too much. And if I give an occasional party for your clients and colleagues. But the only thing that really means something to you is what happens in your work."

"Not true," David said, but without real conviction.

"True, David," Carolyn answered a little sadly. "Look at our therapy. I've really worked to change things about myself. And it's been happening. But you haven't really tried. You say the words, and you have made some gestures to be tender to me; but you are willing to stay the same." She paused, her voice trailing off to resignation. "And I think it's because the quality of our life really isn't important to you." Another pause, this one more significant. "That's why I'm not sure I would even *go* to Boston with you if you decided to now. I might just stay and make my life here and let you go your way."

Dead silence in the room. Claudia, who had not spoken a word, was crying soundlessly, looking from her mother to her father in disbelief. The importance of the moment did not seem to register in Don and Laura, though Don's face was somber.

David's voice was low and firm. "Carolyn, I am not going to let your threats stop me. Just because you don't *like* something doesn't mean I'm going to buckle under."

Carolyn had regained her composure. Her reply was controlled and full of irony. "Oh, I don't think you should. And I certainly wouldn't expect it."

There had not been much opportunity for Carl and me to intervene, but the moment seemed propitious. "Carolyn," I said, "I want to speak to this thing of your being a nobody because I think you're mistaken." Carolyn looked my way, interested. I saw the firm set of her lips and, for some reason, the wrinkles under her eyes. "I don't think there is really any *excuse* for not being a person, and I don't think it really matters whether you are a housewife or have a career or live in Wisconsin or Boston or are married to David or to John Doe." I paused. "I might have been concerned six months ago that you could go to Boston and be no more than David's wife, but I don't think there's much chance of that now. If you'll listen to the power you have displayed in the last half hour, you'll see what I mean. You are *so* different from the timid person you used to be!" Carolyn was visibly pleased by what I had said. "Of course, part of the problem may be the timing of this thing. It seems as if it's interrupting not only your search for a career, but your therapy, too."

"That's true," Carolyn said quietly. "I hadn't thought of that as part of my being so upset."

Suddenly Carl laughed lightly, making us all turn toward him. "Yeah. This character"—gesturing toward David—"may have found a new job just in time to keep from becoming a patient himself. Or to keep you, Carolyn, from getting too much stronger, for God's sake." David grinned at Carl, as though found out. "My apologies, David," Carl continued, "but we could always refer the two of you to a therapist in Boston."

"I'm not sure I'm going there," Carolyn reiterated very seriously.

"Oh, I'm not disagreeing with that," Carl said. "If the two of you want to choose this way of splitting up, that's your business. But I don't think you ought to fool yourselves that there is only one way of looking at your situation."

"What do you mean?" Carolyn asked.

"There are a lot of interpretations you as a couple could put on this job offer," Carl replied. "The interpretation you have chosen seems to be an old one in marriage, that only *one* of you can be a person. The other has to be a subsidiary. And the offer of this job looks as though one of you will have to sacrifice himself or herself for the sake of the marriage. But I don't think that's true. I think that whatever you do, you can *both* be individuals, and you can probably also work out a viable marriage."

"But if I give up now," David said, "I may lose an awful lot."

"Nothing essential to your personhood," I said, crossruffing with Carl's play. "Unless you use this as an excuse to stop trying to be yourself." I smiled, remembering Carl's earlier challenge to Carolyn. "I suppose you could turn the job down and become an alcoholic, and that would make Carolyn sorry for 'forcing' you to stay where you are."

Carl: "Or you could admit that moving right now is not good timing for Carolyn and look for the job you want in a couple of years."

I addressed Carolyn. "Or you could agree to go to Boston but insist that you are going to graduate school the way you talked about a couple of weeks ago and that David is going to have to pay for somebody to help with the housework. And take every other weekend off from the job." I couldn't help teasing David about his overwork.

"Yeah," Carl said. "This is all so symbolic. Which one of us is going to *win*. But it doesn't have to be that way. There are lots of ways to solve these problems." He paused deliberately before ending. "But you also have every right *not* to solve the problems, to conclude that the marriage is never going to work." Though there was more talk before the hour ended, that was essentially the final statement.

We had one more meeting before the scheduled two-week trip to Boston during which David was to be interviewed by the corporation and then visit his family for a while. If the grim silences in this interview were any indication, our words about possible solutions had not really registered. David was doggedly insistent on going, and Carolyn, though now much quieter, was as angry as before about the possibility of their moving. The intransigence of their positions struck us as ominous. Some powerful force impelled a separation in this marriage, and no words of conciliation or rapprochement seemed indicated. So we didn't try. We sat with the family while they brooded about their future. Again, Claudia was the only one to cry, her silent tears unacknowledged by anyone in the room. There was little Carl and I could do but be present with them while they found their way through time and events.

Two days after David was to have departed for Boston, Carolyn called me. She had obviously been crying, and her voice was still a little hoarse. "Could I see you and Carl once while David is gone?" she asked sadly.

"I'm sorry, Carolyn," I said. "I think it would be a mistake. This situation is too delicately balanced for us to risk taking your side. We may be too involved with you already, and that may be part of the problem. As hard as it is, you should try to tough it out." My words were firm, but I had little doubt that she heard my sympathy for her dilemma.

"I thought you would say that," she said, not at all bitterly. In fact, she seemed relieved. "I feel better anyway. I just needed to hear your voice."

CHAPTER 17

The Terrible Choice

I suspect that the decision is made in the dead of the night. Whether it arrives after a glacially slow accumulation of coldness or bursts forth in an unexpected storm of anger, this moment is usually preceded by a long and tortuous history. A relationship that once seemed warm, clear, as safe as the day has changed, apparently unalterably, leaving the partners wandering separately among dark and confusing passageways of a house they hardly recognize. Lost from each other, trapped within the enclosure itself, they live in this space until it becomes an airless hell. Only when one of them is willing to brave the solitary plain outside does a door become visible. It is an opening both essential and dreaded in any meaningful relationship, one to which the partners resort only with the greatest sense of pain and failure: exit; divorce.

Divorce statistics have been kept in this country since 1890, and with the exception of a few interludes, the incidence of divorce has climbed steadily since then, rising more than 300 percent between 1890 and 1970. Since these statistics merely describe marriages that end and since people can marry any number of times, the statistics are usually cited in the context of those marrying for the first time and those remarrying after a divorce.

Generally these statistics have moved in parallel, declining during the depression years, then rising to a peak in the years immediately following the Second World War. Then the number of couples marrying for the first time began a gradual decline that continues even today. For a time divorces and remarriages declined, too. But about 1960 the divorce rate began to climb. For a decade the remarriage rate followed the divorce rate upward as divorced individuals found new mates. Since 1970 the divorce rate has accelerated dramatically, but the number of couples remarrying has not kept pace. An ominous sentence in a scholarly article summarizes the outlook: "The decrease in first marriage rates and increase in divorce rates cannot continue indefinitely, because the pool of divorce eligibles would eventually be used up." In other words, if present trends continue, at some point there will be no one left married! In 1967, approximately a half million divorces; in 1975, more than a million. For most of us these are not mere numbers but anguish: for ourselves, our friends, our relatives.

What are the odds that the average couple will divorce? Predictions are difficult to make: not until death finally separates a couple can we be certain they will not have elected to divorce. A commonly cited estimate is that three or four of every ten marriages will end in divorce. Paul Glick and Arthur Norton made such a prediction in a study published in 1973, focusing on a group of women who married between 1940 and 1944. As figures on actual divorces accumulate, it appears that their estimate was low. If current trends continue, substantially *more* than one-third of marriages will be terminated in a court of law.

Speculation among social scientists about the sharp increases in divorce covers a wide range, but certain themes emerge. Sociologists point out that there is a new clause implicit in the contemporary marriage contract; in contrast with the old utilitarian marriage agreement, it promises sexual satisfaction, romantic love, companionship, and security. Carl and I would add that it also holds out the hope that marriage will be a kind of psychotherapy, a balm for past wounds and misfortunes in the family of origin. Couples believe the promises, expect them to be fulfilled, and are bitter when they are not. Rather than question themselves or their expectations of marriage, many couples hold fast to the dream, concluding that they have merely *chosen the wrong person.* They divorce to keep alive the possibility of this special relationship created by fate rather than by hard work and to free themselves to search for it with someone else.

In actuality, second and third marriages have a poorer probability of success than the first, and evidence is accumulating of a high incidence of depression among the divorced. The fact that individuals are not rushing into remarriage as rapidly as before may be evidence that experience is winning out over naïve optimism and teaching caution.

If there is a single predetermining factor in divorce, it is probably that individuals marry before they have firmly established a sense of independent selfhood. While research indicates that couples that marry at a later age have a much greater chance for a durable marriage, chronological age is not the only variable. The more decisive question is whether at the time of marriage both individuals have passed through a certain *psychological space* in which they grappled with life alone, depended only on their own resources, and discovered that they could win the battle against their own fears. Each partner needs to have discovered that he or she can bear the fundamental anxiety of being a single biological entity in a rather frightening world. In the process of "bearing it," the person gains a certain amount of self-confidence, self-awareness, and self-loyalty—all important precursors to being able to make a solid commitment to another person. Even if childhood has been difficult, this period of autonomy can be a kind of "therapy through life experience."

By marrying too soon, many individuals sacrifice their chance to struggle through this purgatory of solitude and search toward a greater sense of self-confidence. They glance at the world outside the family and with hardly a second thought grasp anxiously for a partner. In marriage they seek a substitute for the security of the family of origin and an escape from aloneness. What they do not realize is that in moving so quickly from one family to another, they make it easy to transfer to the new marriage all their difficult experiences in the family of origin.

The choice of mate may well be the most decisive act of every person's life. People who decide to marry are doing more than making two individual decisions: they are borne along by an interpersonal process that is more powerful than either of them. The choice of mate appears to be incredibly "accurate" in the way it brings together the essential forces in two lives—their histories, their present state, their yearnings for the future. Irrespective of pleasure or pain, the *meaning* of the lives is summarized in the choice of mate.

Continuity and change are the dual themes in every marriage decision. Each person needs to find something familiar *and* something new in his or her mate. As the young man looks at his wife-to-be, he senses unconsciously that in some ways she is very much like him and very much like various members of his family of origin. This "recognition of the familiar" stirs in both partners when they are together, and it is a powerful component in their mutual attraction. Their relationship allows them to feel safe, "at home." The more satisfying their experience of growing up has been, the more likely are people to choose a partner who provides them with a sense of continuity with that experience. Whatever the nature of this early family life, everyone has a profound need to maintain the sense of identity developed in the early years; invariably, there are close links between the old family and the new mate.

But even if our growing-up experience has been satisfactory, we all are *somewhat* unhappy with ourselves and with our family of origin. Unconsciously we attempt to marry someone who will bring into our lives new personal qualities, new experiences, new ways of relating. In forming our own families, we want to solve some of the problems that existed in the families we were brought up in. If my family couldn't fight openly, I may want to marry someone whose family *can* fight. If I am a shy introvert, I may marry an anxious extrovert. Through the choice of partner we try to bring new "information about living" into our lives. We yearn to be "whole"—psychologically complete—and we look to marriage as a partial answer to that craving.

Why do some people choose partners who precipitate panic in them, who embody, in fact, some of their worst fears? We have already partially answered this question: the need for a sense of identity is so strong that it overrides issues of pain and pleasure. The abused child often clings to the abusing parent rather than go to a foster home, and he later grows up to abuse his own children even though he hated the treatment he received. The pattern one knows is . . . the pattern one knows.

Some marriages are begun with an implicit, unconscious plan for a later divorce. The origins of the "plan" are intimately related to complex problems in both families of origin. Considering the agony involved, it seems strange that two people could enter into a contract which they secretly intend to break. But it may be the only way they see of solving a problem.

Couples can arrive at a divorce crisis through a variety of routes that are too numerous and too circuitous to trace here. Though couples may divorce after two months or after forty years, the average length of the marriage that ends in divorce is seven or eight years. Divorcing couples list a wide variety of complaints about their marriages, but Carl and I find a certain commonality in the interaction sequence that precedes many divorces. The process is similar to that which we have witnessed in the Brices.

At the beginning of the marriage both partners are quite insecure, and they "merge" their separate abilities and needs into a tightly dependent unit. For a while the pact works. Both people feel reassured and protected by their "pseudotherapeutic" agreement.

As they begin to feel that something is seriously wrong, their misgivings first take the form of a vague sense of being crowded and constricted by the marriage. Maintaining an intense dependency takes a great deal of work. Since neither can risk rejection, both individuals decide they must suppress many of the feelings that threaten to displease the other. Compromising their own needs in order to please each other is easy enough for a while, but after several years marriage begins to feel like an enormous set of demands within which they both have a sense of being small and insignificant. The set of demands in which they feel *engulfed* is really a two-sided dependency, but in their minds the jailer is Marriage.

Sooner or later they also feel *abandoned*. As we have seen, amateur psychotherapy between partners works well for minor stresses, but the time inevitably comes when it must fail. This typically occurs when both partners encounter major stresses *at the same time*. She is at home alone with two young children and feels both panicked by the responsibility and depressed because of her isolation from the world of other adults. Simultaneously he is seized by self-doubt as he scrambles frantically to "succeed" in the career world. He comes home discouraged, hoping that she will be sympathetic and nurturant; she awaits his arrival with the same hopes. At the time when both need it most, there is simply no "parenting" available.

Serious stress makes the couple feel tightly bound together; it also makes them feel alone as they discover the limitations in their ability to help each other. If both partners have early life histories of engulfment or abandonment, and if they have not been through an appropriate individuation from their families of origin, normal marital stresses can reawaken some of the latent terrors of childhood. The marriage begins to feel like a replica of the families they grew up in, and it threatens to push them back into some of the more alarming aspects of being children again. Most people are willing to consider divorce only to protect something both terribly important to them and fragile: their sense of identity.

Couples can arrange themselves in all manner of complicated patterns around the themes of engulfment and abandonment. When pressures build—and almost any major life stress will do—both partners may panic in fear of engulfment, or they may feel simultaneously rejected as each asks the other for help. If their major vulnerabilities are somewhat similar, at least they have some likelihood of understanding each other's dilemmas. When their conscious fears are different, however, as in the pattern when one partner is supersensitive to abandonment and the other is supersensitive to engulfment, it may be very difficult for them to achieve empathy for each other.

This is especially true since each person's defense mechanisms exacerbate the problem. When she feels abandoned, it is natural for her to seek closeness, but her attempts aggravate his already-aroused fear of engulfment. The "enemy" is not only the immediate crisis bearing down on them as a couple, but each other. When the two of them are anxious, they do not speak the same language; sometimes they wonder if they live in the same world.

The couple have been through a great deal by the time they arrive at a therapist's office with a fairly clear sense that divorce is likely. They have long ago given up compromise and accommodation and shifted to angry coercion in an attempt to get each other to change. They have repeated perhaps literally a million times the despairing cycle: "You change." "No, you change!" While each has given up hope of getting the partner to change, they have, in fact, both changed—rather secretly. Through the innumerable challenges of their years together—bearing and caring for children, earning a living, coping with practical emergencies, making friends— they have gained a measure of self-awareness and self-confidence. The strictures of marriage appear to prevent them from openly enjoying this embryonic sense of themselves, but at least they have the courage now to consider abandoning the prison which for so long has seemed essential to their survival. In fact, it appears to them that only through leaving marriage can they finally "grow up" and "be themselves."

The positions regarding engulfment and abandonment have become rigidly established and mutually intolerable. The person who wants to leave has been elected to be the voice of individuation and adventure, and this is often the person more fearful of engulfment. The partner more afraid of rejection represents the conservative principle, arguing for stability and togetherness.

The couple have also unconsciously created and seized on some justification for the split, a cause around which further to polarize and to escalate their war: his affair, her job, his mother—the issue itself matters little. The divorce process represents a hunger in both of them to be "born again," to leave behind a "sense of family" that denies their personhood. At last and at whatever cost, they are determined to become two people.

The contract which we therapists establish with the couple considering divorce is perhaps the most crucial element in our work with them. Negotiating the contract is a delicate business since the question of "divorce or not" is explosive. If we offer to help them rebuild their marriage, we risk undermining the partner who desperately wants to end it. If we offer to help them work out the divorce, we seem to betray the partner whose very life appears to depend on staying married.

We explain to the couple that the basic problem in their marriage is probably a lack of individuation, of dual personhood, and we usually do not need to look very far to find evidence to support this claim. We point to the repetitive cycle of conflict and to each person's helplessness to resist his or her contribution to it. We assert that many divorces are merely pieces of legal paper that do little to change the couple's massive entanglement with each other. So *many* couples are legally divorced but emotionally still married; they simply carry on their marriages internally or through their children.

If (and we say it big) they are going to get a meaningful divorce, one that includes psychological as well as legal freedom to leave each other, they will need the same thing that is required in a good marriage: *real* individuation. Whatever they do about their marriage, they will need to disentangle their massively intertwined thinking processes; they need to create a sense of genuine autonomy. "Let us help you with individuation," we offer. "When you have achieved that goal, *then* decide what to do with the investment in your marriage. If you wait to decide, you will have a sounder basis for making a decision." In this way we avoid taking sides, and we allow both partners to find hope in the work. We also set ourselves a task that is appropriate for the therapist—psychological change, not decision making about reality. We believe that the decision to divorce, like the decision to marry, is sacred to the couple. *No* outsider should take from them the delicate compass that guides their most vital decisions. Since they must walk the path, they should set the course.

Negotiating the contract is difficult for us. It is even harder to keep our part of it by remaining absolutely neutral about whether or not they in fact *do* divorce. Since it is what we have done in our own lives, we know that our intuitive prejudice is probably in favor of their staying married and working it out, so we may warn the couple that our determination to stay neutral may waver at times. Carl usually adds with a smile, "You'll have to watch me on the other account, too, because I may unwittingly encourage you to divorce so that I can participate in it vicariously. That way I can learn what it is like!"

Our approach to family therapy remains fundamentally the same whether the presenting program is a divorce crisis or some other dilemma. Even if a marriage is ending legally, a "limited partnership" is desirable as the couple continue to parent their children. Whatever future the marriage has, we hope that the *quality* of their relationship will improve. In fact, it is common for a couple to negotiate a "friendly" divorce through being in therapy: they come to understand the psychological forces that have conspired against the marriage, they "forgive" each other, and though admitting with a sigh that living together could probably not work, they move apart without too great bitterness or a profound sense of failure.

When the issue is divorce, membership at the meetings can be complicated. As always, the children are involved: they need to understand why the divorce is occurring, to be perfectly clear that it is not their fault, and to be reassured that both parents will remain in their lives. Their presence also pressures the parents to be a trifle less infantile.

If either partner has a lover, we often ask that the lover be brought to therapy. The lover is invariably an amateur therapist, and if we are to compete with this relationship, we need access to it. In some instances the two lovers may agree to postpone their affair for a while to allow time to work on the marriage. The lover may decide what was his difficulty with work? He kept getting fired. And why did he get fired? For stealing. Though the boys had not known about the thefts consciously, they certainly *had* discovered a way of keeping this mother involved with their father through imitating him. They were working to break up the second marriage and to get their parents back together, and the divorced parents were found to be cooperating in a variety of subtle ways.

These second-marriage therapies may be nightmarishly complex, with the participants including a couple, their own children, his children and her children from their former marriages, one or more ex-spouses, and assorted relatives. We do not assemble all these people as an exercise in grandiosity, but because they are *all* fighting with one another and usually injuring one or more children as they do so. The only way to stop the fighting is to get the people together. The therapist needs a lot of patience, a certain amount of stoicism, a sense of humor, and a co-therapist!

Work with the divorcing family is so demanding and difficult that it will probably become a subspecialty as family therapy evolves. It is difficult to imagine a situation where help is more badly needed than when families are going through the immense pain of a "relationship death." If any sort of "rebirth" is to follow this experience, it will be much more likely if families receive assistance with this most difficult process.

to enter therapy with someone else, often with his or her own spouse. Sometimes the affair is such a profound involvement and so obviously the next marriage that the lover stays in for the duration of therapy. This is tense work indeed, but it is better than having the powerful drama take place covertly. The level of tension is considerably less if *all* the protagonists agree to stop sexual relationships for the time they are in therapy.

In every family's therapy we would like access to the family of origin, but it is particularly advantageous when there is a question of divorce. The parents are often overinvolved in trying to help, and because they are so partisan, they make the stresses worse for the couple. We ask both partners to bring their families of origin for at least a few sessions, and we prefer more involvement if it is possible.

The extended family's participation tends to stop their "meddling" in the nuclear couple's problems, and it brings more positive contributions as well. There is probably no better way for a therapist to develop a sense of insight and empathy with regard to the two partners than through meeting with their families, and if we can "understand"—in both the emotional and intellectual shadings of that word—we may be able to sensitize the couple to the background of their own dilemmas.

Extended family members do not come as patients, but as "consultants" to the younger family's therapy. Invariably, however, the interviews activate conflicts in the extended family that have been buried for many years. Ghosts and carefully guarded secrets emerge, and tensions rise. Since many of the younger couple's problems are carried over from the two families of origin, the reawakening of extended family conflicts may make for *less* tension in the "patient" marriage. If husband is terrified of wife's dependency on him, it can be a dramatic revelation to him to learn that much of the excess emotion in his reaction comes from his fear of his *mother's* dependency on him, and it is very difficult for him to escape facing the link if the two women are in the same interview with him. As the relationship between the problems in the extended family and the problems in the marriage becomes more obvious, the younger couple may develop for a time a sense of having a "common enemy" in their families.

These extended family conferences do more than stir up conflict, however. Relationships with the families of origin are often *improved* as disagreements are aired and at least partially resolved, and this "warming up" gives the couple a sense of feeling less isolated from their families. The warmth that is generated in these conferences can be of great benefit to the couple. If wife is divorcing her husband in part because he seems rejecting and cold like her father, she is less likely to see the husband in so narrow a light if her relationship with her father is more affectionate. Even a slight improvement in a relationship with a parent can be tremendously significant since these are the relationships that formed the model for all subsequent ones. Often the extended family conference is low-key; it may seem uneventful to the unpracticed eye. But a few words, a glance, a softer inflection of voice can be very meaningful when they come from a parent.

As therapy progresses, certain themes may need more emphasis than they would if the couple were clearly planning to remain married. We may need to be assertive about our view that the problems are caused by both partners; nothing is so futile as months of listening to a couple weight the evidence regarding who is more to blame for what. We may also push to get the couple to see that *both* have ambivalent feelings about the relationship. Even though one partner may "specialize" in grieving and the other concentrate on angry withdrawal, both partners usually care about each other, and both are uncertain about whether they want the relationship to continue. If the partners can acknowledge and share this two-sided ambivalence, the sense of polarization may be lessened.

Almost all couples need to learn to fight more constructively and to resolve their differences, but there are always some who are simply not going to be able to settle their major conflicts. The best such couples can seem to manage is to avoid them and perhaps each other. They need to learn how *not* to fight, and that means learning to resist the bait that each offers the other. Only as individuation proceeds and as each partner gains more self-awareness and self-control can this difficult goal be achieved.

At some time during therapy there is usually a moment of decision. Shall they, or shall they not, divorce? If the therapist is prudent, he will simply "be there" while the couple struggle with their agony over the decision. When it is made—and we are never sure which way it will go—there is plenty of work to be done. If their decision is to stay and fight it out, psychotherapy proceeds, but with a new

sense of purpose. At last the couple have a congruent image of what they want: a better marriage.

The same sense of relief and renewed purpose may accompany the decision to divorce, though the remaining work is different. There is grieving to be done—and *everyone* grieves, even the therapists. The couple must surmount their panic about the brave new world of aloneness as they divide property, plan new living arrangements, new jobs, new lives. Simultaneously, there is a different sort of alarm as the couple learn that they are "trapped" by their children into a continuing relationship. They may be truly frightened as they realize how profound their ties are to each other, how very difficult it is to get divorced when there are children. I think much of the bitter fighting in divorce comes out of this panic, in which both partners mutter silently, "I want out, but I can't seem to get free!" The sense of imprisonment that followed them out of the family of origin and into marriage dogs them still.

Carl and I deal gently but firmly with the couple's anxiety over this issue. We tell them that their intuition is probably correct: when there are children, it is almost impossible to get divorced in the sense of feeling truly "free." They can never withdraw the irrevocable trust established in their children. But they can, if they work hard, not only preserve the investment they have made in their children, but add new people, new experiences, new life to what has gone before. And then we set our shoulders to the intricate challenges of helping them do just that.

Not all our work with divorce concerns the couple actively engaged in getting a divorce. We often work with couples years after an "unresolved" divorce, frequently in the context of the second marriage. Even though legally married to someone else, the partners have remained emotionally married to each other, transmitting their communication through their children.

I remember a poignant consultation interview with a family in which ten-year-old twin boys had been arrested for stealing earthmoving equipment! Their delinquent behavior had been steadily escalating for several years, and it was succeeding in driving mother and stepfather apart as they disagreed about how to deal with the boys. The mother revealed the key to the delinquency when she, with great reluctance, agreed to tell me why she had divorced the boys' father. She had become tired of supporting him, she said. And

CHAPTER 18

David

Psychotherapy is a rhythmic process, and long pauses between interviews, like those during the hour itself, are always significant. During the weeks when David was away, I occasionally found myself thinking about recent events in the family and wondering about the various possible outcomes.

The sudden offer of a job in a distant city had fallen on the Brices' marriage like the blow of a stonecutter, threatening to split their relationship. The structural flaw in the relationship had been there from the beginning: a set of "rules for living" that were rigid, repressive, and emotionally "safe." These rules—their inheritance from their respective families of origin—were dictated by anxiety, dependency, a commitment to selflessness, a need to keep life muted and restrained. The price they paid for emotional security was a kind of emotional death.

Carl and I had repeatedly urged David and Carolyn to take more risks with their relationship: to be more separate, to share difficult feelings, to be crazier, to allow more spontaneity. We invited them to live life as it is, not as they thought it should be, and to risk the confusion, the terror, the passion, the fury that exist under the surface of all our tame, planned existences.

We realized that "opening up" might mean disaster for the couple. So much bitterness had been accumulated and carefully stored, so many desires postponed. To break the brittle surface of their conforming lives was to risk unleashing forces no one might be able to control. Small wonder that they had procrastinated for so long.

Now, though, one could fairly hear the whistle of the hammer as it fell through the air.

The couple had chosen to strike at the inertia in their relationship in a manner that is increasingly common. Like many women today, Carolyn Brice heard and responded to an invitation to "find herself." While family therapy was an immediate stimulus that encouraged her search for change, a woman's group or the quest of a friend might also have spurred her on. Women everywhere now seem to have the growing edge in the family, while men like David drift on in roles with which they are not entirely happy, but which they have no pressing incentive to change. Both partners were offered the same invitation, but only Carolyn responded.

Family therapy exists in a society where a great many women are attempting psychological growth, and the changes they are making are exciting. The women's movement is a powerful force in almost every family we see, and both therapy and therapist must somehow respond to it. Therapy does not write the agenda for change; the client does. Even if the Brices had not been in therapy, Carolyn would probably have been the one to make the first move toward individuation. But in the volatile atmosphere of contemporary family life, the fact that a family is in therapy can make a great deal of difference in the *outcome* of such a move. When a wife-and-mother tries to make some of the complex changes called liberation without any collaboration with her husband and children, she may succeed in gaining personhood only at the cost of great bitterness and guilt. The most expensive sacrifice may be the marriage. But if the family, especially the couple, can work together through these agonizing transitions, the outcome may be positive. While wife-and-mother is the pioneer, everyone in the family can achieve both a sense of individual autonomy *and* a sense of closeness and unity.

Carolyn Brice took advantage of therapy. She began to look for new levels of energy in herself, to search for new alternatives for action, and to seek a new sense of self-acceptance. Carl and I were important in this quest, but in essence the journey was hers. We had accompanied many patients on similar quests, and though she was often in great despair and unable to look further than her immediate pain, we could see the process of the person in evolution. This "leading edge" of hopefulness in our perception of Carolyn was, I think, very useful to her. As an individual she became much more alive.

It is a recurrent temptation, however, to think only of the individual. Was Carolyn really on a separate quest, or was her growth no more than the issue which the couple had intuitively chosen as a point on which to diverge and perhaps to divorce? Carl and I, pleased by Carolyn's progress, had always remained uneasy about David's lack of involvement in therapy. We had chided him to get started on his own self-search, but to no avail. When he introduced the possibility of a job in Boston, he startled us all. Carl and I remembered all the times David had pulled back from us in the therapy hour. By resisting change, had he in effect been pulling back from the marriage? Was the Boston development his declaration of war?

The couple construed this development ominously. Carolyn felt that moving would disorganize her still-tenuous hold on a world outside the family, and she was loath to make a change. David, always ambitious in his career, interpreted his wife's stance as a request that he give up something extremely valuable to him, perhaps identity itself. The prospect of the move raised a primitive fear in both partners: that this was a decision which only one of them could win. Yet the existence of an element of contest was evidence that the old pseudomutuality was gone. Now, at least, there was the hope of individual fulfillment, if not the conviction that such fulfillment could be enjoyed by both partners.

The competitiveness which the possible move awakened also revealed the couple's *anxiety about change.* Just as Carolyn was "elected" to seek a heightened personal experience, David was "chosen" to block or inhibit this creative thrust. And both were uneasy about change. They merely specialized in opposing ways in which to express their ambivalence about growth.

It is tempting to blame David for undermining Carolyn. After all, a move now would disorganize her efforts, thrusting her back into the role of corporate wife. It would also safely remove her from the insidious influence of these therapists who were helping her disrupt the family structure. But in this formulation we forget that Carolyn is part of the "plot," that she is actively participating in writing the entire script.

As we have repeatedly emphasized, it is the *marriage* itself which is often in charge of the individuals:

1. Carolyn is elected to make a move for personal growth.
2. David cooperates for a while, but eventually he becomes anxious, if not jealous, and makes a countersuggestion (let's move to Boston) which signals his wife to surrender her initiative.
3. Carolyn agrees to be threatened by his message and to look at the possibility of giving up her own growth. She complains, however.
4. David's initiative to change jobs has two components. One is an attempt to block Carolyn's effort at growth. The other is an initiative on his own behalf: he looks on the new job as a source of growth in his life. When Carolyn complains about moving, David feels that she is defeating *his* attempt to change.

It bears repeating that the couple in this dilemma have developed a symbolic language for threatening each other and that both *agree* to let the other partner's individual initiatives inhibit them. What they do not see is that the real enemy is not their spouse, but their own *internal* blockage, which is usually an injunction or prohibition learned from the family of origin. Carolyn blames David for defeating her, but she endows him with that power. And he gives her the same power over his own growth. In this way both manage to escape responsibility for their own failures. They have constructed a "delusional state" in which the power to change is always seen to reside in the other person.

Breaking this cycle is a difficult task for everyone involved. The couple must do much more than learn to communicate. They must increase their awareness and acceptance of themselves; they must "discover" their own separate lives. One partner is usually elected to be the first to break the marital symbiosis, to be "disloyal" to the marriage in order to create a new loyalty to self. This person needs support in making this shift, and the therapist is the logical person to turn to. A lover, relative, or friend may misunderstand the couple's larger agenda and be drawn into a misguided advocacy of the individual. It is important to support the individual's search for self, as Carl and I did with Carolyn. But it is also important to realize that the family system is thrown out of balance by the individuation and that other family members need help, too. The mounting anxiety in the "immobile" spouse is an especially critical element. As these sometimes dramatic shifts are attempted late in the therapy process, the therapists must be available to everyone in the family and to all the relationships. At such a time we are more aware than ever of the need for co-therapy.

Carl and I were sure that Carolyn's "break" with the marital impasse was a firm one. Whether David would accept the challenge and begin to work on his own growth remained in doubt. The real question was whether he could risk becoming a "patient," a co-voyager in search of self. Carolyn appeared to have passed the point where David's decision could jeopardize her commitment to being a person. Whatever the cost, she was determined to fight for herself. But the survival of the marriage seemed to be balanced precariously on David's willingness to change.

Two weeks passed, and we did not hear from the Brices. A third week, and still no word. Then on Friday, at the end of the third week, Carolyn called Carl and asked for an appointment. We met the family the following Tuesday, the first week of June. It had been nearly a year since our first meeting and almost a month since we had seen them last.

Everyone came. As they filed into Carl's office, I had a fleeting sensation of the passage of time, as though this family with whom I had had such a feeling of intimacy, for whom I had felt so responsible, were now a group of strangers. It was as if we had all been one family for a while, but the Brices had now recaptured their own destiny and were living it independently of us. There was a certain coolness between us and them.

As I looked at them during the initial "social" conversation of the hour, I tried to guess what had happened in the interim, and in doing so, I realized that I was seeing everyone in a new light. The break in our meetings had jarred my habitual perceptions of the family, and I found myself examining critically some of the most visible results of their year. Laura looked, if anything, less "happy" than when we began therapy. But when we started, she was very much her mother's little girl, and this special protected status had sequestered her. She was now more separate from Carolyn, much more serious, and much more aware of the family and of her surroundings. I missed the little girl, but I liked the slim, pretty young person I saw poised on the edge of the sofa, visibly fretting about her family.

I realized with something of a start that Don was quickly overcoming an angry period of his adolescence. He was taller, thinner, and more serious. His voice was a little deeper, his frame becoming long and fine like his father's. I had always thought of Don as a pudgy youngster whose desultory, pouting, unhappy approach to life was characterized by confused sarcasm. Gone, now, was much of that unpleasantness. He seemed organized, open to his experience, and much less defensive. His sarcasm was still present, but it was modified by an undertone of thoughtfulness and concern. Don sat alone in one of the two center chairs, slouching, of course.

Claudia was sitting with her mother on the sofa to our left. Her hair was freshly washed, and it spread in profusion down around her shoulders. She wore a flowered print T-shirt and jeans skirt. Though she was as serious as everyone else in the family at the moment, she was not tense, and she looked almost radiant. I suspected that some of this contentment was related to the obvious closeness between mother and daughter. The long and terrible estrangement was over.

Carolyn wore an outfit very similar to her daughter's, though the skirt was a little less casual and probably more expensive. I found myself wondering when she had cut her hair; it was short and curly, and the new cut made her look younger. Although Carolyn was obviously upset with David and studiously avoided looking at him, she seemed to me to be doing well, considering the ominous over-tones of the couple's estrangement. She appeared composed, strong, *alive*. Still angry, but not depressed and not defeated.

But oh, David. He looked tired, stressed, old. His jaw was set grimly, and he had the air of a man anticipating an endless series of trials. I had always seen David as a good-natured, excessively rational avoider of anything emotional. This was the first time since we had known him that he looked depressed. I felt vaguely, if somewhat guiltily, pleased.

Don was the first to speak following the silence that announced the beginning of the session in earnest. "Dr. Whitaker," he said, "the kids in this family seem to be doing fine, but the parents, well, that's a different story." A trace of the old sarcasm, but mostly worry.

Carl allowed himself to smile in the face of the bleak news. "Well, after nearly twenty years, it's about time they got serious about marriage." Don laughed slightly, but this moment of good humor found no response in the family.

Carolyn glanced at Claudia, as though to reassure herself, then looked at me. "So *much* has happened since we saw you last." She seemed to be trying to arrange her thoughts. We waited, saying nothing. A moment of silence; then she added, still delaying, "What was going on when we had our last appointment?"

Claudia smiled at her mother. "Daddy was leaving us."

"Oh." Carolyn was momentarily confused; then her voice regained its firmness. "Yes. Well, I think that week was the most difficult one that I've ever lived through." She was looking at Carl now. "When David left, we were barely speaking. We had had several bitter fights about the job and moving, and however we tried, we couldn't seem to make up after the fights. We felt more and more separate, angrier and angrier. The word 'divorce' had come up several times. And then he left." She paused, remembering the time with distress. "I guess I wasn't prepared for his leaving, even though I knew it was coming. When he went to the airport, I just couldn't believe that it was happening, that he was really doing it. Then I looked around at the house and my three children—suddenly they felt more like mine than ours—and I felt as alone as I have ever felt in my life."

David interrupted, sounding angry. "I wasn't exactly enjoying myself."

Carolyn: "Well, at least you had somewhere to go. I just had to sit there and see you walk away. There's a good deal of difference between leaving and being left." I could feel the conflict growing.

"It didn't feel too different to me," David said dejectedly, apparently trying to resign from fighting.

"Could you go on?" Carl asked Carolyn.

"Well, it was just horrible. I sat around for a week thinking about what I would do if we divorced. The more I thought, the more depressed I got. I could see myself with three kids and no marketable job skills to speak of—they hired *six* teachers in this town last year! Then I began to be angry about all the years I had been a housewife and a mother and what it had gotten me. I felt horribly dependent on David, and I *hated* the feeling." A pause, the family silent around her. Carolyn looked to her left at Claudia; the two exchanged a brief, warm glance. "Then something happened—several things actually. I called you, Gus, and even though you didn't say anything particularly significant, I could feel a nice quality in your voice. Support, concern. Just talking to you was helpful." Again she thought back. "This was about the end of the first week." Another silence. "Then Claudia came in the kitchen one night after supper, and I was sitting at the table with my face in my hands. I guess I must have looked pretty discouraged. Claudia sat down with me and put her arm around my shoulder and asked me, in a very tender way, what the

matter was." Carolyn's voice trembled slightly. "I couldn't help it—
I just broke down and cried, and Claudia comforted me as though she
were *my* mother." The two women—it occurred to me that both
were women now—looked at each other again, Claudia extending
her hand and grasping her mother's tightly, each holding the other
in a steady gaze. For a moment no one spoke, and in that silence I
felt quiet triumph. Whatever other troubles the family still had, this
handclasp was a victory for mother and daughter and for the family.

Carolyn resumed. "Claudia was marvelous. She said that even if
David and I divorced, she felt that everyone would survive, even
me." A significant pause. "She didn't really think it would happen,
though." Now I felt the tenderness between the mother and daughter being undermined by the continuing conflict between husband
and wife, a distress so powerful and so pervasive that it undercut any
other event in the family. I could hear the anguish in Carolyn's voice
as she plainly contrasted her daughter's love with what she felt was
her husband's *lack* of love. Try as she might, she was no longer
praising her daughter; she was punishing her husband.

The crosscurrents of warmth and anger in Carolyn confused me.
I still didn't know what had happened between her and David.
"Then what?" I asked.

"I began to feel better," Carolyn said assertively. "I looked
around me again, and I decided that perhaps I could do it. I could
get a job, and I could survive. I didn't feel exactly buoyant, but there
was a strange sort of scared exhilaration in facing the possibility of a
divorce. This was the weekend after the first week. I had had no word
at all from David." Carolyn hesitated slightly, frowning. "Then, on
Monday night, he finally called. The conversation was stilted, but it
wasn't as bad as I had anticipated. David talked enthusiastically
about the city and all its cultural advantages and Cambridge and the
Charles River. He said the job looked promising, and with that I felt
a sinking feeling. Then he said he had talked to the firm about my
reluctance to move and had told them it would be a difficult decision
for us." Carolyn waited, emphasizing a turning point in her description. "And suddenly it occurred to me that he had said 'a difficult
decision for *us*,' as though he were really telling the company that
my objections were something that he was taking seriously. That it
would be the two of us making the decision. And I felt pleased. After
all my crying and fighting, maybe he had heard me and was actually

taking my complaints seriously! It was all very indirect, but there was a conciliatory tone in David's voice. He didn't say he missed me or that he was sorry, but I just got a vague sense that something had changed in him. He didn't sound so cold, and he didn't sound adamant about anything." Carolyn looked cautiously at David, and he glanced away from her.

"Where were you in all this?" Carl asked David.

"Feeling hard pressed on a number of fronts," David said soberly.

"Can I finish?" Carolyn interrupted. "I very much want to hear David's side of this discussion, but I would like to finish mine first." Definite, strong. I remembered how tremulous and weak her voice had been when we started therapy.

"Sure," Carl said.

"We had a couple of phone conversations after that. And each one got better. David spent a few hours looking at houses in Cambridge, and he had even called a couple of colleges about their social work programs." She smiled faintly, breaking the train of her story. "I hate to admit it, but I've gotten interested in this psychotherapy business and have been thinking about getting a degree in social work." Then she resumed the other line of her account. "I began to feel almost excited about the thought of moving to Boston. Both David and I felt it, a sort of lightness. I don't know how the change came about, from such bitterness and all that talk of divorce to both of us laughing on the phone and fantasizing about the move. It didn't happen all at once; it was a mood that just grew." Carolyn paused, perhaps confused by her own inconsistencies. "By the time David came back I was feeling great. I decided to meet his plane, and I got all the children together, and we went out, very excitedly. Laura had even made a little sign, saying, 'Welcome home, Daddy.' " Both parents looked at Laura, who was delighted by being mentioned. As Carolyn talked, the family warmed to her retelling, and the mood in the room lightened.

"I had made him his favorite dessert, rhubarb pie," Claudia boasted.

David cleared his throat somewhat officially, saying good-humoredly, "And, I might add, I brought your mother some flowers."

"Well . . ." Don said skeptically.

"A very impulsive thing for me to do, you understand," David said, boasting mainly to Carl.

"Well, I was touched," Carolyn said seriously. She thought for a moment, then smiled slightly. "It was a great reunion for a recently divorced couple."

"So where does all this current anger come from?" I asked.

"I'm getting to that," Carolyn said, becoming more serious again. "We had a wonderful weekend. The whole family got excited about the prospect of moving, and we sat around looking at pictures of houses and chattering about Boston. David and I were awkward with each other at first, but we got over it. When we finally went to bed that first night, we had a really *good* sexual experience. The best in many years. The same thing the next night." I was impressed by her ease in talking about their sexual relationship with their children present.

"So what ruined all this good sex?" I persisted.

Carolyn turned toward David swiftly and angrily, directing her remark more to him than to us. "Please ask *him.*" A strong, silent pause. Then she faced us again and completed her accusation. "I don't *know* what happened. I felt marvelous. And then David began to pull back. He started to look depressed. He wouldn't talk. And nothing I could do would influence him. Now he's silent, uncommunicative, sullen. And all I can conclude is that he has changed his mind about *me.* Somehow it isn't good enough that I am willing to give up my *home* and *friends* and *community* to make this job possible for him!" She was really angry and visibly hurt by what she perceived as a very significant rejection. Her anger rose, suffusing her words and spilling out over them. "I mean, I don't know what he *wants!* What more can I do than I already *have?*"

"You sure sound hurt," I said awkwardly.

"You're damn right I—" Carolyn couldn't finish. Tears filled her eyes, and she closed them, attempting to close her face too so that we would not see its anguish. The pain twisted her features as she fought against her need to cry. Gradually she won, calming herself, and eventually, after what seemed like a very long silence, turning back to us. "I've felt myself ready to attack him, to plunge screaming back into another round-robin fight with David. But I decided that I will not do that." Her voice peaked with the emphasis, straining again to resist crying. "I will not plead with David *anymore* to love me." The statement had a kind of ultimate gravity, as though she had gone as far in a certain direction as there was to go. It was no longer a question of volition, but of reaching the end of the line. "So I have retreated, too." Silence, heavy silence. "And here I sit, waiting." I thought she had finished, but she hadn't. Her concluding remark was level and factual. "I am not sure how much longer I can wait."

Of one mind, Carl and I faced David. He looked a hundred years old. Carl spoke for both of us, gently. "Sounds like it's your move, old man."

David faced Carolyn, his accuser, his voice soft but intense. "Carolyn, it isn't *you.*"

"So what *is* it?" she said, loving and angry and impatient.

David shook his head slowly, looking aside. "This is so difficult."

"Shall I guess?" Carl offered. His tone was enigmatic and suggestive of a shared secret. David looked down, as though not wanting to see what was coming. Then he nodded. "Something about your parents," was all Carl said, and all he needed to say. David did not so much sigh as groan, a breath that spoke of great effort and great discouragement. Then he raised his eyes and addressed Carl. As he began to speak, I realized that for the first time in a year's therapy, we might hear David say something really personal.

"The trip to Boston was a very strange experience," David said hesitantly. "I felt as torn up about our differences as Carolyn did— very depressed and very alone." The slightest catch in the flow of his words as he said "depressed" betrayed the feeling he still managed to keep hidden beneath his words. "But I had the interviews to focus on, and I had to put myself together. I had trouble sleeping the first few nights, but gradually I began to get involved in looking at the job. I had some of the same experience that Carolyn did. I was at first horrified at the thought that we might get divorced. Then I got accustomed to being away from her, and I found that I wasn't so panicked. I began to think that I could live through it if I had to. Then that strange thing happened of our getting back together; it's something I still don't understand, but it was very nice."

"We call it an existential shift," I interposed.

David turned his head slightly to look at me, his steel-rimmed glasses glinting as they reflected the light from the window. "What's that?" he said.

"Sort of like a sea change," I returned. "The two of you got up the courage to diverge, to face the possibility of leaving each other." I paused, thinking about their days apart. "And you actually did separate. You went through a kind of ritual divorce. The important thing may have been the discovery, in both of you, that you could live with a breakup. You could survive it." I looked at Carolyn to make it clear that I was talking to her, too.

"And that allowed us to get back together?" Carolyn asked, having guessed my point.

"That's right. Knowing that you could live without each other allowed you to *experience your caring*. The tide turned because you could now *choose* to be together or apart. You had the sense—again I suspect present in you both—that you *had* to be married because of your duty to the kids or your dependency on each other." I stopped again, allowing the family time to assimilate the idea. "But you couldn't have that experience of choice until you both went off onto the ocean, as it were, alone. You first had to get the self-respect of being able to face life alone." A silence which signified understanding, acknowledgment.

Then I realized that I had moved the focus away from David, as if I had also been anxious about his trying to be personal and had cooperated by taking him off the spot. Carl, noting this, too, gently moved our attention back to David. "You were talking about your part in this change. You said a 'strange experience.'" He was alert as always to a significant phrasing that provides a clue to hidden experience.

"It was." David sighed, looking depressed again. "The whole job offer was strange to me. The people were very polite, even enthusiastic about having me. But there was something in the whole situation that made me uneasy. Something didn't fit." He stopped, thinking. "Then, after the interviews were over, I went to visit my parents. They live in a suburban town about ten miles from the city. And they were fine, too, at first. But somehow they were just *too* interested in my taking the job, kept asking about it and almost pressuring me for an answer about whether we would move. And I began to get a little anxious. My parents always make me nervous, though, so that wasn't anything new. After a while I dismissed it."

"How do they make you anxious?" I asked.

"Well, they each take me aside separately under the guise of just having a friendly chat. But what inevitably happens is that they wind up telling me how terrible the other one is. My mother complains that all my father does is play golf and go to meetings of the various boards of directors that he serves on. And it's true. He's always gone.

But although my mother is sort of cowed around my father, she can be very critical of him, sort of picking at faults. And she can certainly find them. So in some ways I don't blame him for being gone."

"But then he gets you aside, too," Carl reminded David.

"He's worse than she is," David said, anger in his face. "He tells me what a sick woman she is, implying that it is psychological but not really saying it. She's a hypochondriac, according to him. He tries to get her to stop smoking. He thinks she drinks too much coffee. And he is furious at her because she won't go to bed with him. That's really why he's so angry at her hypochondria—because she uses her 'ills' as an excuse." David's face reddened as he talked, and his voice gained strength, rising in volume and pitch. He seemed much more alive as he talked about his parents.

"No wonder you get anxious," Carl said casually, "you're being asked to be your own parents' therapist."

David replied, "It was worse this time because my sister is moving. She and her husband have lived near my parents for some time; in fact, I think my sister has never really broken away from my mother. But her husband was suddenly transferred out west, and it has left my parents very upset. My sister is pretty upset, too, actually. Well, my mother would cry to me about how thoughtless my sister's husband was to 'uproot her' and move her across the country, and my father would ask me to try to help my mother accept the move, and I would get more and more confused." David's speech was becoming less organized as he continued.

Carl, quietly but assertively: "Does your own panic make more sense to you as you talk about this change in the family?"

"What do you mean?" David said.

"That your parents are hoping you will come in and mediate their struggles now that your sister may get free." Carl was matter-of-fact.

"I hadn't thought of that," David admitted. "But it makes sense. They certainly pulled on me pretty hard." He paused, thinking about the idea. Then he looked up at us again. "I haven't told you the worst of it." Silence in the room, the children listening carefully. "When I got back home to my own family, this family"—and he glanced at his wife and children as though to reassure himself of their existence—"I was able to shake some of this sense of trouble with my parents. I was even able to get back some of my enthusiasm about the job. And I was delighted to be back with Carolyn."

"Well, what *happened?*" Carolyn asked plaintively and much more lovingly than before.

"I'm coming to that." David warned her away. He paused. "I was sitting in my study after I got home, three or four nights after I arrived, going over some of the company's papers." He stopped, drawing back from the pain which he anticipated. "And there, on a list of the company's board of directors, was my father's name!" The room fell silent. Then, slowly, tears rose in David's eyes, crested his eyelids, and coursed down his cheeks. "He was behind the whole damn thing!" David said at last, his tears sudden and all too brief. Quickly he caught himself, reining in his grief by becoming angry. "It wouldn't have been so bad if he had *suggested* to me that *I* apply for the job. But to set it up behind my back like that as though I were a child or someone he could manipulate!" A red, teary, little boy's face, full of hurt. "When I think of what those people at that company must think of me and of my father, I shudder! Why they went along with that ridiculous game, I don't know."

I spoke gently. "Whatever the facts, David, your feelings about your father seem pretty darn painful." It was an idiotic statement of the obvious, but it was the only way I could think of to make contact with him.

David addressed me with an incredulous, restrained rage, feelings clearly directed at the absent father. "I have worked my *ass* off for twenty years to try to make myself into somebody he could respect, to please him. And nothing has *ever* been good enough! And I've always had to stay away from him because if I let him near me, or anything that I'm doing, he'll take it over. Just look at the way he did this—manipulating me *across the country* into a job that he had set up." Rage, helpless and random for its lack of an appropriate target.

Carl's comment was delicately bland. "Well, they certainly need you."

David looked confused. "The company?"

"Oh, they probably do, too, but it was your parents I meant."

"Well, I don't need them. I feel very bitter." David looked exposed, worn, weary with the long fight against his feelings. He also looked relieved, glad that it was finally out.

Carolyn's voice was soft and caring and a little hurt. "Why couldn't you tell me this, David?" she asked.

He looked toward his wife, his eyes still red from crying, with an expression that was strangely new. "I don't know, Carolyn. I'm sorry. I know you were confused." Silence, but a good one. "It was just too much."

"I think I can help with that," I said to Carolyn. Her face was open and attentive. "He was probably feeling so cornered by his parents and so locked into their struggle that he couldn't risk getting in a dependent position with you, too. Bringing that kind of big problem to you would have been to risk feeling one-down to you at a time when it seemed dangerous." I smiled, changing my mood as I thought of a parallel. "Besides, he comes from a secretive family."

Carl smiled, betraying his own secret. "Somebody also had to turn down the marriage thermostat after all that good sex," he said jocularly. A flinch of recognition in David and Carolyn. "Say, I've got an idea," Carl added, enthusiasm growing in his voice.

"Uh-oh," Don said, "watch out!"

"Quiet, shrimp," Carl returned. "I'll clean the wax out of your ears with my pipe cleaner."

Claudia brightened, glad for the opportunity to speak. "Yeah, Don. That'll improve your hearing."

"I don't know about you guys either," Carl continued offhandedly, referring apparently to Don's warning. "Let you away from therapy for a couple of weeks, and all hell breaks loose. Divorces, reunions, family wars! Wow." A quality of dissimulation in Carl's voice, as though he were putting off getting to his point.

"Well, what's your suggestion?" David asked, bluntly but warmly.

Carl: "That you get your entire family to agree to fly here for a family conference, or two, or three. And that you use us to get at this whole mess on your side of the family."

The family reacted physically to the suggestion; we could see them tense. Silence. More silence.

Don laughed. "Granpa? You gotta be kidding, Whitaker!"

"Jesus" was all David could say.

Claudia said earnestly, "I think it would be great. I really do." Then she laughed lightly. "We could have it on the Fourth of July."

"Independence Day?" Carl asked.

"Fireworks," Claudia retorted. "Especially you and Grandfather," she said fondly to Carl.

"Oh," Carl said a little defensively, "we grandfathers might hit it off all right. You never know."

The tone of the meeting was loosening; we were ending the

session. I suddenly looked at David and realized how changed he was. For so long I had thought of him as efficient, reasonable, and as essentially unreachable. I could never find much in him to care about. Now he was much softer, humbled by his grief and anger, as human as everyone else in his family. Then I realized that I had never seen the wounded, vulnerable part of my own father and that even though his death had made it impossible for me to cross that bridge, at least I could say something to *this* father.

"David," I said, my tone of voice catching him off guard. "I'm awfully glad that I got in touch with the part of you that was visible today. You seemed very human to me, and I just want you to know that I am feeling a lot closer to you." I suppose I was really thanking him for his gift to me. He seemed to appreciate it, and smiled in reply. We were at an end, the family rising noisily and gladly toward their exit.

CHAPTER 19

David's Family

At last David was at the edge of being involved in therapy, though he was certainly not at peace. He slept poorly. In a panicky telephone call to Carl he asked, "How *can* I ask my parents to come for a conference?" The dread of confrontation.

Carl said firmly, "Ask them to come to *help us help you.* We don't want to make them patients, but we need their help." And it was true. Once David had been willing to look at the troubles in his family of origin, the logic of their becoming involved in the therapy was irresistible.

Mustering his courage, David telephoned, returning to the next interview with a sense of disbelief. "They'll be here next week. They can stay several days, and they're bringing my sister, too." He looked at us with anxious bewilderment. "They didn't even hesitate."

"Parents rarely do," Carl said, "when they really get asked."

The expanded family arrived for the interview talking excitedly to one another, full of the newness of any family reunion, but huddling together in the face of impending stress. They took their seats quickly and a little awkwardly. The room felt overfull. Carolyn was squeezed on the couch to the left with Laura and Claudia. Don took his usual center chair, leaving the other for David's sister. David sat with his parents on the couch to the right. Without anyone's having planned it, David's family of origin was sitting together.

It is a disconcerting experience when real people walk into your office to sit beside—and disrupt—the images you have formed of them. I had imagined David's father as bald, stocky, and abrasive.

Perhaps that's my image of the tough-talking businessman. In actuality, Arthur Brice strongly resembled his son: fine-boned, handsome, his precise, tanned features accented by a thin mustache. He wore an expensive summer suit and sat with an aura of stiff, almost frail dignity. He obviously was a person who expected to be treated deferentially, and he seemed to feel much out of his element in a psychotherapy interview. He shared with David the quality of being in retreat from any strongly personal encounter.

I had pictured David's mother as thin and feeble. Instead, she was slightly overweight, also very well dressed, and pleasant. Appearing both friendly and shy, she had extended her hand to Carl when she entered. The lines of tension around her eyes and a quality of agitation in her voice gave evidence of a complex and troubled person. Elizabeth Brice was being brave in the face of her fear of the interview and what it might reveal.

The sister, Barbara, was perhaps forty, a touch plump like the mother, and though she looked depressed and angry, she was able to change moods quickly, breaking occasionally into a strong smile. During the superficial banter at the beginning of the interview I noticed that she had an appealing laugh.

We talked about the hot June weather, disconcerting for everyone. Then the rigors of air travel. A joking question from David's parents about the whereabouts of Carolyn's parents—would they eventually be coming, too? Carl and I said that we hoped so. It would have been good to have had them at this meeting. Maybe next time. And that remark, referring to a next interview, was sobering enough to precipitate a silence.

David was clearly uncomfortable, sitting between his parents on the couch. "Can I switch places with you?" he asked his sister. An awkward, public transition. He sat on the edge of his new chair, facing his parents and sister. He took a deep breath, exhaling suddenly. "Whew!" he said. "I don't know what to do." Before Carl and I could reply, he launched out at his parents. "I guess I'm really still very angry about what happened when I came to visit you and this whole thing about the job. I know that you set it up, Dad, and I'm furious about it." The father and mother winced under the attack. They had obviously anticipated it.

"David," I said firmly, "can I stop you?"

He looked startled, but a little relieved. "Before you get into this war, could you hold back to give Carl and me a chance to know your family?" I knew David had banked on support from us to give him the courage to launch into his parents, but I could also see impending disaster for the interview—the parents becoming defensive and guarded, feeling scapegoated. Unless Carl and I were allowed to develop some relationship with them, so that we could give them support, the session might leave nothing but bitterness in everyone.

"OK," David said obediently, relieved again.

Carl addressed the father. "Mr. Brice, could you tell us how you see the family from your point of view?"

David's father was glad to be able to evade his son's anger for the moment. "Well, I don't find much fault with it." Then he glanced at David. "My son obviously does find something wrong, though I'm not clear yet what it was—or is."

Carl persisted. "How about the way *you* see the family? I'm not trying to blame you or diagnose you—I just want to try to get to know you." Tension, uneasiness, mistrust. The first interview, all over again. Except that this time, one member of the family was on our side; so much so, in fact, that we had to restrain him.

Carl was chipping away at David's father, inventing questions, trying to make some contact with an unlikely candidate for family therapy. "How did you guys meet?" he said, glancing at the couple. At a dance in their hometown. "What was it like? Did you fall in love slowly or all at once?" The father's posture relaxed slightly as he described their courtship, smiling once or twice at his wife sitting beside him. The questions came gently and steadily, and gradually the dignified older man warmed to Carl. Many of them were routine and noncontroversial, vehicles for conversation, points of information.

"How do you see the stresses in the family as a whole?" Carl asked the father.

"Well," he said, "I suppose lately we've been through the stress of my retiring. I guess that's a problem for every family." A pause. "And my wife has been upset not only with me and my retirement, but with our daughter's decision to move to another city. Across the country, actually."

The mother smiled. "Don't let him fool you. He hasn't really retired. He just plays more golf between meetings of the various boards he serves on." She was describing *him*, of course, just as he had talked about *her* problems.

"You sound unhappy about it, but sort of resigned," I said to the mother.

"I had dreams of our spending some more time together," she replied, warmth mingled with regret. "But it just doesn't look as if it's going to happen." I was becoming more aware of a pairing of force and passivity in David's mother. She had taken the conversation away from her husband, yet she was also acquiescent and compliant toward him.

Carl wanted to get back to the father. "How do you see this distancing process?"

Arthur Brice was apprehensive and tense, but he didn't know how to avoid Carl's questions. "My wife and I have a pretty good relationship, I think, but it has its strains. I do think she has felt for many years that I was married to my career, so to speak. I have felt that she has been too concerned about her health and that she frets over the children too much. Children! I talk as though they weren't middle-aged. But in some ways Elizabeth has never seen the children as growing up. They are still her children."

"So neither of you has been able to retire from your life's work and simply enjoy each other?" Carl suggested. The father made no reply. "Can you hear that you tend to talk about her side of the problem and she talks about yours?"

Arthur looked disconcerted by the observation. "Well, yes," he admitted grudgingly. "But I don't see what this has to do with David and Carolyn. I thought we came here to help them."

"Their relationship is partially modeled on your marriage," I interjected. "You and your wife are the only model for marriage that David has." I allowed a brief silence to punctuate the statement. "And we assume that it will be useful if they can take a look at their inheritance from this side of the family. Of course, the same thing holds for Carolyn's family, too."

"But how can we alter any of this?" the older man persisted. "We're a little too old to change."

Carl and I were functioning in close synchrony, taking alternate lines in the dialogue with the family. He moved now with clarity and force, his voice eager with possibility. "If your family—you and your wife and David and Barbara—could risk increasing the intimacy in your relationships with one another, it would make it infinitely easier for David to risk doing the same thing in his own family."

"How is that?" Arthur asked.

Carl: "Because the thermostat in David's head, the mechanism that tells him how intimate he's allowed to be, was set a long time ago by you two. And if he's going to raise it, it's a lot easier for him if you agree to help by raising your own thermostat along with him. That way he doesn't have to be disloyal to the implicit rules in the family. It's very difficult to be unfaithful to your family's rules."

"I don't think we impose anything upon David," Arthur Brice said, becoming defensive.

Carl answered, "I didn't even imply that you did. But since he learned the rules from his family once upon a time, maybe you could help him change them or at least give him permission."

"He certainly has that." Still defensive. "He can do anything he likes."

Rather than pressure Mr. Brice further, I turned toward David's sister. "How do you see the family's struggles, Barbara?"

"Oh!" she exclaimed, smiling broadly and gesturing as though to brush away my question. "We're a mess!" The contrast with the father's denial was so dramatic, and her statement so abrupt, that the group laughed. Barbara sobered slightly, obviously anxious, and added, "At least I am."

"Go ahead," I said, delighted with her honesty.

She turned quickly toward her mother, who was sitting beside her. "Mother, I want to say this to you." A pause as she gathered courage to continue. "I know you are upset about my moving, and I am, too. But I *have* to do it. I am going with my *husband* to a new *job.* And I wish to hell you wouldn't make me feel so *guilty!*" She was smiling and almost crying at the same time. The statement was sudden and surprising, yet clearly something that she had planned long in advance of the interview and couldn't wait to deliver.

The mother started, tears rising to the edge of her eyelids. Her voice trembled. "I know you have to, darling. I think I *accept* it. But it isn't easy." She stopped abruptly in order to avoid crying outright. When she regained control, she said to her daughter, "I don't see how I make you feel guilty."

"Oh, Mother!" Barbara said with both fondness and exasperation. "You're so incredibly nice! You do all *kinds* of things for me, like taking care of the children and running errands and helping me pack. And I know there are some things that you resent, but you will never say it! And if I ever get mad at you for anything, you just apologize. It's as if you won't stand up for yourself!" She puzzled a moment, looking for the right words. "And I have to try to guess what you're mad about so that I can change what I'm doing. I really never know where you are, Mother. I just wind up feeling guilty about myself and almost everything I do."

The mother's reply was passive and apologetic. "I'm sorry if I do that, Barbara. I guess I can try to change it."

"Can you see that as an example of what she was talking about?" Carl asked.

"What?" the mother asked.

"Your statement. You apologized for yourself then, rather than say where you were or take a stand." Carl gave her a moment to grapple with this idea. "Because what Barbara seems to want you to do is just that—take a stand. Say 'I am,' so that she is free to define *herself* as separate, too." Another silence. "What you have now is a muddle of two people who can't really be separate. Sounds as if you are always in each other's hair."

"Yes, we are!" Barbara said emphatically.

Silence, the mother hesitating while she searched for a response. Then she spoke to Barbara. "There *are* things that I resent. I resent that you let your children run in my living room when you come to visit. And I resent the language you let them use."

Barbara's return was quick. "And I resent your giving my children lectures about their manners when they are at *my* home. I'll admit that they sometimes misbehave when we're at your house, but when they are at home, they are my responsibility."

"All right," the mother said, half-smiling, "I'll refrain from comments when we are at your house, if you will ask them to behave better at mine." Definite, firm.

Barbara turned toward Carl and me. "I can't believe this. Something actually got settled!" A half-sad, whimsical smile. "Now that I'm leaving."

"Or trying to," Carl reassured her. "Leaving home is such a difficult process." He was implying that there was much more to be done. A pause, then a shift in tone to words that were quieter. "I'm not sure it's just leaving that you're after either. But the freedom to separate from one another and to come back together and be closer than ever. But also to have the relationship person-to-person rather than mother-to-daughter."

I would like that. It sounds ideal," Barbara said wistfully. Then she looked at her mother. "Still, it's sad, leaving." Tears again in the mother's eyes as she looked away.

Her anguish was so visible. "A big loss for you," I said to her gently.

Elizabeth Brice looked at me—age, grief, pain, fatigue in her face. It was the face of defeat. "It certainly is hard," she said with difficulty, not wanting to cry. Still, there was a quality of flatness in her voice that said she was not ready to share her feeling openly. It was not surprising since the interview had barely begun and she didn't know us. Realizing that it was not the right moment to relate to the mother's pain, Carl turned toward David.

"And where are you in all this?"

"Still angry with my father."

"And I don't understand why, David," the older man said, again defensive. The group was shifting focus, drawing away from the mother's resigned sadness as though it truly frightened them.

"Well, let me see if I can say it." David was scared, but too angry to stop. Like his sister, he had a long-planned agenda waiting. "I'm still mad about this job thing, Dad. I know that you helped set it up, and I felt terribly manipulated and, well, *underestimated* when I found out about it. As though I weren't good enough to get a job by myself!"

"David, if you would just calm down a minute." Mr. Brice waited. "Now I *did* hear that the company was looking for an attorney, and I did suggest your name. But I told them to leave me out of it entirely after that."

"But, Dad, there is no *way* that a member of the board of directors of a company can avoid being a factor when that company is considering his son for a job!" David was no longer merely angry; there was pleading in his voice. "I wasn't angry that you had suggested me, but I was damn angry at the way you did it. If it had all been out in the open, I probably could have accepted it. As it was, I felt that it was my own achievement that they were attracted to, only to find out that it was something that you had arranged; and it was too much."

The father was contrite. "I'm sorry, son. I guess I made a mistake. I think it *was* your own achievement that they were considering, though I can understand your reluctance to believe that."

David's anger seemed diminished by his father's apology. "You just don't understand my feelings about you, Dad. I've always held you in awe. All my life I've worked to do something you could value, that would please you. But I've always felt a need to stay at some distance because I didn't want to be in your shadow." Silence. "And this time it felt as if I were being tricked into *living* in your shadow. I felt like a five-year-old kid again."

"I'm sorry, David. I don't want to be held in awe, and I don't want anybody living in my shadow." He looked depressed. Then the slight flicker of a smile. "Besides, it's getting pretty thin these days. I'm getting old."

Carl addressed David. "Can you see this as the thing we were talking about before your parents came? It's the shadow he cast when you were a *kid* that you're afraid of. He doesn't have that kind of power over you anymore." He waited. "You're really struggling with images of each other."

David smiled as he replied to Carl. "I feel a little less frightened of him already, having said what I did."

"You think it's your dad's *covert* anger that you are afraid of— what you don't see but suspect is there?" Carl asked David.

"I rarely get angry," the father said.

Carl looked at him skeptically. "On the outside." A pause. "But David may do the same thing with you that Barbara does with her mother—try to guess at what's inside you and make it even bigger than it is. You don't help any by being so secretive about your inner life. Playing it cool and hiding your subjective world is a good way to play chess or poker or to run a corporation. But if you carry that over into your home, it doesn't work. And it's not much fun either."

"But how likely is it that somebody my age will change?" Arthur Brice asked testily.

Carl was curt. "Well, give up on yourself if you like, but don't assume that it holds for everybody. I'm not so much younger than you, and I think I'm still growing. I hope I always will be." The group watched attentively as Carl fought with the father. "I think you're missing a vital part of life if you stay factual and cool with your own son, not to mention your wife." More silence. The content was not the real issue in the struggle. Carl's voice was rough, almost scolding; he was asserting dominance, saying, "Even though I am somewhat younger than you and certainly not as rich, I am still more or less in the older generation. Within this realm, I am more grown-up, more mature than you."

"Perhaps you're right," Arthur admitted.

"What was it like with your own family? Did you have the same struggles with them?" Carl was moving a step further. Having defined the father as one-down, he was now offering to help, searching for the child in the man.

Arthur sounded depressed again. "I didn't know my father really. He was an immigrant, and he worked at two menial jobs during most of my growing-up years. I saw him rarely, though I had an enormous amount of respect for him. He was firm and meant what he said, and I never questioned him."

"Think you and David have been any closer to each other than you and your father?" Carl asked suggestively.

"I think so." Guardedly, not knowing what was implied.

Carl: "But one reason it was difficult for you and David to get together is that you didn't have a model for closeness with your own father." Carl waited, then had a thought, adding briskly, "Except through work. Your dad worked his ass off because he had to. And one way you could feel close to him was to do the same thing. And David is the same way. He even deliberately sees it as a way to please you."

"Well, what's so wrong with work?" the father asked warily.

"Nothing," Carl said warmly. "I'm guilty of it myself. Except that if you live to work or see your life only in terms of your work, it's a big problem." He looked at David's mother. "It's the same as if your wife sees her personhood as tied to being a mother." But he could feel the man's resistance growing, and he didn't want to fight. "How about your parents' marriage?" Carl asked, switching the topic. "What was it like?"

"Again, I know so little," Arthur admitted. "They were civil, but pretty distant. He had his world; she had hers. They never fought, but then they never talked much either. I suppose there wasn't time."

Carl drew the father out slowly and easily. "So this companionship marriage that your wife is looking for isn't something that you ever saw between your parents. Do you think her parents had it? Or were they sort of quietly divorced, too?" Carl was working hard to avoid putting Arthur on the spot now, giving him a chance to talk first about his parents and now about his wife's parents.

"They were the opposite, I think. They both were teachers and a very close couple." He glanced at his wife, who nodded in affirmation. "I would say too close, inseparable." He was reluctant to talk about his wife's family, and she finally relieved him by taking up the conversation.

"He's right. They were always together and terribly protective of each other." A reflective pause. "And of us kids, too, I suppose. We were a very close bunch." She was both nostalgic and mildly disparaging as she described her family's closeness, as though she now saw something negative in their relationship. She looked warmly at her husband. "Arthur has always liked the fact that we could touch each other in my family—we hug and kiss a lot—but he is scornful of how dependent we are."

Carl was enjoying the warmth that was beginning to emerge. "I suspect that you are an expert on his family's problems, and he is an expert on yours." A moment's hesitation, a shift in emphasis. "Still, it sounds like one of the many reasons you married each other—his family could be separate, and yours close, but each family needed some of what the other had."

As Carl eased the older couple into talking about their parents' relationships and their own, covering ground that is by now familiar to the reader, I had the sense that a critical point had been passed. They had relaxed their defensiveness and joined the therapeutic process. Carl became a sympathetic force for them, no longer an accuser, an intruder, or a threat. The difference was perceptible chiefly in the altered tones of voice—a softening, a blending of tones, a feeling of people moving easily together rather than abrasively and in opposition. Finally, a silence that was like coming upon a quiet pool in a forest. Momentarily, a sense of peace.

From this mood I took some of the calm with which I asked a question of Elizabeth. "You said 'was' in referring to your parents. Are they not still living?"

"No," she said, "my mother died of cancer about five years ago, and my father died a year after she did." She waited. "We all said he died of a broken heart, that he couldn't live without her. It was a heart attack that he died of, actually."

"Being that much in love is pretty scary, isn't it?" I suggested rather than asked. It was not surprising that she had married an independent, isolated man. Part of her didn't want to be as dependent as her parents had been. I was so conscious of her sadness now, and I wanted to console her. I suppose my voice confessed my intent. "Another loss for you."

"What do you mean?" She sounded a little fearful.

"It's no *wonder* you're sad. You've lost a lot in the last five years —your parents, the dream of being closer to your husband when he retired, and now your role as a mother and grandmother. You didn't mention a job, and I suppose it's pretty hard to find a very meaningful life at the bridge table." I paused. "Sounds as if you are pretty much alone."

My sympathetic but abrupt listing of the essential facts of her life was too much for her. Tears appeared in her eyes, and she could not fight them back. Crying silently, she looked at me briefly, then away, out the window. "I certainly am," she admitted, bitterness in her voice. Then she retreated. "But no more than a lot of women my age. A lot of my friends' husbands are gone." I realized that she wanted to talk about her marriage but didn't know how. Mr. Brice sat stiffly upright, looking embarrassed and solitary.

"Think maybe your husband feels as alone as you do?" I asked.

"He couldn't." Bitterness again. She looked toward me again, anger fast replacing the grief in her face. "He is so busy he doesn't have *time* to feel alone."

"Yeah," I said skeptically, "but all that stuff is no substitute for a marriage at this time of life." After a brief wait I continued. "Think maybe he gets elected to stay away so the two of you don't have to face the panic of being close?"

The wife was openly angry now. "I *want* more closeness in our relationship!"

I countered. "But you might also be suspicious of it. You implied that your parents were too dependent on each other."

"No danger of that with us," she replied. She resisted my effort to implicate her in the marriage dilemma.

"I'm not trying to blame you," I said quietly, "but if both of you could take responsibility for the distance, it might be easier to solve than if you insist that he take all the blame."

"I think she *is* too dependent," Mr. Brice blurted out, encouraged by my remark. "If I let her, she clings to me like a . . . a"—he searched for an acceptable word, then finally said what apparently had occurred to him first—"leech."

The word struck his wife painfully, and she flared. "I object—"

"Just a minute, would you?" I interrupted her, turning back toward her husband. "You are doing the same thing she is—blaming the other person. "Can you talk about yourself? What do you feel like when your wife depends on you for something?"

"Well, she—"

"Not that way," I interjected. "Say 'I.' 'I feel. . . .' "

It was a new language for the father. "This is difficult," he confessed. "I feel . . . angry."

"Anything else?"

He thought. "Upset, maybe."

"Anything else?"

"I don't know. Confused."

"Can you say some of this to your wife? Tell her what you feel?" I felt very uncomfortable pressuring the older man, but I persisted.

"I feel angry, sometimes upset, and confused." He spoke these words to his wife somewhat mechanically, but the fact that they were so difficult to say made them meaningful.

"Does that sound different to you? Better than being called dependent?" I asked Mrs. Brice.

"It certainly does," she said, obviously surprised by her husband's words. I was about to ask her to make the same kind of statement to him when Arthur interrupted me.

"I still don't understand what all this has to do with David and Carolyn. My wife and I have problems, but we live with them." He sounded angry, probably because I had pushed him. I had expected the anger; in fact, I was a little surprised that the couple had let me intrude as far into their life as I did. They were not, after all, the "patient."

I was increasingly puzzled by Carl's silence but was too hard pressed to stop. Suddenly I caught Claudia's eye and realized what the amused expression on her face meant. "Claudia," I said, smiling slightly, "have you ever heard an argument like this before?"

She was delighted and broke into a grin. "It is a carbon copy of one of my parents' arguments. Just a little more civilized."

"So?" Mr. Brice said, unconvinced.

I faced him, trying to keep my good humor. "One of the ways we try to resolve the problems that we inherit from our families is to repeat them when we grow up and form our own families. Claudia is right. The fight you and your wife just had is almost identical to a major argument between David and Carolyn. Carolyn even had some of your wife's resignation, until she began to make some changes."

The old man would not give up easily. Claudia was also right that he was a real fighter. "But how can we help *them?*" he reiterated.

At last Carl stirred, clearing his throat. "If you and your wife could resolve some of your differences and get together, David might not have to move his family across the country to save the two of you." Coming as if from nowhere, the remark caught the father off guard.

"Save us? I don't see that."

Carl: "Of course. He senses the trouble and wants to help, and the two of you find an excuse like this job to get him to come." Carl tilted his head characteristically to one side, pursing his lips in a way that expressed skepticism. "And it might indeed help bring some more life into your lives. Especially if he could get Carolyn to come along. She might teach your wife something about how to get over making husband and kids the center of her life. She might even teach her how to fight." A pause, punctuation. "But I'm not sure it's necessary for them to move. The two of you seemed to come alive together today. Maybe you can do it without them."

"I would certainly hope so," Mr. Brice said archly.

Carl softened his tone, still addressing the father. "Well, I think you ought to be concerned. I was worried when I heard how depressed your wife sounded today. I wouldn't be surprised if she had been incubating fantasies lately about how she was going to die."

Mrs. Brice blanched. There was not much question about the accuracy of Carl's intuition. "Could you share the fantasies?" I asked gently. "How had you thought you might die?"

She looked pale and frightened, her eyes not focused clearly on either of us. "I have been thinking a lot about dying. I have had the recurrent thought that I was going to have a stroke." The room became very quiet.

"That's the way I think it happens," Carl said. "We *decide* to die." Only the sound of automobile horns, soft and almost musical, drifting in the open window from a nearby street. Carl's voice had a slight cast of optimism in it as he resumed. "Of course, you could decide to live as well as to die, you know."

The mother glanced at Carl briefly but lovingly. Then with the slightest of smiles she looked at her husband as though to find out what he felt about what she had said.

"I agree," I said. "I think that's where you ought to look."

The older man's anger and defensiveness were gone. He looked sobered by his wife's revelation and by our suggestion that she was depressed enough to think of giving up. "I guess I hadn't known you were so depressed," he said.

"I didn't tell you," Elizabeth replied, her face kind.

The room had that sense of rest that comes only when something of real significance has happened. Carl spoke to me. "You know, I feel sort of apologetic that we have pushed the two of them so hard today, but I think you and I intuited the same thing that David did—that his parents have a real crisis. Why else would he be willing to move across the country and risk losing his wife?"

"I agree," I said seriously.

Barbara stirred. "Do you think it's my fault? Is it because I'm moving?"

"Goodness, no," Carl said. "It's not anybody's fault. Besides, they don't need you guys. They need each other."

David seemed shaken by the interview and worried about his parents. "I guess I find myself wondering what my parents can do or what I can do to help them."

Carl spoke firmly. "I think we ought to meet tomorrow and work on this some more. It's a good question, David, but the time is getting short. Let's deal with it tomorrow."

Mr. Brice addressed the group. "I think maybe everybody is too worried about us. Elizabeth and I have some problems, but while I don't think we are going to have any catastrophes, I don't think we are going to do a lot of changing either. We've pretty much lived our lives, and they haven't been so bad."

Carl good-humoredly looked at Mr. Brice. "I wish you wouldn't give up on yourself and your wife so easily." A moment's hesitation. "I hope you won't be offended by this, but I can't help telling a story. It has been running through my head the whole hour, and I want to share it with you partially because it has meant so much to me." Everyone waiting, Carl's smile reflected in their faces. "Back when I was a resident in ob-gyn, before I went into psychiatry, I did a routine physical for a seventy-six-year-old woman. In the course of the interview I asked about her sexual life. 'Do you and your husband still have sex?' I asked. She looked instantly wounded, and I wondered if maybe I had used a dirty word." Carl paused, stiffening in his chair and throwing his head back to demonstrate the woman's posture. " 'Dr. Whitaker,' she said, 'my husband and I have been married for *forty-five years,* and our sexual relationship has improved for *every one* of those forty-five years. And if we live to be ninety, I expect that it will be better still.' " Carl waited again, listening to the group's mood, glancing at the older couple and at David and Carolyn. "And I think that's really the way it can be. It may take some work for the rest of us mortals to get there, but I think that kind of increasing intimacy is really possible—though I don't think it has an awful lot to do with sex. Sex is just where it gets expressed. Our investment in our marriage goes up every year, and it's just a question of whether or not this increase in 'voltage' gets expressed as stress and anger or in the way that couple experienced it. But the chance for it to be warmer every year is there for all of us." Carl had heard the couple's pain about what they both knew they were missing.

Don's voice seemed to rise disembodied from the group, an exquisite monotone, perfectly timed. "Did anybody ever tell you you should have been a preacher, Whitaker?"

Laughter, welcome and good.

The meeting the next day was relatively uneventful, but more supportive for David's parents. A gentle, thoughtful exploration of the family's history, its moods, its patterns of living. At the end of the second meeting Carl and I suggested that Mr. and Mrs. Brice contact a therapist in Boston and continue work on their relationship. We offered to give them the names of family therapists we knew there. Having recovered their composure, they said good-bye to us warmly. Several weeks later we had a call from them; they wanted the names of some therapists.

The interviews with his parents were critical for David. The changes that took place through our contacts with his family convinced him to become a "patient" in a very real sense. He began to look forward to the sessions, and as his participation in them increased, the talk of moving to Boston simply faded.

CHAPTER 20

Ending Therapy

David and Carolyn's decision about their marriage seemed to turn on the question of whether David would make a commitment to therapy or at least to change. It took a lot to shake his stolid, functional view of life: the shock of Carolyn's leap into growth and her tenacious grip on the gains she made; David's disillusionment as his parents tried to manipulate him; and finally, seeing his own parents' problems break into the open in the extended family interview. Not until David's parents began to work in therapy did he finally allow himself to become "a patient."

His decision was more than an individual act. It reflected his parents' "permission" for him to grow, and it was a response to what he heard in the subtle undertones in Carolyn's voice—her insistence on being a person, which meant that he too would have to be a person for the relationship to work, and her real desire to sustain the marriage. While David's "commitment" was the symbolism through which the *couple* expressed their decision to remain married, the actual decision making was far more deeply buried, in fact inaccessible, and I assume that we can never know its true nature.

Both their parents' marriages had "endured," a model for sticking it out that was undoubtedly useful during the times of greatest crisis. That heritage might have worked against David and Carolyn, however, if their parents had stayed married primarily out of fear of divorce. In spite of their many problems, both of the parent marriages must have been founded on real caring. Though they lost touch with it for a while, David and Carolyn had this caring, too, that bond for which there is no substitute.

Maybe they were just smart. They looked at how much they had invested in each other and guessed how difficult—if not impossible —it would be to start again.

It may have been the children, who were opposed to a divorce and who were in the thick of the fight. Their vote was a unanimous, if usually unexpressed, "stay!"

Carl and I never tried to sway them—in fact, we tried very hard *not* to pressure them; but they must have been influenced by our belief that the initial choice of partner is made through remarkably accurate unconscious process that takes account of their often unconscious mutual needs. Perhaps our dedication to hard work was also appealing to this duty-bound couple. Certainly they could sense that we saw hope for their relationship.

However it happened, David and Carolyn's marriage began to come alive. Like spring, the changes came slowly, a leaf at a time. They required work, and there were numerous chilly setbacks; but there was something in the couple's growth that was beyond volition, a quality of movement so subtle and so pervasive that it seemed more the product of a change of season than of deliberate effort.

Therapy continued for eight months after the interview with David's family, and the marriage was the focus for most of that time. For several weeks the couple relaxed and enjoyed the experience of getting back together. Then some of the old conflicts resurged. This time, however, Carl and I insisted that David and Carolyn confront these relationship problems where they were now centered—within the two individuals. We did not ignore their relationship, but we pushed to gain access to each person's struggle *with himself.* As more of each partner's insecurity and self-doubt was exposed, the blaming pattern collapsed; they went from arguing with each other to being somewhat depressed.

Increasingly, therapy consisted of two parallel "individual" therapies. While we still met with the whole family, we spent most of our time working with either David or Carolyn. Sometimes the hour would be shared by the two of them; at other times the whole hour would be spent with one or the other. The "scheduling" was entirely intuitive—it depended on who managed to get the floor. Sometimes there were jokes about equal time.

Of course, the focus was not exclusively on the two adults as individuals. Conflict bubbled up spontaneously from various quarters: between the parents; between the parents and the children;

between the children. We attended to whatever issue seemed pressing. Therapy became "easy," a flowing, natural process to which
everyone was committed. At last, we were all moving with the current.

After it became clear that Carolyn and David were going to stay
married and that the focus on the adults was boring for the children,
we suggested that they come only when it seemed appropriate to
them or their parents. We essentially relinquished control of the
structure of the therapy sessions to the family.

The younger children were relieved by this decision and came
less often, but Claudia attended regularly for some time. When the
children came, they brought their usual wit and good humor, and
they learned something vital to their later lives: how conflict in marriage can be resolved. Of course, we all kept in touch with their
problems, too. If Don and his mother had a fight during the week,
he would usually appear at the next session to work on it.

The reader may find it curious that we did not shift to meeting
separately with David and Carolyn as they focused on their "individual" concerns. After all, isn't the privacy of a one-to-one interview
conducive to honest self-expression? In fact, I did meet alone with
Carolyn in the last two months of therapy, but it was useful to continue to meet with the couple for a considerable period after the
divorce crisis passed.

The marriage problems were far from over, of course. We would
work "individually but together" with David and Carolyn for several
weeks, and then suddenly a conflict would erupt between them. The
couple was surprised and distressed by the intensity of these fights,
but Carl and I expected them. The greater individuation in the
marriage and the increased commitment to the relationship gave
them the freedom to heat up their arguments with less sense of
danger. It was finally safe to be *really* honest, and on some days I am
sure their honesty could be heard all the way down the hall in the
Psychiatry Department.

These conjoint meetings also helped strengthen the couple's
agreement to stop being each other's therapists. While it was a little
embarrassing for David if his jaw began to quiver and tears streamed
down his face as he wrestled with his problems, it was useful for
Carolyn to sit "helplessly" and observe. She discovered not only that

she was unable to help David with certain problems, but that she did not need to. He was learning to be his own therapist.

In part because she did not have to *do* something to help, Carolyn could relax and "be with" David. Absolved of being responsible for him, she was freed to understand him better and to feel closer to him. Rather than be a pseudoparent (and child) to her husband, she became a fellow traveller, a peer. Though the timing of these changes was complex, they did occur in both partners. David too began to see Carolyn as "just a person," divesting her of some of the images of threat in which he had clothed her for so long.

As old angers were discharged and new ones were dealt with more promptly, the couple's fights became brief and direct. It was also increasingly difficult for them to fight seriously. "How can we fight if we keep breaking into snickers?" Carolyn half complained. Carl and I deserve some credit for the couple's levity, because we spent a good deal of time teasing them out of their serious, over-deliberate way of approaching their problems.

We also began to see in therapy some highly significant "little things": they glanced at each other more often; they sat together; occasionally their hands touched. As one might expect, their most intimate talks occurred outside the therapy hour, but the sense of warmth accompanied them to therapy. They did not *do* anything dramatically different; they *were* different. It was as though somewhere the sun had come out, and the room gradually lightened.

We were never able to get Carolyn's family to come for a session. She visited them several times to try to talk to them more personally, and she carried on a long and complicated correspondence with her mother; but we regretted not having direct access to her family. David's family returned twice more, and the sessions with them were productive.

Eventually David grew bored with the meetings. His life seemed satisfactory to him, and he had other things to do. Even Carolyn had no pressing complaints against him; he was taking much more time away from work and was more loving and attentive toward her. The two of them had begun to take weekend trips without the children, and these trips wrought a virtual revolution in the couple's sexual life. David was also beginning to develop a strong relationship with Don since they had discovered photography as a mutual interest.

I don't remember when or how we decided that it was appropri-

ate to let David go and to honor Carolyn's request to continue individually. David seemed to be doing well; the marriage seemed to be
doing well; there were no visible problems in the children's lives. It
just felt right.

Carolyn chose to work with me, and I met with her for two
months. For the most part, the sessions were fairly casual, almost
anticlimactic, but they did contain some intense and tearful moments. Carolyn had been fighting off periodic depressions for many
years, and I encouraged her to stop fighting. "Let them happen," I
advised.

At first she was afraid that she might be swallowed up in these
moods that rose in her so unpredictably. She approached cautiously,
becoming a little more depressed each week for several weeks. Then
one week she seemed almost immobilized, desolate. She looked as
though she were being drawn down into her chair. I don't remember
my exact words to her, but they were mainly a statement of concern,
something like: "You sure do look sad."

Carolyn started crying in a way that was different from her earlier
"breakdown" into tears. Then she had been under intense stress;
now most of her everyday life seemed satisfying. This grief was con-
tentless and ancient, a long, gentle, but extremely painful crying for
the anonymous injuries, probably out of her childhood, that had been
consciously forgotten. She did not so much express these feelings as
allow herself to experience them, wave after wave of the deepest
kind of psychological pain.

When it happened, there was little I could do but be there. I sat
silent and helpless while she cried, able only to care about her. When
her crying had finally diminished and she looked up, I reached over
and touched her hand, saying, "At least it isn't endless."

After that day Carolyn seemed less afraid of her sadness. The
moods did not stop coming, but she learned that she could allow
herself to feel depressed, to cry, to ride down into the feeling and,
eventually, out on the other side. The depressions came less frequently and were less intense. "You know," she said once near the
end of our sessions, "I sometimes think I enjoy being depressed. It's
like a season that I might miss if it didn't come."

Carolyn and I finally stopped meeting because she felt much
better. She realized that someone with her childhood history of intense attack by a parent probably would have a struggle with depres-

sion for the rest of her life; but now she felt that she had a perspective on the problems and that she could do something about them. We said good-bye a little sadly, knowing that we would miss each other. Like everyone else's, Carolyn's therapy was imperfect—she left with problems. But she also left with a sense of pride in what she and the family had accomplished, and with the knowledge that any of them could return to therapy at any time.

Approximately a year after my last interview with Carolyn and nearly two and one-half years after we had first seen the family, Claudia was on campus and dropped by at Carl's office. He had only a half hour before his next appointment, but it was enough.

At first Carl thought that Claudia had come for help, possibly even to enter therapy. She had just finished her first semester at the university, but it had not gone well. She had been eager to start college and had pushed to finish high school early; but her dreams of college life proved unrealistic. The classes were so large that she felt lost in them. She missed the family but hated herself for spending every weekend at home. She had no idea what she wanted to study. "I don't know why I'm going to college," she said.

After a lot of worry and talk with the family Claudia had worked out a plan. David's work had taken him to Europe a number of times, and he had become friendly with the family of a Parisian business-man who had a daughter about Claudia's age. Claudia would go to Paris and live with this family for a semester and a summer, and the father would try to find her a job there. Claudia brightened as she talked about her plans, her hard work on her French.

"Great!" Carl said. "So what's the problem? It sounds very exciting." Then he made a guess. "Don't tell me your father is enthusiastic and your mother has cold feet!"

"Exactly," Claudia said.

"So what's new?" Carl asked. "You and your dad were always hatching plans together. Why don't you do what you want to do and let them stew with each other?"

"Well, it's not so much that," Claudia said. "Mom is a little worried, but she accepts my going. I don't really know what it is. Maybe I'm just scared."

"Sure," Carl replied, "I would be, too." He looked at her quizzically. "You think you feel guilty about abandoning your poor old parents?"

"Maybe," Claudia said tentatively.

Carl: "Don't. They'll miss you, but they'll probably be glad to get rid of you."

Claudia's laugh, aggressive and delighted, betrayed the same impulse. She would be glad to go.

They chatted for a while about the family, and there was no dramatic news. Carolyn had decided against social work school because she thought that becoming a therapist or even a caseworker would be too upsetting for her. Instead, she had become deeply involved in the women's movement and was also taking university courses that interested her—art history, the psychology of women, modern poetry. Claudia spoke of her mother with fond admiration, a striking change from the bitterness she had felt at the beginning of therapy. Claudia's adventurousness was plainly modeled in part on her mother's new exploration of the world outside the home.

Claudia saw her father as gentler and more relaxed, if at times a touch depressed. He seemed to have relinquished some of his ambitions and to be enjoying life more. David had always been Claudia's idol, and Carl sensed a new distance between them. Claudia appeared to realize that her relationship with her father was a little dangerous: if she were to win her freedom, she would have to gain more distance from him, and she wondered if perhaps that wasn't the real reason she was going to Paris.

Don was in high school, playing in a rock band, getting, as usual, mediocre grades, and staying out of trouble. "He smokes a little pot," Claudia said, "but so does everyone else at his school." She paused reflectively. "He's a neat guy. But he has it a lot easier than I did at his age. I guess my parents are much more relaxed about a lot of things. They know about the pot, and they don't even hassle him about it." She looked a little sad as she thought about how troubled her own high school years had been.

Claudia said that Laura was "disgustingly all right." She got good grades in school, and everyone liked her. "Laura is still too dependent on Mother and a little spoiled by all of us, but Mother's outside involvement is helping. Laura is forced to be more independent."

The marriage? "Their relationship is not as good as it was when they stopped therapy," Claudia said, "but it is basically all right. They fight, but then who doesn't? Before therapy I guess we all thought that fighting was wrong. Now we hardly think anything about it. It's just part of living with people."

Carl could hear his next family outside the door. "Enough of this having fun," he said. "I've got to get to work." He often used this remark to terminate a session, and it probably meant that while beginnings are hard work, even the beginning of the next session, endings are also difficult. It is hard to stop. Claudia rose to her feet, gathering her books. She looked satisfied; she had received permission from an "uncle" to run away from home.

Carl couldn't resist a little advice. "For now, the only person you really need to be faithful to is you." They smiled at each other.

Claudia hugged Carl tightly. " 'Bye, Carl." And she was gone.

When I heard about it, I was sorry that I had missed the meeting with Claudia. But I'm not sure I needed to be there, just as Carl didn't need to be at my sessions with Carolyn. After such a therapy experience, we carry it with us everywhere—a portable, interior family, always available. Whatever happens to any of us will touch all of us.

CHAPTER 21

Forum

All presentations of ideas, however thoughtful, are bound to raise specific questions and sometimes doubt. Skepticism is a healthy response to any assertion, and it helps establish a valuable dialogue. In this chapter we attempt to answer some of the questions and doubts which we have encountered from a number of fronts: from professional and lay audiences to whom we have lectured, from our students, and from those who read this book when it was in preparation. It is likely that some of these questions will have also occurred to the reader.

Q: *I'm not clear when family therapy is an appropriate treatment, and when it is not. There are so many "therapies" today, and deciding when a particular approach is indicated seems very difficult.*

Before talking about types of therapy, we should make a more fundamental distinction between types of therapists. When a therapist looks at a human problem, how does he conceptualize that problem? The therapist's view of psychological causality guides his every action, shaping the way in which he uses particular methods and techniques. In fact, his view of the problem determines *what he is trying to change.* If he sees the problem as primarily within the individual, he will move to help that individual. If he sees the problem as involving a set of relationships, he will in all likelihood try to influence that network of people.

The major problem we see in the individual approaches is that they fail to take account of the powerful *interdependence* between family members. Even if the family is very unhappy, the members are intensely loyal to its world—to its emotional tone, its set of rules, its esprit, even its unconscious "plan" for the future. It is very difficult for individuals to change, *and maintain that change*, if the family does not change, too. Working with the whole family not only avoids challenging family members' loyalties to one another, but it allows us to draw upon this charged involvement as a therapeutic resource.

In our view, working with the family system is *always* the best approach to therapy, and the more family members who can be involved, the better. It doesn't matter who has the presenting problem or what the problem is—whether it's a child who wets the bed, an alcoholic husband, a couple considering divorce, a wife who is depressed, a runaway adolescent, or a capable student who is failing in school. The "symptom" is merely a front for the family's larger stress. The greatest therapeutic power lies in tackling the binds, conflicts, misperceptions, inequalities, and hungers in this most intimate of groups. We believe that helping the individual gain insight into his past is less efficient than helping him restructure his current family relationships.

A systems orientation does not dictate a particular membership at meetings. Murray Bowen, for example, often meets alternately with individual family members, though he is constantly *thinking* of the family system as he works. What makes him a family therapist is his goal: helping the entire family to change.

Some therapists concentrate on the couple as the most important subsystem in the family, and even when the identified patient is a child, they may bring him or her in only briefly. These therapists assume that the primary dynamics of the family reside in the marital relationship and that if the parents change, the child will be helped —sometimes without ever appearing in therapy. Other therapists may treat a larger group. Peter Laqueur, a psychiatrist in Vermont, works with groups of four or five families, forming a "therapeutic community" among these families that may continue to meet for many years. Ross Speck, a Philadelphia psychiatrist, convenes a "network" around the identified patient, and sometimes it is difficult to identify the nuclear family at these meetings for all the extras in the cast—teachers, friends, neighbors, distant and not-so-distant relatives.

Carl and I agree with the majority of family therapists in making the nuclear family our primary client. This group has a combination of separateness from the larger extended family and an intense interdependence among its own members that make it a natural unit. While we find it extremely useful to involve the extended family and sometimes other people close to the nuclear family, the nuclear family is our real client.

Q: *Must the family always be two parents and their children? Aren't there other perfectly valid forms of family life? What about the couple that has been living together for a year? Or the married couple without children? Or the divorced parent living with his or her children? What is the relevance of family therapy to these relationships?*

We do not make rigid rules about what constitutes a family, though questions regarding who should be present at meetings can be quite complex. Generally we start with a primary client which consists of a group of people *who live under one roof.* This is usually a two generation nuclear family, though we certainly think of the married couple without children as a family. The family that lives together may also include an aunt or uncle, an elderly parent, or, in the case of the single parent, a lover. Carl and I are reluctant to begin therapy without an agreement that everyone who lives together will participate.

A secondary group consists of those who are important influences in the lives of the nuclear group. We see them as *consultants* in our work with the nuclear family, and a number of circumstances must be weighed in deciding when to involve them. We know, for example, that we will probably not be able to bring in the extended family until we have built a good relationship with the nuclear family, but there are some situations, as when the grandparents live next door and support the family financially, where we must insist that they participate from the beginning. It is a very unusual family that does not have a number of "outside" relationships that can be of valuable assistance at some time during the therapy.

The postdivorce family often presents us with difficult problems regarding membership at the meetings. The divorced mother with custody of her two children may ask for therapy only for herself and the children, but it may be necessary to involve her ex-husband if the two of them are to cease the usually covert warfare which they carry on through their children. Though in the beginning the ex-spouses often resist the idea of meeting together, a surprising number agree to work together for the benefit of their children.

We also work with unmarried couples who live together. These relationships have many of the qualities of marriage, including intense transference involvement; but they do not have the legal bonds that sustain some couples through the turmoil of a stormy therapy experience. Sensing this lack of formal, contractual "support," many unmarried couples approach therapy cautiously.

Q: *How do you decide which members of the larger family grouping to involve at the start of therapy? What sequence usually follows that decision?*

Ideally, we would like to start with the largest system we are able to assemble, then work with progressively smaller subsystems. For example, if we discover there is a war going on between the two families of origin, it is preferable to start therapy at that level. We want to relate to the most global system first, then move on to the smaller subsystems. After the two branches of the family are no longer at war, we concentrate on the nuclear family that initially got in touch with us. When the children have been disentangled from the couple's problems, we may work for some time with the couple. When there seem to be *no* further pressing relationship battles and when our allegiance to the entire group is well established, we can then work with individuals. But individual therapy should be like the Ph.D.—the last stage in training. Individual therapy is for the person who has learned to live with others and now wants to work further on living more comfortably with himself.

In practice, the sequence is usually not so tidy. We often must work with the nuclear family for some time, for example, before they trust us enough to bring in their families of origin, and before they are convinced of the advantages of doing so. The sequence of various membership "groups" in the therapy of the Brices is fairly typical, though occasionally we work with families that are willing to begin therapy by assembling a very large network. A couple we saw recently was willing to bring both of their quite large families of origin to the first interview, a total of twenty people.

Q: *You speak of first resolving interpersonal conflict, then going into*
individual work. I thought it was the other way around—that
you can relate to others only as well as you can relate to yourself.

That's the assumption which the individual therapist makes. It
presumes that the person who comes for therapy *is* an individual,
someone who is able to plunge freely into the process of change. We
family therapists see the person being referred for treatment as
someone who *looks like* an individual, but who is really the agent,
and the prisoner, of a family system. Before people are psychologically accessible to individual treatment, they need to be liberated
from the tyranny of a highly stressed symbiotic system.

We think that individual therapy can be divisive if it takes place
before family treatment. If there is a serious marital problem and one
of the partners goes for individual therapy, this therapy not only may
make the other spouse feel suspicious, but can also create an even
more serious imbalance in the marriage. Marriages are delicately
balanced creations, and any marked asymmetry in the partners'
growth can increase a sense of alienation and distance.

We try to initiate a balanced sequence of growth. We attempt to
help the family achieve individuation of the *generations.* We hope
to create a "sense of the individual" in the family by freeing the
individuals from their crippling entanglements with one another. As
the reader has seen, it is not an easy process. We may work for
months to disentangle a particular relationship, the marriage usually
being the last and most difficult project of all.

There should come a time when the group has given up on their
attempts to force one another to change and when they are ready to
use the therapists to generate self-change. This period is somewhat
like parallel, or rotating, individual therapy, in that family members
intuitively take turns "being the patient." These "public" individual
encounters between therapist and patient also deepen and intensify
the encounters that take place between family members. As a more
adequate model for both closeness *and* separateness develops within
the family, the atmosphere of the meetings becomes intimate *and*
free.

At the end of therapy the family should have resolved their major
relationship conflicts, and the individuals should really *be* individuals
in a psychological sense. The conflicts that remain are then of an

intrapsychic nature, remnants of past experience that continue to trouble the person. If the husband wants to work on his compulsive self-doubts, then there is reason to meet with him individually. If his wife wants to come along, fine. If she is bored with the process or too busy with her own world, fine. By now, there is little danger that individual meetings will fragment the family because a fundamental sense of openness and trust has been established, and the person coming to see the therapist is at last coming as an individual.

Q: *How long does the family-wide growth process take? It sounds as though it might go on forever. Don't many families stop therapy before they are really finished?*

The length of therapy is highly variable. Some families come for only a single interview and appear to change as a result of the one encounter. Others families work for four or five sessions in order to resolve an immediate crisis. Families can work for a year or for three or four years. Many variables influence the duration and depth of the family's therapy: the seriousness of the problems, the degree of courage or ambition that the family brings, the amount of distress pushing them to change, the quality of their previous therapy, the degree to which the therapist can identify with their problems, and the length of time that has elapsed since the problems first arose. We try to respond to the family's immediate needs and to go as far and as deeply as *they* want to go. Carl likes to compare himself to a piano teacher, offering to help the family reach whatever level of "skill" they choose. Many want only to play popular tunes. Some families want to play Beethoven well. And the latter may take a while.

Q: *How does the family know when therapy is over? And how is termination handled?*

Toward the end of therapy, the relationship between therapist and family becomes less professional, more person-to-person. The atmosphere can turn casual, even humorous. There may also be moments of quiet poignancy when the therapist feels deeply involved and openly shares his own feelings. He may reveal significant aspects of his own life. Eventually, the sense of there being "something to work on" dissipates, and the sessions are spaced out in time or become irregular.

At the very end of therapy there is often a sense of grief over the loss of a significant relationship. Carl and I always leave the termination process entirely in the hands of the family, expressing our willingness to reconvene the family whenever the need arises. The door is always open.

Q: *What if the family approach sounds appealing to me, but my family is reluctant to get involved in therapy? Am I out of luck?*

Hardly, although some of the problems in assembling the family may be complicated enough to require the therapist's assistance. Here are some preliminary guidelines.

If your family balks at participating in therapy, it is probably because they are afraid of being blamed or afraid that serious "hidden" problems will come to light. Father is likely to be the most resistant member since he often feels uncomfortable in the "sharing feelings" realm; he may also sense that the children are mother's allies.

Some therapists may be willing to start with less than the whole nuclear family, but Carl and I believe that it is a mistake to begin without at least those family members who live together. It is worth waiting and struggling to assemble this group at the first meeting. One meeting without father, for example, can make him even more defensive and suspicious than he already is, and it can seriously prejudice the therapist's perception of the family.

Tell your family honestly about the problems that you have—"I'm depressed all the time and I don't know why"—and ask their help in solving *your* problems. If they can see themselves as helping you, they may be much less defensive. With time and some relationship-building, the therapist may be able to get the family to broaden their agenda to include changing the whole system.

While it is not realistic to expect a therapist to take the initiative in persuading your family to enter therapy, he can be available over the telephone to answer the questions of skeptical members. Sometimes just hearing the therapist's voice over the telephone can alleviate some of the family's anxiety.

If your family adamantly refuses to enter therapy, you are left with an agonizing dilemma. It is painful enough to have your attempt to get help rejected by the family; now you must weigh the complicated decision of whether to seek help alone. If you do decide to enter therapy individually, you can be assured that if you begin to change, your family will be both upset and heartened. They may *then* be willing to reconsider their decision. Stay open to the possibility that your family can change. Even if it is necessary to bring in a co-therapist because your therapist has become too biased to your point of view, or to start again with a neutral therapist, it is worth the effort.

Q: *What if I don't have an entire family or my family lives a great distance away?*

If your family has been fragmented by separation or divorce, it is often possible and important to reassemble it in order to achieve some closure of unresolved problems. Ex-spouses can work productively together in therapy for the benefit of their children if they understand that the agenda is intended to improve existing relationships, not to reestablish old ties.

If several key family members are dead, your experience with them can often be reconstructed. Involve the family members who *are* available. If father is dead, his brother may help you see your family in a new way. Search for scrapbooks, photo albums, diaries, and friends who knew the missing member or members. A therapist can often help construct a role-play of critical scenes or work in other ways to re-create the presence of the missing member.

If your family lives at the end of a long-distance telephone line, there are several alternatives. Perhaps the family can come for as long a visit as possible; most therapists can clear blocks of time for such visits. A day or two of "marathon" sessions with the family can be enormously significant, as valuable as several months of less concentrated work. These extended family encounters are most useful at the beginning of therapy, before the family has become suspicious of being talked about and before the therapist has formed a stereotyped view of them. If the family can give their "permission for therapy" at the beginning of therapy, those involved will feel much less guilty about being disloyal to the family's implicit rules.

It is also important to realize that in spite of popular lore, you *can* go home again. In fact, for the couple or individual in therapy, it is very important to do so. It is probably best to go without your mate and to let yourself relax deliberately and experience "being a child again." Facing the risk of becoming dependent on the family once more can be anxiety-producing, but it can also rekindle a valuable sense of closeness with the family. If you simply allow yourself to live with them, you are bound to learn things about your relationship with your family, especially if your therapist has helped sensitize you to what to look for. Don't worry, you won't *stay* dependent on them.

It is very important to get to know the members of your family of origin as *people* because they form the model for many of your other relationships. While having them come to an interview is probably best, and a visit home in person is second best, modern technology opens alternative possibilities. You might buy an inexpensive cassette tape recorder and send it to your family. Tell them the questions that interest you and ask them to talk about them. What were your parents' lives like before you were born? (That way they don't have to feel guilty about what they did for you in your infancy.) What was mother's family like? Father's? Send the recorder to the grandparents and ask the same questions. If approached nonjudgmentally, people are surprisingly willing to talk about themselves, and as you listen, you may loosen your grip on the stereotyped images of family members that you have held for many years.

Don't forget the telephone. Though it's expensive, it may be worth setting up a conference call so that absent family members can participate in sessions. The therapist can use a speakerphone which allows everyone to hear everyone else. The family member who lives a thousand miles away will be grateful to be included in the interviews.

If you make a decision to involve your family in therapy, there is usually a way to do it.

Q: *What about the use of group therapy for those whose families aren't available? Indeed, what is the relationship between family therapy and group therapy? Aren't the interactions that are revealed in the group as significant as those one finds in the family?*

The major difference between the two types of therapy is that the biological and legal ties that bind the family make the level of commitment much more profound and the "voltage" in the therapy much greater. The ad hoc therapeutic group can develop strong loyalties among its members, and the patterns of interaction that occur in the group have real significance. But it takes a great deal of work and a lengthy investment in time for the group to begin to feel anything like a family, and most groups never make it. Both group and family therapists may use similar concepts, however, in trying to understand their clients. In both approaches the group process and its inevitable schisms and distortions are the primary focus. The group therapist must continually keep in mind that reactions between group members are likely to be displacements for their family experience. As ever, the family is ubiquitous.

When the family is really unavailable, Carl and I prefer to work with a different kind of nonfamily family: the network of friends, associates, and even professionals who interact regularly with the troubled individual. If the college student can persuade his roommate, his girlfriend, and the teacher who referred him to come with him to see the therapist, he begins with a system of preexisting loyalties and investments that is likely to have strong symbolic significance for him. He can begin immediately to utilize the power inherent in this substitute family. The major reason for working with the system is to gain additional therapeutic power, and we think bringing a naturally occurring social system into therapy is far preferable to attempting to construct a relationship system through a therapy group.

Q: *Does the system always have to come to you? Do you ever work in people's homes?*

Some family therapists *always* work in the family's home, a practice that is particularly valuable when the family is frightened about coming to a professional office. This setting has its drawbacks, however: the telephone rings, a neighbor drops by unexpectedly, and the therapist often feels uneasy about being in the family's territory. While Carl and I do meet at a family's home when it is absolutely necessary, we prefer to work in our own offices, where we have more sense of control and security. The family has *so* much power; we need a few professional props to help us feel relaxed about what we are doing. We also believe that in the beginning it is important for therapy to be isolated from the patient's everyday social reality. It is then more likely to be a symbolic experience, one that touches deeper levels of the unconscious. That's also why we ask the family not to talk about the therapy sessions when they are at home and to save their ideas and feelings about the family for the therapy hour. Initially, we want the entire effort to change the family to be focused on the session.

Q: *Isn't that artificial, if not downright impossible?*

It is certainly difficult at the outset. But after a while the family settles into a rhythm in which the fights and struggles become intuitively organized around the sessions. A couple will irritate each other on the way to therapy and bring the fight right into the interview. This happened repeatedly with the Brices, and it's appropriate. It gives the family a safe arena in which to play out their conflicts, and it allows the therapists to relate directly to the family's emotional life.

Q: *In addition to the question of where you meet with the family, what other differences in approach exist among family therapists? Are there separate schools of family therapy?*

The first family therapists were distinct individualists: strong, creative, and thoroughly rebellious. Their differences were obscured, however, by the fact that they had to band together to fight the entire psychiatric establishment. As family therapy has become more widely accepted and as each "grandfather" has trained his own cadre of supporters, we have had the luxury of discovering and airing our differences. National meetings of family therapists are now often contentious, as each group presents its own approach. The competitiveness and diversity of the field are healthy, the very stuff of creativity, but unfortunately they can result in more perplexity for the prospective client. Let me describe some of the major subgroups under the family therapy rubric.

As with all other therapeutic approaches, the psychoanalytic movement has left its influence on family therapy. The psychoanalytically oriented family approach is most often identified with the late Nathan Ackerman, considered by many to be the founder of family therapy. This approach depends heavily on helping the family achieve insight into their problems, particularly the distortions and "holdovers" from past experience. As he initiates a series of one-to-one interchanges with family members, the therapist remains at the center of the interaction, sometimes blocking the family's own exchange process. The psychoanalytic orientation remains strong on the east coast, particularly in Boston, New York, and Philadelphia.

Partly in an effort to overcome what were seen as limitations in the psychoanalytic approach, the "communications" school, which originated at the Mental Research Institute in Palo Alto, California, rejected all references to past behavior and to symbolic issues in the family. These therapists have stressed *current* interaction between family members, especially patterns of communication. Many outstanding clinicians, including the original group of Don Jackson—now deceased—Virginia Satir, Gregory Bateson, Jay Haley, Jules Riskin, Paul Watzlawick, and John Bell, have been associated with this school; they originated some of the most useful early concepts, such as the "family homeostasis," "family rules," and the "double bind." While some of these therapists have in recent years moved into other approaches, Virginia Satir has remained an extremely influential representative of the communications orientation. Her "communication types"—the Computer, the Blamer, the Placater, the Irrelevant—have become easily recognizable figures for all therapists. The need to help families develop clear, consistent, and nonaccusatory communications skills is so obvious, and the contributions of this group so strong, that all family therapists owe them a considerable debt.

The widespread availability of videotape machines has brought a new dimension to the effort to help families communicate more effectively. The family can now review its own performance within seconds of a particular interaction, and the therapist can point out positive as well as negative trends in the exchange. The use of video is becoming commonplace among family therapists, and such practitioners as Ian Alger, Norman Paul, and Fred and Bunny Duhl are developing sophisticated techniques in the use of this exciting new tool.

At times words can be used to *block* the sharing of genuine feeling in the family, and some communications-oriented therapists are using a new technique called "family sculpting" to get past intellectualization and defensiveness. These therapists, of whom Peggy Papp is perhaps the most widely known, ask each family member to position the family in postures that express the way they experience the family. The use of this nonverbal language can help the "closed" family begin to open up, and it can help the overly intellectualized family reach a new level of emotional expressiveness.

The "structural" approach is identified with the Philadelphia Child Guidance Clinic, one of the most highly regarded family therapy centers. These therapists, led by Salvador Minuchin, focus their efforts on changing stereotyped relationship "habits" in the family.

For example, if the mother is engaged in an intense repetitive struggle with her daughter, they may instruct the father to take over all disciplinary functions with the daughter for a while or suggest that he interact with her more frequently. With the mother-daughter conflict interrupted, tensions in the marriage which had been displaced into the mother-child battle are now free to emerge. Mother begins to fight with father, and the therapists can then turn to help the couple with their problems. This example is oversimplified, but it illustrates the planned nature of the therapist's intervention and the focus on changing larger relationship patterns, particularly triangular conflicts. This group has had outstanding success in work with the problems of children, particularly anorexia nervosa, a self-imposed starvation that often ends in death if not treated skillfully. Their techniques are "teachable" and have been influential in the new generation of family therapists.

The work of Murray Bowen is widely respected. Bowen's concept of the "family ego mass" portrays the client family as having low self-esteem and a pronounced symbiotic quality. Using a number of different techniques, Bowen helps the family achieve self-differentiation, and then a person-to-person quality in all relationships. Like many therapists, Bowen works on breaking triangular conflicts down into simpler, two-person dialogues.

The behavioral school is characterized by a strong focus on how family members act, as opposed to how they feel or think. The behaviorist is concerned with changing destructive patterns by altering the behaviors that reinforce these patterns. Mother, for example, may be unknowingly rewarding her child's temper tantrums by paying extra attention when the child is angry. If she can learn to attend when the child is doing something positive and ignore the tantrum, the child will in all likelihood give up the tantrums. While behavior therapy has been used most frequently with children, the same principles are now being used in work with couples. Husband, for example, agrees to stop shouting in return for wife's agreement to stop sulking, behaviors that are particularly provocative for the partners. Many family therapists are critical of the behavioral approach, believing that it is too mechanical and that its simple conceptual framework is not adequate in the face of the family's immense complexity.

While at the Atlanta Psychiatric Clinic, Carl and his colleagues developed an approach to psychotherapy with individual clients that has been labeled "experiential." This approach assumes that insight is not enough. The client must have an emotionally meaningful *experience* in therapy, one that touches the deepest levels of his person. Therapy is seen as a deliberate regression, one in which the therapist participates, though not as profoundly as the client.

Carl expanded this approach to include the family, retaining certain aspects of the individual pattern: the emphasis on personal encounter, the permission for the family to regress during therapy, the therapist's intuitive and deeply personal involvement in a "reparenting" process, and the goal of achieving a caring, person-to-person relationship among all parties at the end of therapy. The fact that the therapist uses his own person, particularly his intuitive self, makes the experiential approach difficult to teach. However, an entire generation of therapists has been inspired by Carl's brilliant interviews at workshops and symposia, and his work is internationally known. Those of us lucky enough to work alongside him as co-therapists have learned the most from him, including the necessity of creating our own styles.

In spite of the emergence of schools of family therapy, the young family therapist is often eclectic, borrowing useful techniques and ideas from a number of sources. The challenge of treating families is so great that we cannot afford to become rigidly loyal to one set of ideas. In order to be really helpful, the therapist must grow *with* the family.

Q: *How expensive is family therapy? I guess I'm thinking especially of your always working with a co-therapist. Doesn't this practice become prohibitive for the family?*

We charge for our time, not for the number of patients. And while rates vary widely, family therapists charge on the average no more than individual therapists.

The Brice family was financially comfortable and well insured, so Carl and I each charged them our regular rates. About half the expense was paid by the insurance company, the other half by the family.

The degree to which family therapy is covered by health insurance varies widely in different parts of the country. Some carriers are very regressive, covering only in-hospital treatment of an individual, and then only if medical treatment such as medication and electroshock is used. Other insurers pay amply for family therapy, even allowing part of the bill to be charged against each family member, thus increasing the benefits. Some insurance companies will not pay an eminent and qualified social worker like Virginia Satir for family therapy, yet will reimburse the family if they see a general physician with no training in family therapy. The relationship between the insurance companies and the entire mental health system is ridden with inconsistency and conflict, and short of a national health insurance system, there seems little hope for change in the near future.

When the family is not well off, there are several options for the therapist. Carl and I often work with a student co-therapist—a psychiatry resident or psychology intern—and while a student cannot be the ideal co-therapist, he or she is still a distinct addition to the effort. Another practice that avoids the double fee is the use of a consultant. I might come in on the second interview with a family that Carl is going to see, and every month or so he might ask me back—just so that he can maintain a perspective on his involvement with the family. The therapist can also defer the fee for a while, or reduce it, or space out the sessions if the family's therapeutic needs permit this.

But even a single, somewhat reduced private fee may be out of reach for many families. The cost of psychotherapy is an issue no less troubling, complex, and controversial than the cost of other medically related services. Serious inequities exist in the quality of care available to people on limited incomes and to the poor. Fortunately, public service agencies such as mental health centers, welfare departments, drug abuse centers, and juvenile courts are beginning to develop greater expertise in family therapy. In fact, as Carl and I travel the country to give lectures and to consult with training programs, we see outstanding work being done in some agencies that serve predominantly poor families. But for the moment, family therapy, like all the other therapies, is most available to middle-class families.

Q: *You and Carl seem to work together very smoothly. What goes into making a good co-therapy relationship? Are the differences in your training important, or is it a more personal matter? What happens when you disagree? What do you do then?*

We do sometimes disagree, though it didn't seem to happen very often with the Brices. When we feel ourselves at cross-purposes during a session, we will often stop our work with the family and turn to settling our own differences. Sometimes it's a little tense, airing our own disagreements with the family present, but in fact, the family learns from watching us talk out our problems.

Co-therapy is a complicated relationship, much like marriage. You have a contract that binds the two of you to trying to help the family, and you must evolve a relationship that includes room for both individuals to be themselves, yet provides some kind of overall synchrony. The formal professional background of the two therapists seems to be relatively unimportant. It *is* important that the therapists like each other and that each bring a complementary interpersonal skill to the relationship—one who can be humorous, for example, while the other is more serious and logical. It's also useful if the therapists grew up in families with different dynamics. This heterogeneous history provides a buffer against either therapist's becoming overinvolved with the family.

Q: *Speaking of the training of the therapist, doesn't the development of family therapy have dramatic implications for the training of the psychologist and psychiatrist of the future? I don't see anything in the systems approach that would necessitate, for example, all of Carl's medical training.*

Looking back, every family therapist finds much in his or her professional training that was unnecessary, though there may be beneficial "transfers" from some of the irrelevant instruction. While Carl does not use his medical training directly, it gave him a valuable perspective on the relation between the mind and the body, and it taught him to take over forcefully in emergency situations. The practice of medicine also makes the physician acutely aware of death, and this awareness may make it less likely that the psychiatrist will avoid facing this issue when it arises in psychotherapy.

On the other hand, the psychiatrist spends an inordinate amount of time learning medical skills that are of little use in any psychotherapy. He becomes biased to thinking in terms of illness and symptomatology, attitudes that must be unlearned as he tries to understand and work with social systems. We still speak of the family as our "patient" largely out of habit, but it is a bad habit. The tendency to compare human psychological distress with physical illness is an often destructive use of metaphor.

The psychologist who becomes a family therapist also finds that much of his training was peripheral or irrelevant. The hours spent studying statistics, research design, neurophysiology, and learning theory may have an occasional relevance to the family, but I have to strain to find it. Perhaps the skepticism inherent in research training provides a useful objectivity. Maybe all those hours I spent learning how to administer tests to individuals taught me to look carefully at the subtleties of thought or behavior. But the skills I need in order to be able to work effectively with families had to be acquired largely at my own initiative and after the "necessary" training was over.

It is possible that the social worker's training is the most appropriate education of all for family therapy since social systems are the direct focus of this field. The increasing emphasis on teaching administrative skills in social work is disturbing, however, and may make the social worker of the near future a less capable therapist than the current graduate.

If the systems approach becomes the predominant treatment for emotional distress and *if* the graduate schools of our country take seriously the job of training capable practitioners, it will cause a revolution in therapeutic training or practice. This transition will be most difficult for psychiatry, in which reliance on the medical model —maintained by medicine's prestige in our society—must be modified. The struggle to make the transition is already in progress, the battle joined.

For those of us with hard-earned graduate degrees, the disconcerting fact is that the family therapist need not have any formal academic training to be effective. Youths from inner-city Philadelphia with no credentials other than a high school diploma have been successfully trained to be family therapists. They work within an agency, they have access to supervision and to continuing training, and they work effectively. The family therapist needs competent training, but much of it can take place on the job. There is no reason why the family therapist could not be any capable, concerned, perceptive person who is willing to work hard and who comes in contact with families: the welfare worker, the probation worker, the minister, the family physician, the housewife who has reared her own children and wants another tough job. Extreme situations might require the consultation or intervention of the psychiatrist, but even this is not inevitable.

Q: *You speak of belief, conviction, anticipation. But what are the facts about the effectiveness of family therapy? Why don't you cite relevant research that compares your approach to the other therapeutic strategies?*

For the moment, *no* therapeutic approach can demonstrate conclusively that it is superior in the long run to any other. Psychological study of the human creature is appallingly difficult, and research on the *outcome* of psychotherapy is even more problematic since so many variables must be "controlled." Should one look at behavioral change or attitudinal change? What constitutes growth, and how does one measure it? Then there is that most troublesome variable of all, the person of the therapist. Research in family therapy, where the unit of study is a group, adds new dimensions of complexity that are truly nightmarish for the researcher.

Although it is too early to make a definitive statement, recent research indicates that family therapy is indeed more effective than individual treatment. There is a good deal of argument about the quality of existing studies, but the majority of those that compare family treatment with individual treatment find the family approach superior. Statistical data now in press report Dr. Minuchin's long-term outcome in sixty cases of anorexia nervosa as 94 percent successful, and the other 6 percent successful with additional individual therapy. This in the face of the fact that previous data on this easily diagnosed systems disorder reveal a 60 percent death rate if untreated!*

More research is under way, but it will be years before authoritative comparisons can be made between various therapeutic strategies. The field is new, the task is enormous, and research grants are not plentiful. Clinicians like Carl and me who want to have research undertaken do not necessarily want or have the right temperament to do it themselves; while really serious researchers know a hornet's nest of difficulties when they see one and often prefer to study simpler, more manageable problems. But now that family therapy is attracting worldwide professional attention, perhaps it will also attract the research effort that it needs. At the moment the person seeking a therapist must make a decision largely on the basis of subjective evidence.

*Personal communication.

Make no mistake about it: family therapists *do* fail in a certain percentage of cases. Carl and I see families who come away from the experience feeling very disappointed that we didn't help them. We see other families who believe that family therapy changed their lives profoundly. The majority fall somewhere in between, finding the experience helpful, but not earthshaking. We are concerned about our failures, and we hope that we are learning from them. We remain excited about family therapy not because it has the answer to everyone's problems, but because of what seems to us the power, the creativity, and the long-term "rightness" of the approach. We don't expect miracles. We work with situations of extraordinary complexity, and we attempt to change patterns that have been many generations in the making.

While families can learn more creative or efficient *processes* for coping with life, their fate is always uncertain, subject to a great many unpredictable forces. Expecting any therapy, especially one as ambitious as family therapy, to produce a definitive "happy ending" is naïve. Looking at the individual for a circumscribed length of time, one can forget this basic lesson, but examination of the course of family history over several generations invariably gives us a vivid perspective on humanity's valiant struggle in the face of enduring problems. Family therapy *can* make an important difference in this continuing life effort. And we hope that in ten years it will make a more powerful and consistent contribution than it does now.

Q: *If I am interested in seeing a family therapist, how do I go about finding someone competent?*

The large network of thoroughly trained family therapists which our society needs simply does not exist at present. While some very large cities may have as many as thirty or forty experienced therapists, many smaller cities have none.

Here are some places to look. Your city may have a private family therapy institute or a university department that offers a subspecialty in family therapy. The usual departments to ask would be psychology, psychiatry, or social work, but other fields such as educational psychology or child development may also have staff members with expertise in family therapy. Academic departments that train therapists may operate clinics where supervised students see families at reduced rates. These departments may also be aware of the most skilled therapists in a community and be able to make referrals to them.

Impartial groups such as your local chapter of the national Mental Health Association can often be helpful,* as can associations of clergymen. The Community Mental Health Center nearest you is certainly a resource to explore, and if it cannot provide family therapy, it may be able to refer you to another agency or to a private practitioner.

The only organization in the nation that accredits marriage and family counselors is the American Association of Marriage and Family Counselors, 225 Yale Avenue, Claremont, California 91711. Membership in the organization requires a master's degree in one of the behavioral sciences, plus two years of clinical experience under the supervision of an approved agency or a member of the AAMFC. A good many family therapists, however, are not members of this organization.

In your search, use the contacts you already have, people whom you trust: your doctor; your minister; your child's teacher; friends who have been in therapy. Get information from a number of sources, and listen for names that repeatedly get favorable comments. Word of mouth may be the best recommendation for a therapist.

If you can't find a family therapist nearby, expand your search to include neighboring cities or towns. It may be worth traveling some distance to find a therapist with whom you can work.

Aside from reputation, what criteria should one use for selecting a therapist? One should not become preoccupied by the therapist's academic degrees since universities have been very slow in providing their trainees with experience in family therapy. Often family therapists have had to seek their own training on an independent basis following their usual academic training programs.

Look for a therapist, however, who has made a specialty of work with couples and families, not someone who engages in this difficult practice casually or incidentally.

The competent therapist will probably have had some kind of intensive training in family therapy, whether the training consists of an organized program in a private family institute, specialized expe-

*For the address of the chapter nearest you, write to the Mental Health Association, 1800 North Kent Street, Rosslyn, Arlington, Virginia 22209.

rience in a university program, or an apprenticeship with an experienced family therapist.

As in any other therapeutic approach, the length and depth of the therapist's experience are critical variables. Research has consistently shown that individual therapists with many years of experience are more competent than their younger colleagues. This is undoubtedly true of family therapy, too, but there are, of course, younger therapists whose eagerness and dedication compensate for their lack of experience.

The most important thing to consider about the family therapist is his or her *person.* And to evaluate that person, you will probably have to work with him or her for a while. Make the best choice possible, and then try several interviews. It may require several meetings to gather an adequate impression of the therapist, for first impressions can be misleading in any relationship. These are some of the questions which you might use in evaluating the therapist:

Is he strong enough to lead the family through difficult moments? The therapist who seems hesitant and unconfident may insist that the family contain its turmoil for his benefit.

Does the therapist seem to understand what is happening in the family? Do his comments "register" on more than a superficial level? Do you come out of each session having learned something new?

Does the therapist seem to care about people and their dilemmas? Whether or not the therapist is a caring person may be both the most important quality to assess, and the most difficult.

Perhaps the best way to conclude a book about a new field is to look at the future. We therapists anticipate working very actively as family therapy becomes more widespread. We expect that in the next decade or two some form of family involvement will become routine in the treatment of all emotional disturbance. Before this change occurs, however, our society must become more aware of the power of the family system both to cripple lives and to expand their potential. Only then will we make the large-scale effort that is needed to train an adequate number of family therapists.

A systems approach to treating emotional disturbance cannot stop with the individual family. The family is often merely the scapegoat of a highly stressed, competitive, and finally rather cruel society. We cannot work with the family system without becoming aware of the power of the governmental system, the school system, and the work system in the life of the family; and though most of us see our expertise as being in work with individual families, we know that there is much in this larger family of humanity that must be altered. Some family therapists will become politicians and social crusaders.

Nor can treatment ever be enough. We hope to see a world where the family's emotional *growth* has a high priority, and where the average family will find no stigma in seeking consultation to improve their creativity, to increase their communication or the level of their intimacy, or to cope with the expected crises of family life. This can happen only when we know just how human we all are, and how alike. Perhaps the commonality of our family experience can teach us this lesson.

Suggested Readings

For those interested in the more technical side of family therapy

Ackerman, Nathan W., Ed., *Family Therapy in Transition*. Boston, Massachusetts: Little, Brown and Company, 1970. (By one of the founders of family therapy.)

Bloch, Donald A., Ed., *Techniques of Family Therapy: A Primer*. New York: Grune and Stratton, 1973. (Includes an article on problems of the beginning therapist.)

Boszormenyi-Nagy, I., and Framo, James, Eds., *Intensive Family Therapy*. New York: Harper & Row, 1965. (Includes some excellent articles on family theory.)

Boszormenyi-Nagy, I., and Spark, G. M., *Invisible Loyalties*. Hagerstown, Maryland: Harper & Row, 1973. (Difficult going, but an important analysis of the loyalty issue in the family.)

Ferber, A., Mendelsohn, M., and Napier, A., Eds., *The Book of Family Therapy*. New York: Jason Aronson, 1972. (Includes a good deal of autobiographical commentary by family therapists.)

Guerin, Philip J., Ed., *Family Therapy: Theory and Practice*. New York: Gardner Press, 1976. (A fine collection of articles covering the history of family therapy, theory, clinical issues, techniques.)

Haley, Jay, *Strategies of Psychotherapy*. New York: Grune and Stratton, 1963. (A classic text comparing various therapeutic approaches.)

Haley, Jay, *Changing Families: A Family Therapy Reader*. New York: Grune and Stratton, 1971. (An excellent collection of articles spanning the history of family therapy.)

Haley, Jay, *Problem Solving Therapy*. San Francisco: Jossey-Bass, 1976. (A practical guide for the family therapist.)

Haley, Jay, and Hoffman, Lynn, *Techniques of Family Therapy*. New York: Basic Books, 1967. (Contains detailed analysis of interviews by four family therapists, including Carl Whitaker.)

Halpern, Howard, *Cutting Loose: An Adult Guide to Coming to Terms with Your Parents.* New York: Simon and Schuster, 1977. (For the general reader.)

Kantor, David, and Lehr, William, *Inside the Family.* San Francisco: Jossey-Bass, 1975; paperback: New York, Harper Colophon Books, 1977. (A systems view of the family.)

Laing, R. D., *Politics of the Family and Other Essays.* New York: Vintage Press, 1972. (A superb collection of lectures.)

Laing, R. D., and Esterson, A., *Sanity, Madness and the Family.* London: Tavistock, 1964. (A portrait of family pathology.)

Minuchin, Salvador, *Families and Family Therapy.* Cambridge, Massachusetts: Harvard University Press, 1974. (The best work on structural family therapy.)

Minuchin, Salvador, et al., *Families of the Slums: An Exploration of Their Structure and Treatment.* New York: Basic Books, 1967. (Pioneering work with poor families.)

Satir, Virginia, *Conjoint Family Therapy.* Palo Alto, California: Science and Behavior Books, 1964. (A guide to treating the family, written in outline form.)

Speck, R., and Attneave, C., *Family Networks.* New York: Pantheon Books, 1973. (A description of network therapy by its most prominent practitioners.)

Watzlawick, Paul, et al., *Pragmatics of Human Communication: A Study of Interactional Patterns, Pathologies, and Paradoxes.* New York: Norton, 1967. (An excellent analysis of communication strategies.)

Zuk, Gerald H., *Progress and Practice in Family Therapy.* Haverford, Pennsylvania: Psychiatry and Behavioral Science Association, 1974. (Quite readable, provides operational guidelines for family intervention.)

Zuk, Gerald, and Boszormenyi-Nagy, Ivan, Eds., *Family Therapy and Disturbed Families.* Palo Alto, California: Science and Behavior Books, 1967. (The strongest articles are in the theory of family functioning.)

Index

About the Authors

Augustus Y. Napier was born in Decatur, Georgia, in 1938 and graduated from Wesleyan University with a B.A. in English. After deciding to become a therapist through a personal therapy experience, he earned a Ph.D. in clinical psychology at the University of North Carolina. During an internship in the Department of Psychiatry at the University of Wisconsin–Madison, he began to work with Dr. Whitaker as a student co-therapist, an experience which formed the basis of this book. Dr. Napier later served on the faculties of the Psychiatry Department and the Child and Family Studies Program at the University of Wisconsin. He now directs The Family Workshop, a family therapy training institute in Atlanta, Georgia, where he works frequently with his wife, Margaret, who is also a family therapist. A frequent consultant, he is the author of numerous papers and of *The Fragile Bond*, published by Harper & Row in 1988. The Napiers have three children.

Carl A. Whitaker was born on a farm in Raymondville, New York, in 1912 and received his M.D. degree from Syracuse University in 1936. After a residency in gynecology, he turned to psychiatry. He trained in psychiatry at Syracuse University and child psychiatry at the University of Louisville, where he was also on the faculty of the Department of Psychiatry. He was chairman of the Department of Psychiatry at Emory University from 1946 to 1955 and helped establish the Atlanta Psychiatric Clinic in 1955. In 1965, he became a professor of psychiatry at the University of Wisconsin Medical School. In 1982, at the age of 70, he became Emeritus Professor of Psychiatry and is now retired. He is the author of two books and many professional papers and has contributed chapters to numerous textbooks. He lives in Neshotah, Wisconsin, where he works in co-therapy with his wife, Muriel, in addition to maintaining a full schedule of workshops in the United States and abroad. The Whitakers have six children and eleven grandchildren.